SOCIAL SCIENCE
RESOURCES IN THE
ELECTRONIC AGE

SOCIAL SCIENCE RESOURCES IN THE ELECTRONIC AGE

Volume III
Government and Civics

**Elizabeth H. Oakes and
Jeffrey D. Greene**

GREENWOOD PRESS
Westport, Connecticut • London

Library of Congress Cataloging-in-Publication Data

Oakes, Elizabeth H., 1964–
 Social science resources in the electronic age.
   p.   cm.
 Includes bibliographical references and indexes.
   Contents: v. I. World history / Elizabeth H. Oakes and Mehrdad Kia — v. II. U.S. history /
 Elizabeth H. Oakes and Michael S. Mayer — v. III. Government and civics / Elizabeth H.
 Oakes and Jeffrey D. Greene — v. IV. Economics / Elizabeth H. Oakes and Michael H.
 Kupilik — v. V. Geography / Elizabeth H. Oakes and Jeffrey A. Gritzner.
   ISBN 1–57356–589–X (set : alk. paper) — ISBN 1–57356–474–5 (v. I : alk. paper) —
 ISBN 1–57356–473–7 (v. II : alk. paper) — ISBN 1–57356–476–1 (v. III : alk. paper) —
 ISBN 1–57356–477–X (v. IV : alk. paper) — ISBN 1–57356–475–3 (v. V : alk. paper)
   1. Social sciences—Computer network resources. 2. Humanities—Computer network
 resources. I. Title.

H61.95.O25   2004
025.06′3—dc22   2003060400

British Library Cataloguing in Publication Data is available.

Copyright © 2004 by Greenwood Publishing Group, Inc.

All rights reserved. No portion of this book may be
reproduced, by any process or technique, without the
express written consent of the publisher.

Library of Congress Catalog Card Number: 2003060400
ISBN: 1–57356–589–X (set)
       1–57356–474–5 (vol. I)
       1–57356–473–7 (vol. II)
       1–57356–476–1 (vol. III)
       1–57356–477–X (vol. IV)
       1–57356–475–3 (vol. V)

First published in 2004

Greenwood Press, 88 Post Road West, Westport, CT 06881
An imprint of Greenwood Publishing Group, Inc.
www.greenwood.com

Printed in the United States of America

The paper used in this book complies with the
Permanent Paper Standard issued by the National
Information Standards Organization (Z39.48–1984).

10 9 8 7 6 5 4 3 2 1

Contents

Introduction

Social Science Resources in the Electronic Age: Government and Civics was designed as a one-stop resource for cutting through the chaos of the Internet to find authoritative, age-appropriate information. The book is divided into five chapters. In the first chapter, "Resources in Government and Civics," you'll find a list of relevant formats and types of resources for your research, with a listing of specific Web sites of interest for government and civics classes.

The second chapter, "Researching Individual Government and Civics Topics on the Internet," provides you with a treasure map to quality information on the Web, which will save you hours of your own research time. Here, we point you to the crème de la crème of Web sites that provide specific information on key topics in government and civics. These topics were chosen based on a review of national curriculum standards and were screened by an expert in civics and government.

For each topic, you'll find an entry that lists and reviews four or five Web sites, giving you all of the goodies you need to know: the name, URL, appropriate grade range, and a thorough discussion of how to use the site for research. When you log on to the Web to find a tidbit about impeachment or to gain a fuller understanding of the Declaration of Independence, you'll now have four or five handpicked sites, as opposed to the thousands that might turn up with a keyword search. In case you choose to conduct your own online search for a key topic, we have revealed which search engine and keywords provide the best hits.

The following chapter, "Materials and Resources for Government and Civics Teachers," reviews a number of excellent Web sites that offer

materials and resources for educators, such as reprinted government documents, lesson plans, and downloadable software. The next chapter,
"Museums and Summer Programs for Government and Civics Students,"
surveys Web sites offering unique online museum exhibits, interpretive
centers, summer programs, mentoring programs, student chapters, and
other interactive opportunities for students of civics and government.
The final chapter of the book, "Careers," turns its attention to Web sites
that provide students with career information in this field. Here, we've
reviewed sites and books with specific career information, as well as sites
for professional associations, academic groups, conferences, workshops,
programs, clubs, and other outlets for students interested in pursuing
work in the field.

HOW TO USE THIS BOOK

There are two ways you can find information in *Social Science Resources in the Electronic Age: Government and Civics*. First you can look
at the detailed table of contents. If you are researching a particular topic
in Government and Civics, you can immediately go to the alphabetical
listing of topics in Chapter 2. You can also use the index, which expands
our coverage significantly. Because we had to limit the number of topics
in Chapter 2, we added as much detail as possible to our site reviews.
These include names of people and countries, events, and other topics
covered in the Web site but not included in our topic list. All of these
have been indexed. Also, don't forget to refer to "The Basics" section
in Volume I of this set for general information.

1

———— ∞∞ ————

Resources in Government and Civics

FORMATS OF RESOURCES

Library Electronic Services

Specialized Databases

A number of topic-specific databases are popular among civics and government students and researchers. The following represents just a handful of those you might find at your library. Check with the library staff to see which databases would be useful for your project.

Public Affairs Information Service Bulletin (PAIS). Selectively indexes periodical articles from over 300 journals, as well as books, government documents, pamphlets, and unpublished reports of public and private agencies.

IAC Legal Resource Index. Indexes over 700 law journals from the United States and other countries "of the common-law tradition."

ABC Pol. Sci. Indexes more than 300 international journals in political science and government.

International Bibliography of Political Science. Indexes documents relevant to political science from thousands of international journals and books.

CD-ROMs

At a university library, you will also find specialized subject indexes such as the *Social Sciences Index* or *Historical Abstracts*. Find out if there are CD-ROM periodical indexes that cover civics, government, or social sciences at your library. Subject-specific CD-ROMs will naturally offer the most complete coverage of your topic.

Unlike print reference tools, CD-ROMs can cross-reference and link information together. Kaplan's *U.S. History and Government Essential Review* is a good example. This CD spans more than 500 years of major historic events, ranging from the signing of the Declaration of Independence to President Clinton's impeachment and acquittal. The program incorporates complete tables of the U.S. presidents and constitutional amendments, as well as a time line of historical events from the country's founding to the start of the twenty-first century. Practice tests can help you track progress and identify areas for further study, while the brainstorming, outlining, glossary, and bibliography programs will improve homework assignments and papers. The CD format allows you to tap into information in a variety of ways. You could begin with the table of contents or glossary, choose a particular chapter, or jump right into reading and practice tests. To gather a collection of information like this, you would have to rely on a variety of print reference books.

There are a number of other affordable CD-ROMs that might be of interest to government and civics students and teachers. McGraw Hill offers *American Government: The Political Game CD-ROM*, which provides an interactive journey through the study, practice, and application of political concepts. An excellent CD-ROM by Multieducator, *We the People: Civics 101*, provides an interactive look at the Constitution, the Bill of Rights, and the role and history of the presidency, as well as information on how Congress and the federal court system are structured. Compton's New Media has created a CD-ROM called *Campaigns, Candidates, and the Presidency*, which covers issues and events that shaped the campaigns of 42 American presidents and their opponents. *Inside the White House*, a CD-ROM developed by The Bureau of Electronic Publishing, takes an insider's look at the world's most powerful institution.

E-mail

If you have a general political or government-related question and want an expert to answer it, check out Pitsco's *Ask an Expert* site (http://www.askanexpert.com/) or visit *AskMe.com* (http://www.askmecorp.com/) for categories that include "Government" and "Politics."

Other online expert resources include sites such as C-SPAN's *Capitol Questions* (http://www.c-span.org/questions/), which offers answers to questions about the House, Senate, impeachment, and more, and *WebPresidents USA Ask-a-Question* (http://www.webpresidentsusa.com/), which also provides homework help, trivia, and an excellent reference bibliography.

Mailing Lists

Two examples of government- and civics-related mailing lists are SocialCapital (http://newhouse.syr.edu/socialcapital/), a list for people interested in using the Internet as a tool for reconnecting people, re-building communities, and re-engaging people in civic activities, including politics; and CIVTALK (civtalk@listserv.syr.edu), a list designed for discussions on the teaching of civics.

To find other mailing lists of interest, check these Web sites:

CataList: The Official Catalog of Listserv Lists (http://www.lsoft.com/lists/listref.html)

Topica: The Email You Want (http://www.topica.com/)

Usenet Newsgroups

A few newsgroups of interest to government and civics students include the following:

alt.politics.elections (Discussion about elections)

alt.politics.usa.constitution (Discussion about interpretations of the Constitution)

talk.politics.libertarian (Discussion on libertarian politics)

To find and subscribe to newsgroups that interest you, check out these two Web sites:

Deja News (http://www.deja.com/usenet/)

CyberFiber Newsgroups (http://www.cyberfiber.com/index.html)

Full-Text Magazines and Newspapers

Two e-journals of interest to students of government and civics include *American City and County* (http://www.americancityandcounty.com/), which offers a voice for local governments. The magazine serves an audience of city and county officials who are charged with developing and implementing local government policy, programs and projects; and *Congressional Quarterly* (http://www.cq.com/), with up-to-the-hour congressional news, including what's happening on the floor, in committee, and around town.

Digital Libraries

Digital libraries are an exciting initiative that's taking place on the Internet. For example, the *American Memory* digital library (http://memory.loc.gov/ammem/ammemhome.html) was created to digitally capture the distinctive, historical American holdings at the Library of Congress. This library includes the *Abraham Lincoln Papers* (http://memory.loc.gov/ammem/alhtml/malhome.html), a collection of incoming and outgoing correspondence and enclosures, drafts of speeches, and notes and printed material dating from the 1850s through Lincoln's presidential years, 1860–65.

Other digitized collections that provide images and documents of interest to government and civics students and teachers are the following:

The Oyez Project (The U.S. Supreme Court Multimedia Database)
http://oyez.nwu.edu/

Maintained by Northwestern University, Oyez provides complete records of Supreme Court cases, biographical information on justices, and a virtual tour of the Supreme Court building.

Franklin D. Roosevelt Library and Digital Archive
http://www.fdrlibrary.marist.edu/index.html

This digital archive provides access to an increasing number of items in the collection of documents, photographs, and video recordings at the Franklin D. Roosevelt Library in Hyde Park, New York.

United Nations Publications Database
http://www.un.org/Pubs/

If you're researching international affairs, this library of United Nations publications will probably be of interest. Here you'll find a comprehensive listing of nearly all United Nations publications with easy hyperlink access.

Visit *Digital Library.Net* (http://www.digitallibrary.net/), *Berkeley Digital Library SunSITE* (http://sunsite.berkeley.edu/), or the *Digital Libraries Resource Page* (http://www.interlog.com/~klt/digital/) for lists of online digital libraries or to read more about digital libraries.

Reference Books

Many libraries stock print editions of specialized reference guides that offer greater depth of information on topics pertinent to government and civics. These include the *Dictionary of Government and Politics*, the *American Political Dictionary*, the *HarperCollins Dictionary of American Government and Politics*, and the *Dictionary of the U.S. Constitution*.

If you're looking for biographical information on important people in government and civics, there are numerous biographical reference books. *The Biographical Dictionary of Congressional Women* and *The Vice Presidents: A Biographical Dictionary* are both excellent specialized guides. Almanacs, such as *The World Almanac and Book of Facts,* contain historical and current facts and statistics that may help substantiate other research you do. Another great source for facts and figures is *Statistical Abstracts of the United States,* which is issued by the U.S. Bureau of the Census in print and CD-ROM formats.

TYPES OF WORLD WIDE WEB RESOURCES

Reference Sites

C-SPAN Congressional Glossary
http://www.c-span.org/guide/congress/glossary/

This URL will take you directly to C-SPAN's excellent congressional glossary—all kinds of terms that come up on the Senate and House floors. Ever want to know what "recede and concur" refers to or what a "companion bill" is? It's all here in short, easy-to-understand definitions.

National Standards for Civics and Government: Glossary
http://www.civiced.org/stds_glossary.html

This straightforward site is part of the Center for Civics Education's home page. It contains a long, but not too long, alphabetically organized list of key words and phrases in civics and government. You will find brief but solid definitions of everything from affirmative action to World Court. Use it as an easy-access dictionary when you need good definitions of basic government lingo.

Political Reference Almanac
http://www.polisci.com/almanac/world.htm

The *Political Reference Almanac* will search for your research topic by word or phrase, or you can use the menu at the right, which contains such listings as "Calendar," "Executive," "Legislative," "Judicial," "State/ Local," "Parties," "Nations," and more. Updated every year, you will find this a great source for up-to-the-minute facts, names, and statistics.

StudyWeb
http://www.studyweb.com/

StudyWeb is a subject guide designed for student researchers who need to find information as easily as possible. With over 141,000 quality Web links reviewed and categorized into numerous subject areas, you can narrow in on a topic for a report, find background material for a project, begin research for a paper, or just increase your knowledge of a particular topic.

The home page for *StudyWeb* is clutter-free and easy to navigate. For starters, click on the "Government and Politics" topic link, which is broken into the categories of "U.S. Government," "World Government," "Related Countries," "Military Science," "Politics," and "Related People." When you enter the "U.S. Government" section, you're presented with subcategories, which include "Civics," "Executive Branch," "Legislative Branch," "Judicial Branch," "Government Agencies," "The Constitution," "Foreign Policy," and more. Under each subcategory, you'll see a list of specific topics or keywords, each accompanied by a selection of relevant Web links. Under "Legislative Branch," for example, we clicked on "How Lobbying Affects Legislation" and found 11 Web site reviews. *StudyWeb* helps you decide if the link is appropriate for your research by giving the site a score for visual interest, describing its contents, and indicating which age group the material is geared toward.

InfoPlease
http://www.infoplease.com/

InfoPlease is the online spin-off of a company that's produced almanac publications and reference databases for more than sixty years. This colorful site lets you tap into a massive collection of almanacs on almost every imaginable topic—chock-full of millions of authoritative factoids.

Click on the subject area "History and Government," and you'll find almanac sections such as "U.S. Elections," "U.S. Government," "Supreme Court," "U.S. Presidents," "U.S. Documents," and more. By clicking on a section—"U.S. Presidents," for example—you will find current and historical facts, biographies, inaugural speeches, contact info for the presidential library system, and tidbits about past presidents, their wives, and kids. In another almanac section—"U.S. Elections"—you'll find extensive details on presidential elections dating back to 1789, such as historical data on voter participation and vote summaries.

You can also search for keywords in *InfoPlease*'s database to come up with an impressive amount of information—more than some general search engines provide. For example, the keywords "Civil Rights Act" yielded 20 relevant hits in *InfoPlease*'s dictionary, feature articles, and encyclopedias. If you know the kind of information you need, you can use a pull-down menu to restrict your search to *InfoPlease*'s dictionary, biographies, or encyclopedia.

For more general research help, click on "Homework Center," a section designed to help K–12 students conduct their research and improve note-taking and writing techniques. This section will also direct students to other study-aid Web resources.

The Digital Librarian
http://www.digital-librarian.com/government.html

This site, maintained by Margaret Vail Anderson, a librarian in Cortland, New York, provides hundreds of links to great resources in government. From "Administrative Codes and Registers" to "WINGS," which is an acronym for Web Interactive Network of Government Services, you will find everything but the kitchen sink here. Although the coverage is superb, the organization is a bit awkward. The government sites are included in a long alphabetical list that does not have search capability, so you have to scroll to find what you want. Some of the topics also may be hard to find due to the fact that they are alphabetized by name of site instead of subject matter. The congressional site that lists all e-mail addresses and other contact information for members of Congress is listed under "Contacting the Congress," for example, instead of "Congressional Contact Information." But despite this minor drawback, this is a site well worth visiting.

If you are looking for world government information, you will find a smattering of sites on this page—big things like the European Union's home page—but for a deeper look at world governments, follow the link for "International," which is found at the top of this page. You may also want to check the pages for "Law," "Politics," or "Statistics," all of which have hyperlinks at the top of this government page.

Commercial Sites

Education World: Social Sciences: Civics
http://www.education-world.com/soc_sci/civics/index.shtml

Education World's internal search engine is for educational Web sites only, which allows you to find trustworthy information without searching the entire World Wide Web. It is a great place for students conducting research for a classroom assignment and for teachers who want to find lesson plans and research materials.

At this particular page, you will get a number of Web site links with complete reviews so that you can decide which sites will be helpful without actually taking the time to go to every site. Teachers will also appreciate the links to lesson plans, standards, and other education resources.

Politics.com
http://www.politics.com/

This lively site offers a great source of information on current issues and political news. (As you might expect, it gets especially lively during presidential campaign years.) The site's "News" section features items such as "Today on the Hill," "House and Senate Roll-Call Votes," and "Off the Wire," a top-notch collection of news headlines from the wires and online papers.

You'll also find a "Directory" section with links to every political Web site you could fathom, which can be a wonderful resource for election information, info on people and organizations, facts and figures, and news/opinions/perspectives. While *Politics.com* offers an evenhanded look at the world of politics, it's not shy about provoking debate. There are sections devoted to editorials, discussions, polls, rants, and even gossip.

The History Channel
http://www.historychannel.com/

Created by A&E Television Networks, the *History Channel* Web site offers a number of resources to aid in your study of government and civics. The site is undeniably commercial, with columns and banners devoted to selling stuff and promoting the History Channel television network. However, it's possible to ignore the promotional clutter and tap into the excellent reference and educational material.

Click on the "Classroom" section to find study guides and teacher manuals on topics such as the American presidency, the Founding Fathers, secrets of the Oval Office, and a lot more. You can also utilize the *History Channel* Web site's search engine for particular keywords. A search, for example, for "federalist papers" turned up several strong essays and encyclopedia entries on the subject, as well as a handful of biographical items on Alexander Hamilton, James Madison, and other key figures.

GovSpot
http://www.govspot.com/

Don't be fooled by the name. *GovSpot* is a *commercial* site that points you in the direction of useful government sites. It's a terrific reference resource for non-partisan government information. Designed to simplify the search for government information online, *GovSpot* offers a collection of government and civic resources hand-selected by an editorial team for quality, content, and utility. (*GovSpot*, by the way, is kin to another frequently recommended homework site, *LibrarySpot.com*.)

Use the main sections—"Government," "News," "Social Services," "Politics," etc.—to find useful factual info, government offices, reports, and statistics. In fact, the "Government Online" section could be called a site unto itself, providing subsections on the executive, judicial, and legislative branches, as well as local, state, and world government. If the subsections let you down, there's also an internal search engine to help you conduct a pinpoint search for info.

Social Studies for Kids: World Governments
http://www.socialstudiesforkids.com/subjects/foreigngovernment.htm

Looking for information on the law, elections, or governing bodies of foreign countries? This kid-friendly site contains all that and more. You will find "No. 10 Downing Street," the Internet home of Britain's prime minister, a site devoted to "Laws of Foreign Countries," and "Visions of China," a CNN special report on China and communism, for example.

If your research takes you beyond the boundaries of what's located at this page, use the menu at the left to connect to pages on "Government–U.S.," "Wars–World," "U.S. Presidents," and other government-related topics.

Government Sites

No doubt about it, government sites provide some of the best information about government and civics that's available on the Web. No matter what particular topic you're researching, you'll want to bolster opinions and theories with good old reliable statistics and facts, which the government generates in abundance. Government sites are almost uniformly well designed, easy to navigate, and have good search tools.

Ben's Guide to U.S. Government for Kids
http://bensguide.gpo.gov/
middle school and up

Sponsored by the U.S. Government Printing Office, this site includes myriad resources for students, teachers, and parents on how the government works. Choose the appropriate grade level (6–8 or 9–12) and you will find games, activities, and age-appropriate information on all kinds of nuts-and-bolts topics about the government and the resources available through the Government Printing Office. There's also a map of the United States, where you can pick a state to study and learn quick facts about its government.

A glossary and a links page for locating other good U.S. government Web sites rounds out the offerings here.

The Constitution of the United States
http://www.nara.gov/exhall/charters/constitution/conmain.html
middle school and up

This Web site, which is part of the National Archives and Records Administration's vast holdings, is a great place to start your research on the Bill of Rights. Although it doesn't go into a lot of detail, it explains the Bill of Rights in the context of how the Constitution was created. You will find biographies of all the major players involved, the story of the Bill of Rights, and a digital version of the original copy of the Bill of Rights.

The best way to dive into this subject matter is to check out this Web site's long (but easy-to-read) essay, "A More Perfect Union" (you will see the link from the home page), which is an in-depth look at the ratification process of the Constitution. There is a section on the Bill of Rights and the role that these first amendments played in getting enough delegates to accept the Constitution. This essay will introduce you to the important figures related to the Bill of Rights—James Madison, George Mason, Thomas Jefferson, and Patrick Henry—and also to the major themes underlying these first ten amendments to the Constitution.

At the bottom of "A More Perfect Union" (and also at the bottom of the home page), you will see a link, "Bill of Rights," that will allow you to access more specific information. You will find another short essay, as well as links that enable you to read the full text of the Bill of Rights (click on "Amendments 1–10") and to view the original document. Click on "Virginia Declaration of Rights" to learn more about this precursor to the Bill of Rights, which Mason wrote for the Virginia Constitutional Convention in 1776 and which served as a model for Madison when he drafted the Bill of Rights.

FirstGov
http://www.firstgov.gov/

Intended to be your first resource for finding any government information on the Internet, FirstGov topics include online services for citizens, businesses, and governments, everything from "Passport Applications" to "Business Laws and Regulations" to "Federal Personnel and Payroll Changes." If you don't see a topic you need in one of the three main columns, try the drop-down menu of topics at the left.

If you are searching for information from a specific government agency, you can search by going to that agency first. Use the menu at the top left of the page. Under "Agencies," click on "Federal," "State, Local, and Tribal," or "International."

The site is a bit daunting when you first arrive at the home page—there's just so much information packed onto one page. But don't despair: it's actually really well organized and easy to navigate.

THOMAS: Legislative Information on the Internet
http://thomas.loc.gov/

The *THOMAS* Web site was launched by a Library of Congress team in 1995 in an effort to make federal legislative information freely available to the Internet public. It has met and surpassed that goal and is now the largest disseminator of national legislative information in the world. Considering the wealth of information here, *THOMAS*'s home page has a pleasing-to-the-eye, easy-to-use format. The site offers the following databases: "House Floor This Week," "House Floor Now," "Quick Search of Text Bills," "Bill Summary and Status," "Bill Text," "Public Laws by Law Number," "Votes in the House and Senate," "Congressional Record," and "Committee Information."

In addition to the databases, the *THOMAS* home page provides you with general information on the legislative process ("How Our Laws Are Made"), a summary of congressional activity, a selection of historical documents, and links to House and Senate directories and Web sites of other legislative agencies.

The Constitution Community
http://www.nara.gov/education/cc/main.html

In case you've ever wondered what possible connection the musty old Constitution has to our lives, take a look at this incredible site. As part of the National Archives and Records Administration Digital Classroom project, the Constitution Community Web site offers lessons and activities that address constitutional issues, correlate to national academic standards, and utilize primary source documents.

Arranged according to historical era, there are more than 35 lesson plans that are informative and useful for teachers and students alike. Each lesson plan provides background info, suggested activities, and bibliographies, as well as an examination of the issue's connection to the U.S. Constitution. These extensive lessons span the revolution (1754–1820s) to the contemporary United States (1968–present).

Executive Office of the President (White House)
http://www.whitehouse.gov/

Want to know about the White House, the President, the First Lady, or even the First Pets? Equal parts substance and fluff, this government site offers a wealth of information. In the "News and Policies" section, you can research policies the administration is focusing on, tap into current news and press briefings, and learn about appointments, nominations, and executive orders. Many of the President's addresses and speeches are available here in audio and video format, and you can also access a photo library. There's also a handy section for the latest federal government statistics, including economic indicators and social statistics.

If you need to fill your daily fluff quotient, check out the "History and Tours" and "First Lady" sections for interesting tidbits.

Timeline of U.S. Diplomatic History
http://www.state.gov/www/about_state/history/

This Web site, which is maintained by the U.S. State Department's Office of the Historian, is a good source of information about the history of American foreign policy. Click on the "Timeline of U.S. Diplomatic History" to access the bulk of this useful material. Select the period of history that interests you: "Diplomacy of the American Revolution," "Diplomacy of the New Republic," "Jeffersonian Diplomacy," "Diplomacy and Westward Expansion," "Diplomacy of the Civil War," "Diplomacy and the Rise to Global Power," "Diplomacy of World War I," "Diplomacy of Isolationism," "Diplomacy of World War II," "Diplomacy of the Cold War," "Diplomacy and Détente," or "Diplomacy in a Multipolar World."

Under each of these headings, you will find a concise explanation of the major events that occurred in each period. For instance, in the "Diplomacy of Isolationism" segment, you will learn that the central theme of the era was disarmament efforts. Each entry also contains the key diplomatic policies of the periods and the people who played an important role in developing U.S. foreign policy.

The Web site also contains straightforward history about the State Department, past secretaries of state, the Foreign Service, and the role of women and minorities in the State Department. Click on "Frequently Asked Historical Questions" on the home page to view. In addition, the "Frequently Asked Questions" section includes a list of "Diplomatic and Consular Posts: 1781–1997" and "Department Personnel: 1781–1997."

Academic and Educational Sites

Birth of the Nation: The First Federal Congress (1789–1791)
http://www.gwu.edu/~ffcp/exhibit/

Created by First Federal Congress Project at George Washington University, this online educational exhibit provides a look at the often overlooked First Federal Congress, the group that fleshed out the governmental structure outlined in the Constitution and began addressing the tough issues left unresolved by the Constitution.

The site explores how our government worked at its inception and how it works similarly today. There are fourteen units, each of which open with a section of the Constitution to which the group of documents relate. These units include "First Federal Congress"; "New York City as the Seat of Government"; "Setting Precedent"; "An Imperial Presidency"; "Creation of the Executive"; "Creation of the Judiciary"; "Amendments to the Constitution"; "Establishing a Revenue System"; "Senate and Foreign Affairs"; "Expansion of the Empire"; "Petitioning the Federal Government"; "Locating the United States Capitol"; "Funding the National Debt"; and "The Compromise of 1790." The units are visually supported by historical letters, newspaper articles, cartoons, portraits, and more. With handy supplemental tools such as bibliographies, lesson plans, and vocabulary lists, students and teachers alike will find the site engaging.

Center for Civic Education
http://www.civiced.org/
middle school and up

The Center for Civic Education is a nonprofit, nonpartisan corporation dedicated to fostering the development of responsible participation in civic life by citizens committed to values and principles fundamental to American constitutional democracy. "We the People . . . Project Citizen" is a program in which middle school students work in groups to learn how to monitor and influence public policy. "We the People . . . The Citizen and the Constitution" promotes civic competence and responsibility among elementary and secondary students through a curriculum focused on the U.S. Constitution and Bill of Rights.

CivNet
http://civnet.org/

This is a great teacher resource, but students too will find an array of resources geared specifically to their needs. *CivNet* is the Web site of Civitas International, which is an organization of civic-education practitioners from all around the world.

Students can use the menu at the left to locate resources such as "Great Documents," a collection of links to the world's great historical documents related to politics and civics. You will also find links to a directory of civic-education students and an index of civics-related Web pages.

Internet Crossroads in the Social Sciences
http://dpls.dacc.wisc.edu/internet.html

The Data and Program Library Service (DPLS) offers an arsenal of data collections that are used by social science researchers at the University of Wisconsin-Madison. This portion of it—*Internet Crossroads*—contains more than 650 annotated links to data-related resources. The site is organized into the following four major sections: "U.S. Government," "U.S. Non-Government," "International Government," and "International Non-Government." Within each of these sections, the links are sorted into categories, which include "General," "Economic/Labor," "Education," "Geographic/Historical," "Health," "Political," "Sociological/Demographic."

Although the structure of the site takes a little getting used to, it can be extremely helpful for researching a topic that crosses back and forth between social-science disciplines.

Legal Information Institute
http://www.law.cornell.edu/

This Cornell University site contains sections on "Constitutions and Codes," "Court Opinions," "Law by Source or Jurisdiction," "Directories," "Current Awareness," and several other topics specifically related to Cornell's Law School and the Legal Information Institute's publications. Each of these sections is subdivided into logically titled sections so that it's easy to locate the right part of the site for your specific research.

There's also a spotlight section on the opening page that lists topics of recent interest in the news. This is a great place to search if you are following a current legal debate. Topics are organized by date, moving from most recent to oldest, and you will find just about everything that's been publicly discussed.

National Election Studies
http://www.umich.edu/~nes/

National Election Studies (NES) offers a gem of a Web site for your research into elections, voter participation, and related issues. Funded by the National Science Foundation, one of NES's primary goals is the improved measurement of public opinion and political participation. With such a goal in mind, NES conducts national surveys of the American electorate in presidential and midterm election years. The group's research now encompasses 23 biennial election studies spanning five decades. Data from these studies cover themes such as expectations about the election outcome; social and religious characteristics of the electorate; political involvement and participation; evaluation of congressional candidates; and more.

A major feature of the site for students, journalists, and the general public is "The NES Guide to Public Opinion and Electoral Behavior," which offers summary data on a whole range of issues. For extensive research, you can even download the entire "NES Guide" to your own computer. "The NES Bibliography" is another useful tool; it lists over 3,000 papers, dissertations, books, journal articles, and other such works that have made use of NES data.

Principles of American Democracy (SCORE)
http://score.rims.k12.ca.us/grade12/index.html

You will want to make this site one of your first stops for researching government and civics topics. Its educational resources truly help make concepts about American democracy tangible and exciting. There are seventeen units in all, each offering Web resources and activities appropriate for in-class use and for research purposes. The topics include "Constitutional Concepts"; "Rights of Citizens"; "Responsibilities of Citizens"; "Legislative Branch"; "Constitutional Amendment Process"; "Executive Branch"; "Judicial Branch"; "Supreme Court Cases"; "Campaigns and the Political Process"; "Levels of Government (National, State, Tribal, Local)"; "Media and Politics"; "Fascism, Communism & Authoritarianism"; "Parliamentary Governments"; and "Dilemmas of American Democracy."

SCORE is a part of a network of Online Resource Centers in California linking resources from the Web to the California curriculum. The goodies you'll find here have been selected and evaluated by a team of educators.

Project Vote-Smart
http://www.vote-smart.org/

You might not expect to see the names of Jimmy Carter and Newt Gingrich as founding board members of any organization, but politicians of all beliefs are supporting Project Vote-Smart. It is a volunteer-driven service that provides information on more than 12,000 candidates for public office. You can find voting records, campaign finances, position statements, backgrounds, and the evaluations of candidates by more than one hundred competing special interest groups. You can also track legislation and find your own political representatives.

Public Agenda Online
http://www.publicagenda.org/

Public Agenda is a nonprofit, nonpartisan research and citizen education organization with the mission to help students understand the major issues facing the nation. "Clarifying Issues 2000" is the Internet election guide that presents issues the candidates are debating and helps young people think through how the election could affect them, their families, and their communities.

Social Movements & Culture
http://www.wsu.edu:8001/~amerstu/smc/abolition.html

This wonderful site is a collection of indexes with a separate page (and separate index) for every major social and political movement you can think of. You will find "Abolition/Slavery," the first one on the long list, "American Indian," "Black Nationalism," "Gay/Lesbian/Bi/Queer," "Globalization," "Media Activism," and much more. Each movement's page offers an extensive index to other key sites on the topic. You will also find general resources on each page, with listings of articles, bibliographies, glossaries, conferences, and courses.

The White House Historical Association
http://www.whitehousehistory.org/

This is the home page for the Historical Association of the White House, not the White House itself. If you want to learn White House history, access primary documents, or research White House historical treasures, this is the site to visit. If taking a tour interests you, you'll want to try the White House Web site itself; it offers the best Web technology for the virtual tour.

Interactive and Practical Sites

ConstitutionFacts.com
http://www.constitutionfacts.com/

As the name implies, you'll find plenty of straightforward factual information at *ConstitutionFacts*. For instance, you can view the entire text of the Constitution, the Bill of Rights and the Declaration of Independence here.

But you'll also be able to have a little smarty-pants fun here, especially in the crossword puzzle section. Eight puzzles—ranging from beginner to expert level—allow you to test your knowledge of the Constitution.

American Justice on Trial
http://score.rims.k12.ca.us/activity/internment/index.html

Designed for an intensive class activity, this site provides you with all the tools you need to create a mock trial. In the trial, you're asked to examine the questions of justice involved when the U.S. government set up zones restricting the constitutional rights of Americans of Japanese ancestry during World War II.

This Web site will lead you in this role-playing project by providing historical background, supplemental reading lists, and specific tasks to accomplish.

Biographies

Presidents of the United States
http://www.ipl.org/ref/POTUS/

Chances are that government and civics researchers will at some point need to learn about an American president. This general Web site is the place to get basic information, as well as referrals on where to look to learn more. All you have to do is click on the name of the president you are interested in from the index. You will then get a brief overview of his administration, along with links to Internet biographies.

Truman Presidential Museum and Library
http://www.trumanlibrary.org/

Although there is more here about Truman than anyone else, you will find information on lots of other presidents, political and military figures, and major events in U.S. and world history, too. You will also find excellent online museum exhibits on such topics as "The American Presidency," "Truman's Presidential Years," Truman's Chryslers," "The Declaration of Independence Road Trip," and more.

The "Kids' Page" has puzzles galore, multimedia collections that include cartoons, photos, documents, and speeches, and examples of student research projects, in case you are looking for a little inspiration to get your own project off the ground.

Economic and Social Policy Institute Sites

These economic and social policy institutes—also known as think tanks—conduct research on economic and social policy issues to inform the public and to influence policy decisions. In the list below, we've included a spectrum of economic and social policy institutes; most have a particular political viewpoint, while a few maintain a nonpartisan approach. If you use one of these sites for your research, keep in mind that its contents might very well be biased in one direction.

American Institute for Economic Research
http://www.aier.org/

The American Institute for Economic Research is an independent nonprofit research and educational organization. Its current areas of focus include personal finance, economic fundamentals, individual liberty, and the role of government.

Brookings Institution
http://www.brook.edu/

The Brookings Institution, established in 1916, is one of the nation's oldest think tanks. As a private, independent, nonprofit research organization, it conducts research in economics, governmental studies, and foreign policy and offers executive education for corporate and government managers.

Cato Institute
http://www.cato.org/

The Cato Institute promotes public policy based on the principles of limited government, individual liberty, free markets, and peaceful international relations.

Century Foundation
http://www.tcf.org/

The Century Foundation is a liberal research foundation that conducts critical analyses of major economic, political, and social institutions and issues. Its current areas of focus include economic inequality, the aging of America, and American foreign policy.

Economic Policy Institute
http://epinet.org/

The Economic Policy Institute is a nonprofit, nonpartisan think tank that analyzes and debates issues relating to economics and developing "a prosperous and fair economy."

Heritage Foundation
http://www.heritage.org/

The Heritage Foundation is a conservative think tank that publishes research on domestic, economic, foreign, and defense policy.

Hoover Institution
http://www-hoover.stanford.edu/

The Hoover Institution operates its think tank on the campus of Stanford University. It is dedicated to research in domestic policy and international affairs and to generating ideas that define a free society.

Institute for International Economics
http://www.iie.com/

The Institute for International Economics is a private, nonprofit, nonpartisan research institution devoted to the study of international economic policy. Its agenda emphasizes global macroeconomic topics, international money and finance, trade and related social issues, investment, and the international implications of the new technologies.

National Bureau of Economic Research
http://www.nber.org/

The National Bureau of Economic Research (NBER) is a private, nonprofit, nonpartisan research organization dedicated to promoting a greater understanding of how the economy works. NBER's research material is contributed by professors across the United States.

National Center for Policy Analysis
http://www.ncpa.org/

The National Center of Policy Analysis (NCPA) is a nonprofit, nonpartisan public-policy research organization, working to develop and promote private alternatives to government regulation and control.

RAND Institute
http://www.rand.org/

The RAND Institute conducts research and policy analysis in a broad range of areas, including national defense, education and training, health care, criminal and civil justice, labor and population, science and technology, community development, international relations, and regional studies.

Map Collections

Historical Atlas of the Twentieth Century
http://users.erols.com/mwhite28/20centry.htm

If you want a good general atlas of the twentieth century, turn to this site. It has hundreds of maps, charts, and graphs dealing with historical topics worldwide. The number of American maps is small, but we have included the site because it links to a superb collection of other sites that are very useful for American history and government research. To find the sites, click on "Links" under "Broad Outline" at the left of the home page. Then scroll down to "America" under "Human History organized by Place rather than Time" and click on "United States."

Images of American Political History
http://teachpol.tcnj.edu/amer_pol_hist/_browse_maps.htm

Images of American Political History concentrates on maps illustrating border changes or showing the results of presidential elections. While the territorial-change maps are inclusive, running from 1768 to 1920, the election maps span only from 1796 to 1968. The collection also contains a few demographic maps, but this is not the best site for demographic information.

Map Collections: 1500–1999
http://memory.loc.gov/ammem/grndhtml/gmdhome.html

Map Collections offers a small fraction of the American maps and atlases in the Library of Congress. But "small fraction" is a relative term; the Library's Geography and Map Division holds more than 4.5 million items. There are hundreds of maps available for downloading from this wonderful site. The site is divided into six collections: "Cities and Towns"; "Conservation and Environment"; "Discovery and Exploration"; "Cultural Landscapes"; "Military Battles and Campaigns"; and "Transportation and Railroads." Each collection contains an overview as well as a history of mapping the topic. You can search *Map Collections* by keyword, geographic location, subject, map creator, and title.

Perry-Castañeda Library Map Collection: Historical Maps of the United States
http://www.lib.utexas.edu/maps/histus.html

The University of Texas at Austin has a wonderful online collection of maps that cover American history from pre-Columbian Indian tribes through the twentieth century. Maps on the site are organized under six broad categories: "Early Inhabitants"; "Exploration and Settlement"; "U.S. Territorial Growth"; "Military History Maps"; "Later Historical Maps"; and "Maps of National Historic Parks." The collection is particularly strong on military maps. The site also links to hundreds of maps on other Web sites.

West Point Atlas
http://www.dean.usma.edu/history/dhistorymaps/MapsHome.htm

For United States military maps, this is your source. This online atlas, developed by the history department of the U.S. Military Academy, is based on a series of print atlases that the department created over the years for its course on the history of military art. It includes detailed campaign maps of most of America's wars. *West Point Atlas*, which is still under construction, covers U.S. conflicts from the colonial period through the 1992–1993 Somalia campaign. The site does not include any narrative, so you will have to look elsewhere to put the battles in historical context.

Primary Sources

The American Colonist's Library: A Treasury of Primary Documents
http://personal.pitnet.net/primarysources/

This is an extraordinary site that is a must-visit for anyone interested in colonial government and history. Compiled by Rick Gardiner, a history teacher, it is a comprehensive gateway to colonial American primary documents on the Web. The site states, "if it isn't here, it probably is not available online anywhere," and that's not an idle boast. *Colonist's Library* is massive. But what makes it invaluable is not just the size but the scope of the material. This is not just another "key documents" site where you find important government documents and political literature. Gardiner has linked any document available online that is relevant to the colonists' lives. Thus the user gets a deep understanding of what molded colonial culture and ideals as well as politics.

The Mayflower Compact, the Stamp Act, and the Declaration of Independence are all here, but there's much, much more. You will find links to classical and medieval authors such as Livy and John Calvin who influenced colonial thought, as well as the texts of Jonathan Edwards' sermons, letters of Plymouth settlers, the transcripts of the Salem Witchcraft Trials, and Daniel Boone's journal. It's all here. This is an incredible site!

Archiving Early America
http://earlyamerica.com/

Archiving Early America contains a wealth of primary source material from eighteenth-century America, often displayed in its original format. This site sets itself apart from other primary document collections by emphasizing newspapers, maps, magazines, writings, and art, rather than just government documents. The documents are here, but you will also find contemporary reactions to important events. The site is a little frustrating to use. You get to the material either through "The World of Early America," a topical index with very broad and sometimes meaningless categories, or through the search feature, which often generates numerous duplicates. But be patient. You will find primary material here that you can't find in most other document sites.

Avalon Project at the Yale Law School
http://www.yale.edu/lawweb/avalon/avalon.htm

The *Avalon Project* features documents from around the world in politics, diplomacy, government, history, economics, and law. Although the site is international, it has an extensive collection of U.S. documents including colonial charters, Madison's notes on the Constitutional Convention, treaties between the U.S. and other nations as well as between the U.S. government and Native American tribes, and annual messages from the President. There is also a collection of documents related to the Sept. 11, 2001, attack on the United States. You can access the material by time period, keyword, or collection. If you don't know the formal name of the document you want, the easiest way to get to the American material is by clicking on "Major Collections" or by going through the "Chronology of American History" found under each time period. The chronology lists the U.S. documents in date order.

Chronology of the United States Historical Documents
http://hamilton.law.ou.edu/hist/

This collection, compiled at the University of Oklahoma, contains hundreds of primary documents from the founding of the colonies to the twenty-first century. It is particularly strong on inaugural speeches and presidential declarations, as well as key legislation. It also contains some poetry and songs such as "Yankee Doodle" and Ralph Waldo Emerson's "Concord Hymn." There are some downsides to this site. It has no search function; you have to scroll down the list of chronologically arranged documents. In addition, some of the links to documents in the late twentieth century are not live.

Civics Online
http://civics-online.org/

A joint effort between secondary school teachers and the faculty of Michigan State University, this Web site provides a digitized collection of government documents that can be helpful to students in their research. You will find such primary source material as treaties, inaugural addresses, photos, maps, paintings, court decisions, and more. A timeline, glossary, and a section called "Civic Explorations" also provide great resources for kids. Teachers and parents will find sections designed specifically for their needs as well.

Core Documents of U.S. Democracy
http://www.access.gpo.gov/su_docs/locators/coredocs/index.html

Want the Gettysburg Address, the Bill of Rights, Abraham Lincoln's papers, Supreme Court decisions from any year, or the *Statistical Abstract of the United States*, for example?

This site, maintained by the Government Printing Office, is the first place to look for important government documents. The focus is on legal and legislative material, but you will also find regulatory and some presidential items as well. Although the site takes you to eighteenth- and nineteenth-century documents such as the *Federalist Papers* and congressional debates, the emphasis is on the twentieth century. Here you can be connected to Supreme Court decisions from 1937 to the present and public laws from 1996 to 2001. You can also research presidential proclamations and executive orders from 1945 to 1989.

History and Politics Out Loud
http://www.hpol.org/

This is a searchable archive of politically significant audio material—campaign speeches, Nixon Watergate recordings, sermons, inaugural addresses, and much more. The archive is searchable by date, by speaker, or by title of the material, so it's fairly easy to locate what you are looking for if indeed you are looking for something specific. If not, just use the "Browse" function and check out the fascinating material here.

National Archives and Records Administration (NARA)
http://www.nara.gov/

NARA is an independent federal agency that oversees the management of *all* federal documents. Although NARA has made only a fraction of its archives available online, you will still find an immense amount of information—all in the form of original documents.

One way to locate documents is to enter into NARA's virtual "Exhibit Hall" (just click on the heading in the toolbar at the top of the home page). You can then browse NARA's considerable holdings. If you are curious about early American government, select "The Charters of Freedom" exhibit, where you can view digital versions of the original Declaration of Independence, Constitution, Bill of Rights, and Magna Carta. The "American Originals" and "American Originals II" exhibits contain some of the most famous documents in U.S. history. Peruse the Louisiana Purchase or view the police blotter that describes President Lincoln's assassination. You can read the soon-to-be-broken treaty of 1868 that recognized the Black Hills as part of the Great Sioux Reservation. Another great exhibit for government students is "The Treasures of Congress," where you can examine documents and photographs that are related to the many issues that have played out in Congress over the course of the nation's history.

For a more focused document search, select the "Search" heading from the home page toolbar. Then simply type in the keywords that relate to your topic. Expect to find loads of documents about well-known historical figures or events. For instance, a search for "Franklin Roosevelt" yielded an audio recording of his speech after the bombing of Pearl

Harbor, telegrams he sent to Navy commanders, letters written to ambassadors, and more. Less-renowned figures, however, will yield fewer results. A search for "Chief Joseph," for example, brought up nothing.

Teachers and students will both enjoy NARA's "Digital Classroom," which can be accessed from the home page. "Primary Sources and Activities" presents educators and students with thematic lesson plans that use specific documents (links to these documents are included).

Also of interest here are the links to related sites, including sites with declassified satellite imagery from the U.S. Geological Survey and records from the National Archives and Records Administration.

Nineteenth Century Documents Project
http://www.furman.edu/~benson/docs/

This gateway leads you to an extensive collection of primary sources that concentrates on speeches, editorials, and political documents important for understanding sectional conflict and evolving regional identity from the 1830s through Reconstruction. Among the wealth of material you will find abolitionist Angelina Grimké's "Appeal to the Christian Women of the South," statistics on slaves and slave families, maps of the 1856 presidential election, the 1860 Republican Party platform, and South Carolina's declaration of secession.

Nineteenth Century Documents Project is a very basic site. Documents are organized chronologically under general heads: "Early National Politics," "Slavery and Sectionalism," "1850s Statistical Almanac," "The Election of 1860," "War Begins," and "Post-Civil War Documents." The site does not contain a search function, but you can use your browser's "Find" function to locate what you want.

Nineteenth Century Documents Project also has a great list of links to related sites. To reach them, just go to the bottom of the page and click on "Lloyd Benson's Past Connections." (Benson is the professor of history at Furman University that compiled the site.)

Speeches
http://www.historychannel.com/speeches/index.html

Here's a great place to hear some of the most important broadcasts and recordings in twentieth-century history. Although the site is international, the emphasis is on American history. You can hear Martin Luther King's "I Have a Dream" speech or listen to Amelia Earhart discuss the future of women in flying. From the home page you can access the speeches through the search function at the left or by browsing the categories: "Politics & Government"; "Science & Technology"; "Arts, Entertainment & Culture"; and "War & Diplomacy." Don't try to access material through "Speech Archives." You will get a message asking you to use the search function.

United States Historical Census Data
http://fisher.lib.virginia.edu/census/

This site provides demographic and economic data for states and counties from 1790 to 1960. Each census can be searched by a number of variables depending on how the particular census was collected and organized. The site also contains a history of the census.

2

⟨∞∞∞⟩

Researching Individual Government and Civics Topics on the Internet

Researching a specific topic on the Internet can be overwhelming. Type a topic such as "affirmative action" into a search engine, and you will pull up hundreds—if not thousands—of Web pages, some of which are only remotely connected to your subject.

This section of the book is designed to help you over this major hurdle to online research. In it, you will find a list of about 150 topics in Government and Civics, such as "abolition," "caste system," and "civil disobedience." For each of these topics, you will see a key term, or several key terms, listed that will make searching the Internet a little easier. For example, under "civil disobedience," you will learn that it might be helpful to search under "Thoreau" and "Gandhi," as well as under "civil disobedience." The best search engine to use will also be listed.

Below these recommendations on how to search, you will see the names and descriptions of Web sites that best cover the topic. Some of the Web sites give basic overviews, some are multimedia extravaganzas, and some make primary source material available to you. Because each main topic is so broad, some of these Web sites will only look at a particular facet of the topic. Use these tried-and-true sites as a jumping-off point, and then follow the links until your heart's content . . . and your paper topic has come into crystal-clear focus.

ABOLITION

Best Search Engine: http://www.google.com/
Key Search Terms: Abolition
Anti-slavery

Abolition, Anti-Slavery Movements, and the Rise of Sectional Controversy
http://memory.loc.gov/ammem/aaohtml/exhibit/aopart3.html
high school and up

The Web site, part of the Library of Congress's *African American Odyssey*, gives you a good overview of the abolition movement and growing sectionalism in the years before the Civil War. The site is without frills but makes up for its plainness by providing excellent information. It's divided into two parts. Part I offers you information on "Anti-Slavery Activists" and "Popularizing Anti-Slavery Sentiment." Click on the former if you want to learn more about abolitionist groups and their leaders, such as Anthony Benezet and William Lloyd Garrison, or about their philosophy. Click on the latter if you want to see examples of abolitionist literature and songs. Part II discusses the Fugitive Slave Law of 1850, growing sectionalism in the 1850s, and the rise of militant abolition, particularly John Brown's Raid in 1859. It also has a section on Harriet Beecher Stowe's *Uncle Tom's Cabin,* which it calls "The Book that Made this Mighty War."

The site has some limitations. There are no links to people and terms, and it doesn't list what's in Part II when you are in Part I and vice versa. But stick to it and you will find a lot of first-class information here.

Africana.com: Abolitionism in the United States or Antislavery Movement in the United States
http://www.africana.com/Utilities/Content.html?&../cgi-bin/
banner.pl?banner=Blackworld&../Articles/tt_278.htm

The *Africana* site is well organized and easy to navigate. You will find a comprehensive essay on abolitionism in the center of the page and many useful links related to abolitionism and the slave era along the right side. You always have the option to search any key word or browse through the site's categories, such as biographies and archives. This site is a great place to research any information pertaining to the abolitionist movement. In addition to many articles and essays, there is also an interactive "Talk Back" forum, which you can use to ask questions or request more information if you need it.

The abolition article addresses many aspects of the abolitionist movement, including religious opposition to slavery, how slavery related to the revolution, and the various activist groups that existed at the time. Click on the right side if you want to read related encyclopedia articles such as the views of anti-abolitionists and the plight of slaves in colonial Latin America. This site also allows you to e-mail any information to friends with one click, or to send the editor your feedback on the article.

ABORTION RIGHTS

Best Search Engine: http://www.google.com/

Key Search Terms: Abortion rights

Abortion + government

Abortion Law Homepage
http://members.aol.com/abtrbng/index.htm
middle school and up

The *Abortion Law Homepage* was constructed for informational and academic purposes, so it attempts to be as objective as possible by presenting a full spectrum of facts and viewpoints surrounding the abortion issue. The Web site is comprised of fifteen sections focusing on abortion-related topics, such as " 'Partial Birth' Abortion Laws," the ground-breaking Supreme Court decision "Roe v. Wade," "Federal Law," and "Abortion-Related Legal Terms." From this site you can download zipped files containing the full text of selected Court cases like *Griswold v. Connecticut* and *Planned Parenthood v. Casey.* You can also refer to the section on "Canon Law" to learn about its influence on the Roman Catholic Church. Here you can also learn how both sides of the abortion debate make moral inferences from the Canons.

The *Abortion Law Homepage* is useful in that it provides you with a lot of facts and tries to eliminate opinions on the abortion debate. However, it also essentially eliminates any additional media, including images and extra links. So if you are looking for a lot of multimedia to capture your attention, you might want to look elsewhere, but if it's hard facts on abortion and the evolution of its debate in America that you want to study, this is the site to use.

The National Abortion and Reproductive Rights Action League (NARAL)
http://www.naral.org/
high school and up

The National Abortion and Reproductive Rights Action League (NARAL) is an organization dedicated to maintaining women's rights to legal abortions. NARAL's Web site is clearly based on a pro-choice perspective. The site is full of useful information and is very clear and easy to use. You can research the evolution of NARAL and the pro-choice movement in America. You can click on "Reproductive Rights Issues" to get an overview of today's most controversial reproductive topics, or on "Links and Resources" for a full list of groups and action networks involved in the debate. You can also refer to various legal cases that have shaped the way America looks at women's reproductive rights. NARAL provides an updated list of current legal and political headlines along the right side of the page. If you want to find out about current legislation in your state or about getting involved on a local level, all you have to do is click on the name of a state for a list of upcoming events, state laws, and a NARAL state rating, indicating how much your state upholds or restricts women's access to reproductive health services.

NARAL also gives you many ways to become involved in the pro-choice cause and a link to various pregnancy help lines.

ACT OF SETTLEMENT (1701)

Best Search Engine: http://www.ixquick.com/
Key Search Terms: Affirmative action

Monarchist.org
http://www.monarchist.org.au/ACTSETTLE.htm
middle school and up

This Web site is a one-stop shopper's guide to the Act of Settlement. Here you can gain an extensive understanding about the Act, how it affected not only the English citizens, but also those of Australia, Scotland, Ireland, and Wales. This site lays out a detailed time line of events that led up to the passing of the Act of Settlement, going back as far as the twelfth century. It includes a crucial discussion of the political climate outside England and explains how it contributed to England's fight for religious sovereignty. You will learn about every important person involved in the struggle, and about many interesting details, like one important stipulation that no heir to the throne could be involved with, or married to someone involved with, the Roman Catholic Church.

This site is comprehensive, and due to an absence of images, links, etc., it may seem a bit boring. But if you want the whole story behind the Act of Settlement and specifics pertaining to the Act, this is the best site to visit.

University of Houston, College of Liberal Arts and Social Sciences
http://www.hfac.uh.edu/gbrown/philosophers/leibniz/BritannicaPages/
   SettlementAct/SettlementAct.html
high school and up

This site, constructed by the University of Houston's School of Liberal Arts, will give you an overview of what the Act of Settlement is, when and where it was passed, and what information it contains. It is very straightforward and contains only one image, which takes you to the actual Act of Settlement text. Although somewhat brief and simple, this site is a way to gain an initial understanding about the history and the regulation of the British throne, including important details like constitutional provisions to which the British monarchy still adheres today. You can also click on any highlighted name to get more information on certain historical figures who played a role in the Act of Settlement.

ACTIVISM

Best Search Engine: http://www.google.com/
Key Search Terms: Activism
                     Political activism

Political Activism Resources
http://www.kimsoft.com/kimpol.htm
middle school

This site is a nonpartisan index of material related to political activism. There are sections of links devoted to the following topics: "Current Issues/Hot Links," "Politics–USA," "United Nations–World Politics," "Environmental Issues," "Human Rights," "Labor Movements," "National Liberation Movements," "Political Parties–Ideologies," and "Political Action Groups." Under each of these headings you will find numerous links to sites that deal specifically with these topics. If your research topic falls under any of these headings, you will want to check out the sites collected here to see if any of them offer what you need.

Radical Times: The Antiwar Movement of the 1960s
http://library.thinkquest.org/27942/indexf.htm

This *Thinkquest* site (created by a team of high school students) does a superb job of exploring different aspects of the antiwar movement and its effect on society and politics. If you are researching the political unrest during the antiwar movement or the effects of the movement on society, for example, this site is a must-see.

You can explore background information on the war, the countercul-ture that sprang up in opposition to the war, the violence associated with some of the activism, and the general campus unrest of the time.

Use the "Perspectives" section of the site to form your own opinions after reading the essays of some people involved in the antiwar move-ment. Access video clips, photographs, and other resources in the "Multimedia Room."

AFFIRMATIVE ACTION

Best Search Engine: http://www.google.com/
Key Search Terms: Affirmative action

Affirmative Action and Diversity Page
http://aad.english.ucsb.edu/
middle school and up

The *Affirmative Action and Diversity* Web site offers a diversity of opin-ions regarding the affirmative-action debate. This will allow you to learn about many different topics surrounding affirmative action without feel-ing pulled one way or the other. Go to the site map to see how the site's pages are categorized. You can click on the "Culture and Af-firmative Action" page to see a list of relevant sub-pages, such as "Extending Beyond Afro-American Experience" or "European and Non-European Cultures." Click on "News and Campaigns" to learn about an important initiative in California that would ban racial classification of students and state employees. Or click on "Changing Definitions of Dis-crimination" to study how our nation's perception of racial diversity has evolved over the years and how it relates to the affirmative-action issue.

This Web site is packed with important information. It will be helpful for you if you want an in-depth analysis of affirmative action. But try not to get bogged down, as the language may seem at times to be rather advanced. As long as you pinpoint which affirmative-action topic you are interested in, this site will definitely provide you with some helpful viewpoints.

ALIEN AND SEDITION ACTS

Best Search Engine: http://www.google.com/
Key Search Terms: Alien and sedition acts

Virginia and Kentucky Resolutions

Sedition Act of 1798
http://www.studyworld.com/sedition_act_of_1798.htm
middle school and up

Think of this no-frills Web site as your first research stop. It doesn't have pictures, links to primary sources, multimedia exhibits, or interactive features. But what it does have is a thorough and tidy description of the Sedition Act of 1798, the events that led up to its passage, and the Act's consequences. *Sedition Act of 1798* hits on all the related topics—Federalism, the Alien Acts, and the Virginia and Kentucky Resolutions. So while you might miss having some bells and whistles on this site, you will appreciate its careful and understandable examination of the Sedition Act. It's also a no-brainer to navigate. Just scroll down the screen.

Virginia Report of 1799–1800, Touching on the Alien and Sedition Laws,
    Together with the Virginia Resolutions of December 21, 1798
http://www.constitution.org/rf/vr.htm
high school and up

This Web site is probably the most comprehensive one about the Alien and Sedition Acts that you could possibly find. It has full text versions of all three Alien Acts, the Sedition Act, the Virginia Resolution, and the Kentucky Resolution. It also contains the transcripts of the debates held in the Virginia House of Delegates in 1798 regarding the Virginia Resolution, the full text of the Virginia Report of 1799, James Madison's commentary on the Virginia Report of 1799, and letters Madison wrote about it.

How are all these documents related? The "Introduction" by Jon Roland explains. Roland links these documents to the feud between the Federalists and the anti-Federalists, a disagreement that colored the creation of the Constitution and jeopardized the early unity of the nation. To access the "Introduction" scroll down the home page until you see the table of contents. It's the first item in the index.

This site also contains explanatory information written by J. W. Randolph, who published the Virginia Report in 1850. Randolph's "Preface" goes over the history behind all these documents, as does his "Analysis." You will find both the "Preface" and the "Analysis" in the table of contents on the home page.

Like the *Sedition Act of 1798* site, this one could use some sprucing up. There are no visual materials whatsoever. It's tough to criticize a site that is so helpful, though. Also keep in mind that the *Virginia Report of 1799–1800* is probably too advanced for younger students. They can get a simpler version of the events in the *Sedition Act of 1798*.

AMERICAN REVOLUTION

Best Search Engine: http://www.google.com/
Key Search Terms: American Revolution

Diplomacy of the American Revolution
http://www.state.gov/www/about_state/history/time1.html
middle school and up

This Web page, put up by the U.S. State Department, focuses on one important aspect of the American Revolution—the diplomacy. The site is organized into seven categories, five of which deal with the earliest American diplomats. Click on the topic that interests you to read a short essay.

You can explore Benjamin Franklin's attempts to gain French support for the colonial uprising, or John Jay's work in Madrid to get Spain to officially recognize the United States. The other categories include "John Adams in Holland," "Francis Dana in Russia," "Robert Livingston," "French Assistance to the American Cause," and the "Treaty of Paris." At the bottom of the page, you can connect to the "Timeline of Diplomatic History" home page, which has summaries of U.S. diplomatic policy in other eras. Click here if you want to read about the "Diplomacy of the New Republic (1784–1800)."

What is great about this Web site is that it addresses a specific—and often overlooked—element of the American Revolution. However, the entries are brief, and might require that you look for additional information elsewhere.

Liberty! The American Revolution
http://www.pbs.org/ktca/liberty/
middle school and up

This companion site to the PBS series *Liberty!* is a great starting point for anyone researching the Revolutionary Era, the period between the end of the French and Indian War in 1763 and the adoption of the Bill of Rights in 1791.

To get a good overview of the period just go to "Chronicle of the Revolution." This takes you to a menu of six key dates around which the site has organized the historical narrative. Clicking on "April 1774," for example, takes you to the section on the roots of the conflict, where you learn about the causes of the Revolution. Clicking on "Philadelphia, 1791" leads you to a discussion of the battle for the ratification of the Constitution and the adoption of the Bill of Rights.

One of the great features of this site is the links to related topics that enable you to expand your research in key areas. From "April 1774," for example, you can click on "Native Americans" to learn about their role in the Revolution or "Diversity" to get an overview of the ethnic makeup of the colonies. From "Chronicles of the Revolution" you can also access a simple time line. This will help you with the chronology of the period, but it does not contain all the key events mentioned in the text, so you will have to use the six key dates to get a good overview of the period. The site also contains a bibliography as well as a great list of links to other Internet resources.

The Revolutionary War: A Journey Towards Freedom
http://library.thinkquest.org/10966/
middle school and up

If you need quick information on the Revolutionary era, you can try this site, which includes primary documents, biographical sketches, and essays on major Revolutionary battles.

To navigate *A Journey Towards Freedom*, use the menu on the left side of the home page. Click on "Infopedia" to access historical material. You will see links there to "Major Battles," "Historical Documents Collection," and "Historical Figures Collection."

The site has a couple of other neat features as well. If you have questions or comments, you might want to explore the site's online bulletin board. Click on "Forum" from the main menu to reach it. Younger students will appreciate the interactive features of the site's games. Go to the "Fun Zone" from the main menu. If you play "The Flames of Rebellion," you can command the colonial or British forces in this strategy and war game. The "British Are Coming" game is directly related to the Battle of Lexington and Concord. You have to guide Paul Revere on his famous ride to Lexington and Concord; if you don't answer questions correctly, the British will beat him to it.

This is not a comprehensive site, but it is easy to navigate and includes the basics. For more in-depth information you will have to look elsewhere.

The War for American Independence
http://home.ptd.net/~revwar/index.html
middle school and up

This Web site is the best place on the Internet to find primary source material related to the American Revolution. If you are interested in reading newspaper accounts of battles, speeches delivered by an anonymous soldier, or touring a "virtual museum" of Revolutionary War artifacts, then set aside some time to tour this excellent Web site. All links to documents are from the home page. Just click on a heading and you will be transported back in time! You can read an advertisement from a 1778 newspaper that offers a reward for the capture of deserters. Click on the "Connecticut Gazette" to read the first published account of a battle (1781). You can access a letter written by a soldier, the text of speeches given by George Washington, and a biography of one of Washington's most trusted commanders. Click on "Virtual Museum" and you can browse through a collection of artifacts, such as a receipt for bounty money, an example of colonial currency, and a receipt for transporting the baggage of the French army. This is a terrific Web site, especially for those of you looking for firsthand accounts of the war, but do keep in mind that it only provides primary sources. You won't find descriptions or analysis of events like you will on the other Web sites.

AMERICANS WITH DISABILITIES ACT

Best Search Engine: http://www.google.com/
Key Search Terms: Americans with Disabilities Act
                        Civil rights

Job Accommodation Network: Americans with Disabilities Act Hot Links
http://www.jan.wvu.edu/links/adalinks.htm
high school and up

The Job Accommodation Network (JAN) is a service of the Office of Disability Employment Policy (ODEP) of the U.S. Department of Labor. JAN's mission is to facilitate the employment and retention of people with disabilities in America. Their Web site includes a very comprehensive section on the Americans with Disabilities Act, which is, by far, the best source of information pertaining to the ADA you will find. The page is divided into five sections: "ADA Law," "Building Accessibility Guidelines," "ADA Technical Assistance Manuals," "Other ADA Materials," and "ADA Enforcement." Each of these subsections contains separate lists of topics you will want to peruse. For example, under "Other ADA Materials," you can click on "Supreme Court Rulings" to study up on important legal cases related to the ADA. Or click on "Guide for Small Businesses" to learn how business owners adhere to ADA laws in America. You can even go to "Commonly Asked Questions About Service Animals" to find out what an employee should do when a disabled person with a service dog comes into his or her establishment. This site's material seems limitless, offering information on virtually everything related to the ADA. It is strictly textual, though, which means you may need to take your time studying it, but if you want the online authority on the ADA, this is the site to visit.

National Museum of American History: The Disabilities Rights Movement
http://www.americanhistory.si.edu/disabilityrights/index.html
middle school and up

The Smithsonian Institution created this Web site as a kind of online museum exhibit. You move through the site as though you were actually walking through a museum. Each image displayed here is accompanied by a summary explaining its relevance, while many images have additional video or audio material for you to preview. The site is divided into twelve sections, which you can access by clicking on any of the blue buttons. Go to *ADA* to learn how the Act, passed in 1990, has led to a more general awareness of people with disabilities, resulting in improved physical environments and better access to communications. You can then click on the *ADA* to view its actual contents, or click on the audio button to hear some excerpts from when the Act was passed and signed by former president George Bush.

The best part about this Web site is the way it combines all forms of media in an effort to create a virtual museum online. Exploration of the site is fully engaging, which makes learning about the Americans with Disabilities Act easy and fun. The downside to the site is that it is not very in-depth. Because it is meant to be a virtual exhibit, most of the summaries are quite short in length, making it difficult to dig deeply into the subject.

AMICUS CURIAE

Best Search Engine: http://www.ixquick.com/
Key Search Terms: Amicus curiae

Tech Law Journal
http://www.techlawjournal.com/glossary/legal/amicus.htm
middle school and up

The *Tech Law Journal* site provides you with definitions of technical terms concerning the regulation and legislation of the Internet. As a result, you can use this site to help simplify and explain some difficult legal terminology, such as *amicus curiae*, a Latin term meaning "friend of the court." In addition to a solid definition of *amicus curiae*, this site also gives you an outline of the process involved in filing an *amicus curiae*, including information about the stipulations involved in filing this legal brief. This rather technical and uncommon legal process is difficult to define in general terms, but the *Tech Law Journal* site does a pretty good job of it. You will walk away with the main idea, but don't expect much more from this site.

ANTI-FEDERALISTS

Best Search Engine: http://www.google.com/
Key Search Terms: Anti-Federalist

                                     Federalist

                                     U.S. Constitution

Constitutional Topic: The Federalists and the Anti-Federalists
http://www.usconstitution.net/consttop_faf.html
middle school and up

The *US Constitution* site includes a "Constitutional Topics" page, which breaks down and explains various subjects that the average American often finds perplexing, such as the historical battle between the Federalists and the Anti-Federalists. How did the two groups come about? What events precipitated their establishments? If you want an answer to theses types of questions concerning the Federalists and Anti-Federalists, this is the site to use. It presents a clear time line of events surrounding the ratification of the Constitution, as well as the major philosophical sticking points between the proponents of the Constitution and the opponents, also known as the Anti-Federalists.

Index to the Anti-Federalist Papers
http://www.wepin.com/articles/afp/

In 1778 the states debated the merits of the proposed Constitution. Those who supported the Constitution defended it in *The Federalist Papers*, which became a classic of American political thought. Those who opposed ratification also presented their position in papers, leaflets, and discussions in the Continental Congress. Because their arguments never appeared in one body of work, it's hard to find a good collection of Anti-Federalist thought. If you are studying these views, go to this simple site. Here you will find almost ninety documents that present Anti-Federalist concerns on issues such as states' rights, direct elections, suffrage, and slavery.

The *Index to the Anti-Federalist Papers* site is very simple and easy to use. Documents are organized chronologically. Just click on the title of the document you want to read.

ARTICLES OF CONFEDERATION

Best Search Engine: http://www.google.com/

Key Search Terms: Articles of Confederation

Ben's Guide: The Articles of Confederation
http://www.bensguide.gpo.gov/6-8/documents/articles/
middle school and up

The difference between the *Ben's Guide* Web site and others pertaining to the Articles of Confederation is that this site offers some simple analysis. In addition to being able to access and study the actual articles, you will get an idea of what our forefathers experienced during its creation. This site breaks down the main points addressed by the Articles of Confederation, which were the apportionment of taxes according to the population, the granting of one vote per state, and the right of the federal government to dispose of public lands in the West. It also discusses the challenges that were faced while trying to govern according to the document. If you want to be able to put the Articles of Confederation into perspective and understand its relevance at the time it was written, this is the site to read.

The U.S. Constitution Online
http://www.usconstitution.net/articles.html
high school and up

Use this Web site to learn about the Articles of Confederation, the basis of U.S. central government prior to the Constitution, and the important role this document played in American history. You can start by clicking on a "Constitutional Topics Page," which leads you to an essay giving you historical background on the Articles and summarizing each of the document's provisions. Here you will get a mental picture of what it was like to live in America at a time when its government policies were still being defined and refined. You will see how America's government was run according to the Articles of Confederation, how people determined what was wrong with the Articles, and what was done to resolve these issues. You can then go back to the home page to read the entire text of the Articles. Finally you can compare the Articles of Confederation with the Constitution by clicking on "Comparison of the Articles and the Constitution" at the top of the home page. This site is virtually all text and not very exciting to look at, but it's a great resource for exploring how the Constitution came about.

BILL OF RIGHTS

Best Search Engine: http://scout.cs.wisc.edu
Key Search Terms: Bill of Rights

The Bill of Rights: A Brief History
http://www.aclu.org/library/pbp9.html
middle school and up

This informative Web site, which is part of the American Civil Liberties Union's (ACLU) site, contains an essay written by the scholar Ira Glasser that provides basic information about the Bill of Rights. The site also gives some background information on the Bill of Rights and why it was so important to getting the Constitution accepted (although the explanation is not as complete as the one you will find at *The Constitution of the United States*). The real strength of this Web site is that it makes the Bill of Rights come alive! What you will get is an understanding of the fact that the Bill of Rights is a *living* document that is recreated and reinterpreted in American courts every day. As this site makes clear, the Bill of Rights isn't just about James Madison and George Mason arguing over long-since-outdated issues. *The Bill of Rights: A Brief History* explains how the document impacts you and everyone around you. You will also learn about the people who were *left out* of the Bill of Rights—women, Native Americans, and African Americans—and how the struggle to apply the Bill of Rights to *all* Americans has been hard fought and even harder won.

In addition to the informative main essay, this site provides opportunities for you to get more information. For those of you who want to see just *how* the Bill of Rights is still being fought over, go to the ACLU's home page (you will see the link at the very bottom of *The Bill of Rights: A Brief History*). From here, select issues from the Bill of Rights that interest you, say religious liberty or freedom of speech, and then read about current cases and legislation that impact these constitutional rights. If you want to learn more about the freedoms protected by the Bill of Rights, click on the links you will find under *The Bill of Rights: A Brief History*'s "Certain Unalienable Rights" section. You can read "ACLU Briefing Papers" on the freedom of religion, press, speech, petition, assembly, as well as on equality before the law.

The Constitution of the United States
http://www.nara.gov/exhall/charters/constitution/conmain.html
middle school and up

This Web site, which is part of the National Archives and Records Administration's vast holdings, is a great place to start your research on the Bill of Rights. Although it doesn't go into a lot of detail, it explains the Bill of Rights in the context of how the Constitution was created. You will find biographies of all the major players involved, the story of the Bill of Rights, and a digital version of the original copy of the Bill of Rights.

The best way to dive into this subject matter is to check out this Web site's long (but easy-to-read) essay, "A More Perfect Union" (you will see the link from the home page), which is an in-depth look at the ratification process of the Constitution. There is a section on the Bill of Rights and the role that these first amendments played in getting enough delegates to accept the Constitution. This essay will introduce you to the important figures related to the Bill of Rights—James Madison, George Mason, Thomas Jefferson, and Patrick Henry—and also to the major themes underlying these first ten amendments to the Constitution.

At the bottom of *A More Perfect Union* (and also at the bottom of the home page), you will see a link, "Bill of Rights," that will allow you to access more specific information. You will find another short essay, as well as links that enable you to read the full text of the Bill of Rights (click on "Amendments 1–10") and to view the original document. Click on "Virginia Declaration of Rights" to learn more about this precursor to the Bill of Rights, which Mason wrote for the Virginia Constitutional Convention in 1776 and which served as a model for Madison when he drafted the Bill of Rights.

Documentary History of the Bill of Rights
http://www.constitution.org/dhbr.htm
middle school and up

If you are searching for primary source material about the Bill of Rights, this is your Web site. It explains the history of the Bill of Rights through documents. Beginning with the "English Bill of Rights," you can chart the development of the ideas that were eventually incorporated in the Bill of Rights. Reading the documents that influenced men like James Madison and George Mason gives you a unique historical perspective on the Bill of Rights. You will also find the text of the "Virginia Bill of Rights," which served as an example for Madison when he drafted the Bill of Rights. This Web site will also allow you to track conflicts that took place in incorporating the Bill of Rights. You can read amendments proposed by various states' ratifying commissions, as well as a letter written by Madison to Thomas Jefferson.

BLACK CODES

Best Search Engine: http://www.lii.org/

Key Search Terms: Black codes

Black Codes and Jim Crow Laws
http://afroamhistory.about.com/library/weekly/aa121900a.htm
middle school and up

Black codes were laws passed by certain southern states after the Civil War with the intention of limiting the real freedoms of the freed African Americans. Former slave owners in the South strongly resisted the idea that newly emancipated African Americans were now entitled to the same freedoms that they took for granted. Black codes were designed to further inhibit these freedoms.

The African-American history Web site offers an explanation of southern black codes and their historical significance. You can get specific information about the codes, such as what was officially permitted and what was discouraged. For example, did you know that blacks were often prohibited from entering towns without permission? In Opelousas, Louisiana, blacks needed a note from their employer to travel from town to town or risk imprisonment. The *Black Codes and Jim Crow Laws* site, provides detailed information like this, as well as general information related to the Civil War era and the plight of ex-slaves in America.

BOSTON TEA PARTY

Best Search Engine: http://www.ixquick.com/

Key Search Terms: Boston Tea Party

American Revolution Home Page
http://www.dell.homestead.com/revwar/files/INDEX2.HTM
middle school and up

This Web site is the place to get the basics about the Boston Tea Party—who was involved, why this act of rebellion took place, and what the consequences were. What's also great about the *American Revolution Home Page* is that it allows you to place the Boston Tea Party in the context of the rest of the events that led up to the American Revolution. This site is informative, easy to navigate, and clearly written. It's a little dull, though, since it doesn't have any interactive features or interesting illustrations.

To read the site's essay on the Boston Tea Party itself, simply click on "Boston Tea Party" from the subject index on the home page. The piece gives you the nuts and bolts of the raid and provides links for more information on related topics. Click on key figures involved in the Boston Tea Party, including Samuel Adams, Governor Thomas Hutchinson, and John Hancock, or on other events, such as the passage of the Intolerable Acts, to learn more.

If you want to get a sense of the chronology of the American Revolution and how the Boston Tea Party fits into it, explore the other topic headings in the index. "The End of Compromise," "The Stamp Act," "The Townshend Acts," "The Boston Massacre," and "The Burning of the H.M.S. Gaspee" all shed some light on why the Boston Tea Party took place. "The Intolerable Acts" and "Lexington and Concord" sketch out the ultimate results of the Boston Tea Party.

The History Place
http://www.historyplace.com/unitedstates/revolution/teaparty.htm
middle school and up

Sometimes, the best way to learn about an important historical event is to read what people who experienced it had to say about it. So if you are looking for primary source material on the Boston Tea Party, you will love this site. From the home page, select "1763–1775: Prelude to the Revolution" from the main index at the top of the screen. This will take you to an easy-to-read and detailed chronology of the events leading up to the American Revolution. You can scroll through this time line or proceed directly to 1773, where you will see a link to "The Boston Tea Party." If you click on this, you can access a description of the event written by a man named George Hewes, who participated in dumping the tea into the Boston Harbor.

Perhaps you need primary documents about events that took place before or after the Tea Party. Then you can simply click on the links from the "Prelude to the Revolution" chronology. Are you interested in the buildup of tensions prior to the Tea Party? Then check out the 1765 "Resolution" that colonists sent to King George III requesting a repeal of the Stamp Act. If you want to explore some of the fallout from the Tea Party, scroll down to 1774, where you can follow the link to read a declaration drafted by the First Continental Congress disputing taxes imposed by the British.

BRANCHES OF GOVERNMENT (SEE ALSO EXECUTIVE BRANCH, JUDICIAL BRANCH, AND LEGISLATIVE BRANCH)

Best Search Engine: http://www.ixquick.com/

Key Search Terms: Branches of government

Federal Agency Directory
http://www.lib.lsu.edu/gov/tree/
middle school and up

The *Federal Agency Directory* is a very straightforward site to use if you want to locate any committee, office, or subsidiary of one of the three branches of government. It is simply a list of names of agencies, divided into five sections: Committees, Executive, Independent, Judicial, and Legislative. Click on any of the listed names to get to a page that will define the department for you or to get to an independent site designed by the department itself.

This site is simply a Web-site directory, so it provides you with nothing but names and links, but it is a thorough list, so virtually any agency or office you may need information on will be found here.

USA Government
http://pittsford.monroe.edu/jefferson/calfieri/government/govframe.html
middle school and up

The *Pittsford-Monroe USA Government Site* is a lot more user friendly than *The White House* site. It contains much less information and is more clearly organized for educational purposes. Begin by clicking on one of the three branches on the left of the page, which will take you to a page explaining how each branch works. On the "Legislative" page, for example, you will find three options: "Congress," "State Legislature," and "County Legislature." Go to the "Congress" page and you will read a simple synopsis telling you what, exactly, Congress does. You will learn the essentials, including how Congress is divided into the House of Representatives and the Senate, and when and where Congress meets. Then you will see a list of relevant links. That's it, other than an option to test your newfound knowledge at the top of every page. The best part about this site is that it's totally straightforward. There doesn't seem to be any pertinent information missing either, which means that you will probably want to begin your study of the three branches of government by visiting this site.

The White House
http://www.whitehouse.gov/government/
middle school and up

Although *The White House* site is the official Web site for the U.S. President's office, which is the executive branch of our government, it also includes an equal amount of material on the other two branches: legislative and judicial. Here you can see how the three divisions attempt to work together to keep America's government going. The easiest way to navigate through this site is to locate the three links at the bottom of the homepage: "Executive," "Judicial," and "Legislative." Click onto any of the links and you will see how each branch is divided into separate entities. For example, click on the "Judicial" page, then on "U.S. Federal Courts" to see a breakdown of the American court system. You can then visit the home pages of these courts to get detailed information about their processes, their members, or about relevant cases.

There is quite a lot of material having to do with the three branches of government in the United States, which makes studying them a bit tedious. *The White House* Web site is the access point for all three branches, but because it's the official site for the U.S. President's office, it's full of a lot of information you won't even need, which means you can get lost easily. Although *The White House* site is a little complex, if you stay on track and locate the right pages, you should find it to be very useful.

BROWN V. BOARD OF EDUCATION

Best Search Engine: http://www.ixquick.com/
Key Search Terms: Brown v. Board of Education

African-American Odyssey: The Quest for Full Citizenship
http://lcWeb2.loc.gov/ammem/aaohtml/exhibit/aointro.html
middle school and up

This terrific site from the Library of Congress's *Online Exhibits* looks at the history of African Americans in the United States through primary documents and photographs. Most of you won't need to use the entire site, which begins its narrative with the introduction of slavery in the United States. However, one section of the site focuses specifically on *Brown v. Board of Education* and the subsequent desegregation of American schools.

To access the material about *Brown* and desegregation, select "Civil Rights" from the menu on the left side of the home page. Then click on "Desegregation," and scroll down the screen to read the excellent essay. As you work your way down the page, you will encounter documents that illustrate the essay's points. Among other items, there's a letter from Thurgood Marshall to the NAACP, a photograph of Marshall celebrating after the *Brown* decision, and material about James Meredith's heroic efforts to attend the University of Mississippi.

Brown vs. Board of Education: The Interactive Experience
http://www.digisys.net/users/hootie/Brown/
middle school and up

The emphasis in this site is on making the case of *Brown v. Board of Education* understandable. There's no legal jargon here. Instead, this site gives you the basic information about the landmark case with a lot of interactive features that makes learning about it fun. This site won't provide enough detailed information to be a single source for more advanced students. But it's perfect for younger students or for those of you just getting started on your research.

The site is divided into five main sections: "Background," "Linda Brown," "The Case," "Thurgood Marshall," and "Conclusion." Each of these contains a multimedia feature that illustrates the topic of the section. In "Background" you can listen to an audio clip of Martin Luther King's "I Have a Dream" speech. Under "The Case" there's an audio clip of Earl Warren announcing the Court's decision in *Brown v. Board of Education*.

CABINET

Best Search Engine: http://www.google.com/
Key Search Terms: Cabinet + executive
                      Cabinet + U.S. government

The White House: President's Cabinet
http://www.whitehouse.gov/government/cabinet.html
middle school and up

The *President's Cabinet* page, part of *The White House* Web site, tells you who's who in the current President's cabinet. If you don't know what a cabinet is, this site also gives you an overview of this executive tradition. You will find that the purpose of the cabinet is outlined in the Constitution as a means to assist the president in decision-making. You can also link to current cabinet and cabinet-rank members, their photos, biographies, and respective Web sites.

CAMPAIGN FINANCE REFORM

Best Search Engine: http://www.google.com/
Key Search Terms: Campaign finance reform

Campaign Finance Information Center
http://www.campaignfinance.org/
middle school and up

Investigative Reporters and Editors is a nonprofit organization dedicated to improving the quality of investigative reporting. The IRE *Campaign Finance Information Center* page focuses mainly on where money goes once it has been contributed to candidates. Here you can gain a better understanding of why there is so much conflict surrounding the issue of campaign finance reform, and why there is such a push to reform current practices. You will learn about problems associated with campaign financing and, specifically, about ongoing investigations into how money is spent and possible unethical practices involved in these political contributions.

The site is pretty straightforward. In addition to current legislative and political headlines found throughout the page, you also have access to campaign financing details, constructed by the Federal Election Commission, such as a breakdown of specific campaign funding sources and the amounts of money given, as well as information on the contributors. You can also click on "Power Search" to track the flow of financial contributions on a state-by-state basis. This site really gives you the whole picture. Use it if you want to know the rationale behind campaign finance reform.

Campaign Finance Reform: A Sourcebook
http://www.brook.edu/dybdocroot/campaignfinance/
high school and up

Created by public policy analysts at the Brookings Institution, this site will get you up to speed on the widely debated issue of campaign finance reform in America. You will find numerous ways to access many different types of information on the topic. Click on "Campaign Finance Reform: A Sourcebook" and you can read an entire book on the topic online. You can also scroll down a bit to choose from many different publications that deal with campaign finance reform. An additional source of information here can be found under the heading "Sources" near the bottom of the page. You can go to "Federal Election Campaign Act," "Key Court Cases," or "Current Legislation" to find out about the latest and hottest political topics. Also, on the left side of the page, you will find various subtopics related to campaign finance reform, such as "soft money," "limits," "congressional debate," and "unions." Finally, the ongoing news headlines updated on the right side of the page are a useful aspect of the site if you are trying to stay abreast of current news.

The downside to this site is that it does not offer you a direct link to the background of campaign finance reform. You can go to any of the publications or books it presents, and then to the appropriate chapter, but it takes a little time to get to specific topics that way. It would be easier if a summary and history page were just a click away from the main page. But even without this extra, the Brookings Institution site is comprehensive, and you should be able to find anything you need on campaign finance reform here.

CENSUS

Best Search Engine: http://www.google.com/

Key Search Terms: Census

U.S. Census Bureau
http://www.census.gov/
middle school and up

For a site that houses an amazing wealth of data, the U.S. Census Bureau's Web site is reassuringly straightforward and easy to navigate. Use the A-Z index if you have a specific topic in mind. Otherwise, you can search by keyword or subject, or delve into the general sections, which include "People," "Business," "Geography," "News," and "Special Topics." If you are looking for data about the population and socio-economics of the United States, this is the preeminent source.

Other good research tools at this site include the "American Fact-Finder," an interactive database that can provide you with data from the 1997 Economic Census, the American Community Survey, the 1990 Census, the Census 2000 Dress Rehearsal, and Census 2000. To get information at the national, state, and county level, you could click on another tool called "QuickFacts."

Just for fun, be sure to check out the population clocks for the United States and the world that reveal, minute by minute, just how rapidly our populations are increasing. The site also provides excellent links to other government sites with useful social, demographic, and economic information.

United States Historical Census Data
http://fisher.lib.virginia.edu/census/
high school and up

This site provides demographic and economic data for states and counties from 1790 to 1960. The easiest way to utilize this site is to start by going to the left of the page and clicking on a particular year. You will then see that the database has been organized into two sections: economy and population. Go to either of these topics and there you will see a list of subtopics that you can choose from. For example, in the year of 1840, if you were to search "Number of white persons 20 years of age and over who cannot read or write," you would find that while there were 521 people in Connecticut who could not read or write, there were almost 59,000 in Virginia.

This database contains some very interesting information. You can search virtually anything you want here. The only thing that can be a bit frustrating is the way the database is set up once you get your search results. Just remember to scroll down for your results and not to get caught up in the sorting options, unless you choose to, at the top of the page. You do have the option of adding new variables, finding proportions, and graphing your results, all of which may come in very handy. If you want to do something like this, you will have to play around a bit to get used to it. If you don't need to get into that much detail initially, though, just keep it simple and you will find a wealth of information on this site.

CHECKS AND BALANCES

Best Search Engine: http://www.google.com/
Key Search Terms: Checks and balances

Encyclopedia Americana: Checks and Balances
http://www.gi.grolier.com/presidents/ea/side/checks.html
middle school and up

The *Encyclopedia Americana* page on checks and balances offers a solid explanation of the term, including a classical perspective on the theory behind the notion. Here you will learn about the separation of powers among the legislative, executive, and judicial branches of American government, and about why it is important to keep these three branches in check of one another.

This site is simple and basic. You will find a very broad definition of checks and balances, but very little detail. However, you can also access the links at the top and bottom of the page to find additional information pertaining to checks and balances, such as specifics on the three branches of government or how a law is passed.

CIVIL DISOBEDIENCE

Best Search Engine: http://www.google.com/
Key Search Terms: Thoreau, Gandhi, civil + disobedience

Act Up: Civil Disobedience Manual
http://www.actupny.org/documents/CDdocuments/CDindex.html
high school and up

The AIDS Coalition to Unleash Power, Act Up, has developed this Web site as a reference manual for civil disobedience and nonviolent activism. The site is divided into twelve sections, ranging from "A History of Mass Nonviolent Action" to "Legal Issues/Risking Arrest." You can read about the evolution of civil disobedience throughout history, beginning with Mohandas Gandhi in 1906 at the onset of the South African campaign for Indian rights. Or you might click on "Civil Disobedience Training" to see a step-by-step guide to developing an action campaign. You can also go to "Jail Solidarity" to learn about strategies designed to effect changes while incarcerated. Essentially anything you might want to know about civil disobedience can be found in this source site.

It is a bit rough in its organization and doesn't go into a lot of detail when discussing the history of civil disobedience. But the how-to information here is invaluable. Act Up has put together quite the activist's guide. Because nonviolence is the basis of civil disobedience, understanding it step-by-step is imperative, which makes this site a necessary stop.

Thoreau's Civil Disobedience
http://eserver.org/thoreau/civil.html
middle school and up

This site is a starting point for any student hoping to understand the roots of the term "civil disobedience." Coined by transcendentalist Henry David Thoreau, it connotes a refusal to obey civil laws in order to induce governmental change, characterized by nonviolence. You can use this site to access the original text of Thoreau's "Civil Disobedience," and to read about ways in which this essay affected politics in America. The best and most useful part about this site, though, is its list of links on civil disobedience. Visit any of these sites to get a clear picture of what civil disobedience actually encompasses. You can go to "Burning Down a Dictator" to read about how the Serbian people reclaimed their country from Slobodan Milosevic in the fall of 2000 by means of civil disobedience. Or click on "King and Gandhi" to learn of Thoreau's influence on these two civil-rights and peace activists. The main point here is that in order to fully comprehend the concept of civil disobedience, you must have clear examples of its manifestations. This site will assist you in this process.

CIVIL LIBERTIES

Best Search Engine: http://www.google.com/
Key Search Terms: Civil liberties
                     Human rights

American Civil Liberties Union
http://www.aclu.org/
middle school and up

The American Civil Liberties Union was founded in 1920 as a small group of civil-rights activists. From then its membership has grown to more than 300,000 supporters. The ACLU remains one of the most powerful forces in the fight for civil liberties in America. Its mission is to fight civil-rights violations on every level. This includes situations of racial or sexual discrimination, sexual-orientation discrimination, freedom of speech or religion violations, and a gamut of other civil rights abuses.

The ACLU Web site is packed with information for students and researchers. Here you can go to "About the ACLU" for a four-page review on the history of this organization. Here you will read about some of the most important ACLU milestones, like the Scopes case, in which biology teacher John T. Scopes was charged with violating a Tennessee ban on the teaching of evolution in school. The ACLU secured Scopes' attorney in this case, and although Scopes was convicted and fined, his later appeal was successful and his conviction was reversed. Also included in the ACLU history section are events and movements like the internment of Japanese-Americans during World War II, school desegregation, the Civil Rights movement, abortion decriminalization, and freedom of speech on the Internet. The ACLU remains one of the most powerful forces in the fight for civil liberties in America.

Also, click on "In Congress" and then on "Civil liberties in Congress" to get an update on the most heated civil liberties issues currently being addressed in the 107th Congress. Here you will read about topics ranging from police abuse to drug policies to the International Women's Rights Treaty . . . the list goes on and on.

Back at the home page, you can take a look at the list of issues to the right. Just click on any of these to get the summary. You will see where the ACLU stands and what it is doing to promote support for its cause. Here you can also get information on joining the ACLU and contributing to its campaigns.

The ACLU Web site is an excellent source of material on civil liberties. All of its campaigns and political actions focus on this subject and everything the ACLU does is displayed in its site for online interest and to promote public awareness. This is a very well-designed Web site with a ton of information and research data. It is a must for those of you interested in American civil liberties.

Amnesty International
http://www.amnestyusa.org/home.html

Amnesty International (AI) is a civil-rights organization that addresses human-rights abuses on a worldwide scale. AI's Web site is very extensive, with information on everything from its origins and history to the most pressing issues currently being addressed. If you are interested in civil liberties and how they are addressed and protected on an international level, Amnesty International is definitely the site to visit.

Go to "About" for some very interesting options that will teach you about the organization's history. From here you can click on "Amnesty Roots," which contains the story of Amnesty's founding and its early roles in the fight for basic human rights. Or you can go to "An Interactive Timeline" where you will take a fascinating multimedia journey through time with Amnesty. This includes the most important events in this group's history, all of which relate to civil liberties. Back at the home page, you can also click on "All Around the World" where you will learn about the thousands of Amnesty branches worldwide and their histories and focus points. Or go to "Heroes and Scoundrels," a report about the five greatest advances and disappointments since founding. Here you will read part of an annual report that details events in countries like China, Zimbabwe, and the United States. By reading this section, you will get a clear picture of today's events in the human-rights arena. You will better understand what activists are working for and against and where the most significant problems lie.

If you want to know about the individuals directly involved with Amnesty International—where the organization's energy and drive comes from—click on the "Profiles" section from the home page. Here you will read individuals' life stories, about the situations that brought them to Amnesty International, and where their energies have gone since coming aboard. Some of these stories are extremely sobering. Many of these activists have joined forces with Amnesty following a time of dire need, a time when they were among the ones whose cases were being fought. For example, here you will read about victims of torture, victims of political or religious persecution, and victims of ethnic warfare. Again, this is an excellent means of comprehending—by firsthand accounts—the reality of situations in which basic human rights are endangered or disregarded.

In addition to these sections, you can always click right on any featured topic for ways to become involved in the particular campaign and with Amnesty International in general. Here you will be given different options. You can choose to send letters of protest to various political representatives. You can learn about getting involved with a local or regional branch of Amnesty. You can also choose to simply get the word out to others, which, as you will learn is the case with all civil-liberties activist organizations, is the most important facet of their work.

Human Rights Watch
http://www.hrw.org/
middle school and up

The Human Rights Watch is an international watchdog for human-rights issues and abuses. HRW was established in 1978. Its main objective is to challenge governments and those who hold power to end abusive practices and respect international human-rights law. HRW is an independent, nongovernmental organization that receives no government funding, directly or indirectly. It is fully funded by contributions from individuals and foundations worldwide.

The HRW site is very extensive. You can pick a country or region from the home page to learn about the human-rights issues faced there. Click on any country name and you will be taken to a separate page that, once again, divides the country into separate regions. Go to a region and you will read a list of issues, news bulletins, alerts, political and legal updates, and calls for support and protest. Click on any of the headlines here for more details.

To learn more about what HRW does, its international reach, and its mission, go to "About HRW" where you will get a synopsis about the organization as well as a list of various projects currently under way. You can go to "The Impact of Our Work" to read about HRW's most prioritized issues and action campaigns. Here you will learn that HRW is actually stationed in war-torn regions or where there is pronounced ethnic, religious, or political tension. For example, read about HRW's presence in Kosovo following the massacres and bombing campaigns there. HRW launched the most extensive emergency effort in its own history there, assisting the thousands of refugees and victims of violence and displacement there.

You might also want to click on the "HRW Annual Reports," sectioned into spans of years, to get the condensed reports. Or go to "Interview with Peter Bouckaert, Senior Emergencies Researcher for Human Rights Watch" to simply listen to a firsthand account of what's occurring with HRW. This sound bite allows students to get personal accounts and interpretations of the HRW and its missions.

The HRW is an incredibly far-reaching organization with involvement in virtually every region in the world. Its Web site is *the place* to visit for firsthand information on its international involvement. You can come here and research events anywhere and everywhere. If it's civil liberties in the international arena that interests you, research this site for the facts. The HRW site will tell you exactly what's going on. Because it's completely nongovernmental, there is minimal political persuasion and pressure here. Its material is reliable.

CIVIL RIGHTS

Best Search Engine: http://www.google.com/
Key Search Terms: Civil rights
Civil rights movement
Civil rights acts

Civil Rights
http://www.wld.com/conbus/weal/wcivilri.htm
high school and up

You've heard the term "civil rights" used a whole lot, but have you ever stopped to wonder exactly what it means? This page can tell you. It's an entry on civil rights from the *West Legal Dictionary*, but it covers a whole lot more than just a simple definition of these words. Starting with a look at the meaning of the term, the essay goes on to explain how that meaning relates to the enactment of civil-rights legislation.

But that's not all. The essay goes on to present a comprehensive overview of the history of American civil-rights legislation, starting with the drafting of the Constitution and the adoption of the Bill of Rights, through the Civil Rights Act of 1866 and the U.S. Supreme Court's decision in the case *Plessy v. Ferguson*, which effectively took civil rights *away* from African Americans, all the way up to the Civil Rights Act of 1991. Although the essay is too complex for younger students, more advanced researchers will get a lot from it.

Civil Rights: A Status Report
http://www.ghgcorp.com/hollaway/civil.htm
high school and up

This vast Web site provides a detailed history of the Civil Rights movement in America. While most people think of the Civil Rights movement as having begun in the 1950s, this site charts African Americans' nearly four-hundred-year struggle for civil rights in the United States. As the author says in his introduction, "We would be remiss if we ignore the earlier struggles that laid an immovable foundation for freedom and equality in America." *Civil Rights: A Status Report* is definitely for more advanced students. The site is dense, comprised almost entirely of plain text, and written at a high level. It's worth the effort, though. *Civil Rights: A Status Report* is an excellent resource that is both thoughtful and encyclopedic. But remember that this is not the ideal Web site to use if you want to find information in a hurry.

Once you enter the site, you will automatically be taken to an introductory page. Scroll to the bottom of that screen to access the "Table of Contents," which contains many chapter headings (arranged chronologically). The site begins with the "Discovery of the New World" and devotes a lot of attention to the history of slavery, the Compromise of 1850, and the rise of the Ku Klux Klan in the South. Although you might want to pass over this material because it's not directly relevant to the modern Civil Rights movement, these chapters do a lot to help put the modern movement in context. It's only when you have a sense of the persecution that African Americans have endured, that you will fully understand the significance of the quest for equality during the modern Civil Rights movement.

If you do want to limit your reading to the modern Civil Rights movement, scroll down the "Table of Contents" until you reach "The Democratic Convention of 1948." The next twenty-five or so chapters cover the period you want. At the end of the "Table of Contents," you will see "Opinion" essays on a variety of topics. These are interesting but not terribly informative. Further below is another section, "Final Analysis," that contains links to essays that give quicker synopses of various eras. The most relevant to the modern Civil Rights movement are "WWII and the Beginnings of Change," "The New Movement Begins," "Change Finally Comes," and "Non-Violence Yields to Chaos."

Spartacus Encyclopedia: Civil Rights 1860–1980
http://www.spartacus.schoolnet.co.uk/USAcivilrights.htm
middle school and up

This site can tell you almost anything you'd ever want to know about the struggle for Civil Rights from the beginning of the Civil War to the dawn of the Reagan era! It has a huge number of links to essays about key figures, organizations, events, and issues in this long-running American morality play. You could spend hours on this site—and because it's so well designed, you'd never get lost.

Spartacus Encyclopedia: Civil Rights 1860–1980 breaks its offerings up both chronologically and between people and events/issues. But all of the information is accessible from the home page. You just need to scroll down to get to the sections that interest you. To learn about the NAACP, for example, look for the heading "1900–1980: Issues and Events" and find NAACP in the alphabetically arranged list. Following the link will take you to an essay about the history of the organization that has a tremendous number of links to articles on the people and issues important in the organization.

Another cool feature of many—but not all—of the other essays on the site is the selections from primary source documents at the end. You will be able to read comments from various contemporary figures (including Frederick Douglass, Abraham Lincoln, Andrew Johnson, and Supreme Court Justice Salmon P. Chase) on whether African Americans should be allowed to vote.

Timeline of the American Civil Rights Movement
http://www.wmich.edu/politics/mlk/
middle school and up

This is a great site if you just want to get a handle on the key events of the modern Civil Rights movement! Unlike *Civil Rights: A Status Report,* this site is perfect for younger students—or anyone who wants to learn the basics about the Civil Rights movement. As its name suggests, *Timeline of the American Civil Rights Movement* condenses the Civil Rights movement into an easy to digest time line that highlights the key events of the period.

The time line runs down the left side of the home page. All you have to do is click on the events that interest you. The topics are "Brown vs. the Board of Education," "Montgomery Bus Boycott," "Desegregation at Little Rock," "Sit in Campaign," "Freedom Rides," "Mississippi Riot," "Birmingham," "March on Washington," and "Selma." Once you click on a topic, you will be able to read a short essay about it on the right side of the screen. Photographs are included in the essay. From some of the essays you can also access primary source material. For instance, from the "Birmingham" section you can click on a link to read Martin Luther King's "I Have a Dream" speech.

CIVIL RIGHTS ACTS

Best Search Engine: http://www.google.com/
Key Search Terms: Civil rights acts

Civil Rights: Law and History
http://www.usdoj.gov/kidspage/crt/crtmenu.htm
middle school and up

If you only visit one site on the legal and historical aspects of American civil rights, let The U.S. Department of Justice Web site for students be that stop. It's simple. The site is divided into a full range of sub-pages, including "The Establishment of the Civil Rights Division," "Education," "Voting," "Employment," "Americans with Disabilities," and "American Indians." The important feature of this site is its treatment of all issues that relate to civil rights. It is a good reminder that constitutional rights and the effects of our Civil Rights acts extend to a very diverse array of cultures in America.

Click on "Education" to find an outline of Title IV of the Civil Rights Act of 1964, prohibiting discrimination in public schools. Also, read about James Meredith, the first black American to attend the University of Mississippi (a result of a Supreme Court ruling followed by President Kennedy sending 16,000 federal troops to the university campus for assistance and backup). Or click on "American Indians" and discover that there are more than five hundred and fifty American Indian tribes that have tribal governments that are recognized by the United States in a government-to-government relationship. Read on to learn of a lawsuit filed by the Department of Justice against a school district in Utah for not having a high school in the remote community of Navajo Mountain. This lawsuit was the first time the Civil Rights Division had ever enforced the education statutes on behalf of American Indians.

Civil Rights Movement
http://blackhistory.eb.com/micro/129/80.html
middle school and up

This site addresses the Civil Rights movement in general but includes detailed information on the Civil Rights Acts as well. It is presented in the form of an article, which begins by discussing America's initial attempts at a Civil Rights Act in 1875, during the Reconstruction Period, and concludes with talk of affirmative action and increased African American involvement in government. This site doesn't miss anything of importance. It does a good job of laying out a time line of events and includes definitional links along the way for reference. If you want more information on the Civil Rights Act of 1964, just click here for another full page of material on this act that generated so much protest and debate in America. Specifically, learn about the test case, *Heart of Atlanta Motel v. U.S.*, which was the first Supreme Court case challenging the constitutionality of the act.

EEOC: 35th Anniversary
http://www.eeoc.gov/35th/index.html
middle school and up

This site has a ton of information to help you research this topic. It was launched by the Equal Employment Opportunity Commission (EEOC)—the government agency that was created by the Civil Rights Act of 1964—to celebrate its history. *EEOC: 35th Anniversary* provides a comprehensive overview of civil-rights legislation in America. This site has a lot of material drawn from a variety of perspectives to help you with your research. The photographs, video clips, and other primary source documents will make the subject come alive. The time lines, essays, and interpretive material will allow you to understand the significance of the Civil Rights Acts and to put the historic legislation into their historical contexts.

To begin your online journey into the history of civil-rights legislation, choose one of the topic headings from the home page: "History," "Milestones," "The Law," "Voices," or "Visions." You will probably find the "History" section to be the best place to learn the specifics about the various Civil Rights Acts. The "History" section is further subdivided into eras so you can focus your research more closely. Select from among "Pre-1965," "1965–1971," "The 1970s," "The 1980s," "The 1990s," and "The 2000s." Within each of these areas, you will find photographs, videos, and links to other documents. For instance, you can read the Civil Rights Acts of 1964 and 1991, the Equal Employment Opportunity Act of 1972, excerpts from President Kennedy's famous 1963 speech about civil rights, and the audio file of the elder President Bush's speech before he signed the Americans with Disabilities Act.

The other sections are also good resources. If you select "Milestones" from the home page, you can access an excellent interactive time line. For a brief look at the laws enforced by the EEOC, click on "The Law" from the home page. The "Voices" section (click on the heading from the home page) gives you a cool behind-the-scenes look at the EEOC's history. You can read (or listen to) several oral-history projects involving the EEOC, in which EEOC personnel and people outside the agency reminisce about important events.

EEOC: 35th Anniversary is clearly written, easy to use, and a breeze to navigate. It's also one of the few Web sites out there that concentrates on the history of modern civil-rights legislation as a whole. Its only downside is that it sometimes focuses a little *too* closely on important events within the EEOC (especially in the "History" section) that might be of less interest to the general reader. Nevertheless, you will love the breadth and depth of this site's offerings and its many interactive features. Just remember that it doesn't cover the two nineteenth-century Civil Rights Acts. For information on those, use a site like *Spartacus Encyclopedia: 1860–1980* (discussed below).

Spartacus Encyclopedia: Civil Rights 1860–1980
http://www.spartacus.schoolnet.co.uk/USAcivilrights.htm
middle school and up

If you are interested in the modern Civil Rights Acts, you will probably want to approach this site by cruising down to the heading "1900–1980: Issues, Events & Organizations" (it's most of the way down the very long home page). There, you can click on the links that interest you. Obviously you will want to hit "Civil Rights Act (1957)," "Civil Rights Act (1960)," and "Civil Rights Act (1964)." The 1964 Act receives the most coverage here, but the essay on the 1960 Act has a link you should follow to learn more about President Lyndon Baines Johnson, who was instrumental in securing the passage of the Civil Rights Act of 1964. Just clink on the "Lyndon Baines Johnson" hypertext in the essay. You should also take a look at some of the other key laws passed during this period, such as the "Voting Rights Act (1965)" and the "Immigration Act (1965)." And don't skip links such as "NAACP," that will tell you about groups that played important roles in working to enact and put into practice the guarantees made by the Civil Rights Acts.

You should then back up to the section dealing with key people of the era. Look for the "Campaigners: 1900–1980" heading, and then click away. Most of the essays have embedded links to the key people, places, and events covered in them, and you will quickly come to recognize how interconnected the various twentieth-century efforts to achieve civil rights were. One thing to keep in mind—because this site ends its coverage in 1980, it has no information about the Civil Rights Act of 1991. Oddly, it also overlooks the Civil Rights Act of 1968. But given the breadth of *Spartacus Encyclopedia: Civil Rights 1860–1980*'s other offerings, these are only minor inconveniences.

CLASS SYSTEM

Best Search Engine: http://www.google.com/
Key Search Terms: Class system
                       Social class

All Politics: In Focus, America's New Class System
http://www.cnn.com/ALLPOLITICS/1996/analysis/time/9602/26/
    class.system/index.shtml
high school and up

Nicholas Lemann's article for *Time* magazine, called "America's New Class System," is what you will find at this address. It's about how the people of this country divide themselves not only by money but also by paths to success. Read it and see what you think. It's not really an introduction to class systems, but it will provide you with some historical background on class in America, as well as an up-to-date look at what new forms class segregations take today.

People Like Us: Social Class in America
http://www.pbs.org/peoplelikeus/resources/top.html
middle school and up

This PBS site is designed to give kids, teachers, and parents some food for thought on the word "class" and the many ways in which social class affects our lives. It's an overall resource page, so once you arrive, you will have to browse at the options and pick the way in which you'd like to explore.

Options include "You Are Where You Live," a site where you can type in your zip code and then receive and ponder a printout of "the kind of people who live there, as well as the kinds of cars they drive, the food they eat, and the magazines they read." Find out if you are like your neighbors. "Class Markers," another option, is a list of diverse links that reflect the interests and pursuits of America's many social classes. Expand your own class horizons! This is the place to learn about polo ponies, double-wide mobile homes, and café latte, among many other things. "Educator's Resources and Bibliography" is geared toward helping teachers find the resources they need to teach about social class in the classroom, but if you are a student, you might find the bibliography of books on social class interesting, especially if part of your assignment is writing a book report. "Essays" is your final option on this thoughtful PBS page. It brings you a list of links to articles and essays by writers as diverse as Barbara Ehrenreich and David Brooks. If you are still hungry, this is more food for thought.

COMMUNISM

Best Search Engine: http://www.google.com/
Key Search Terms: Communism
                                    Marxism

Blacklist
http://www.otal.umd.edu/~rccs/blacklist/welcome1.html
middle school and up

To understand the political ramifications of the communist movement in the United States, visit this intriguing site on the Hollywood Ten. Beginning in 1947, the House Un-American Activities Committee (HUAC) began to investigate communism in Hollywood. As Sen. Joseph McCarthy would later, HUAC operated by getting witnesses to provide lists of other supposed communists in an effort to secure more lenient treatment for themselves. Of the many people summoned before HUAC, the Hollywood Ten (10 influential screenwriters, novelists, directors, and producers) gained the most attention.

This site tells the story of the Hollywood Ten by focusing on the case of one of the Ten, Adrian Scott, a screenwriter and movie producer who refused to answer HUAC's questions, was imprisoned for this, was blacklisted, and was unable to find work again in the United States until 1968.

For an overview of the Hollywood Ten and discussions of the events and their trials, read all three links in the "Hollywood Blacklisting" section of the table of contents. To learn about Adrian Scott and to read his testimony before HUAC, click on the links ("A Brief Biography" and "HUAC Testimony") that are listed below his name in the table of contents on the home page. To access primary source material, including photographs and letters, go to the links in the "Archives and Resources" section.

Cold War International History Project
http://cwihp.si.edu/default.htm
high school and up

This is a phenomenal site and a must-visit for anyone researching communism in the larger perspective of the Cold War. Established at the Woodrow Wilson International Center for Scholars, the Cold War International History Project (CWIHP) disseminates new information and perspectives on the history of the Cold War, especially new findings from previously inaccessible sources in the former Communist world.

You will want to look at the *CWIHP Bulletin*, which publishes recently released and translated documents found in archives of former Communist countries. These documents are accompanied by brief introductions by leading Cold War historians and archivists. You can click on "Virtual Archive" to search for documents by keyword or browse the subject headings, which include "Rise and Fall of Détente," "Arms Race," "Cold War Leaders," "Le Duc Tho," and dozens of others.

Political Systems
http://dspace.dial.pipex.com/town/street/pl38/sect2.htm
middle school and up

Although not an academic site, this one appears to be fairly objective in its treatments of the various political systems of the world, and it's more comprehensive than other similar sites. You will find a good list that is divided into two main categories—the collectivists and the individualists—and then subdivided by specific political system. Systems discussed include autocracy, communism, conservatism, democracy, fascism, imperialism, monarchy, pluralism, plutocracy, socialism, theocracy, anarchism/nihilism, liberalism, libertarianism, objectivism, capitalism, and republics.

Once you've read this overview of the systems, you will probably want to locate further resources on a specific system. Some of the descriptions contain links to pages that discuss the political system in more depth. If you don't see any links to the system you want to explore, simply check out the other sites listed below or do a keyword search at Google.com.

The Red Scare
http://www.spartacus.schoolnet.co.uk/USAredscare.htm
middle school and up

How did U.S. government officials react to the possibility of communism taking root in America? This Web site answers that question. *The Red Scare* gives you all the details of official Washington's first reaction to communism. In the process it tells you a lot about the early history of communism in the United States. *The Red Scare* is easy to navigate and has many links for you to follow to learn more about important American communists and their enemies in the U.S. government.

The Red Scare focuses on a narrow period of American history—from 1917 to 1920. The Russian Revolution had successfully overthrown the czarist regime in Russia in 1917, when President Woodrow Wilson appointed A. Wilson Palmer as his attorney general. Palmer was convinced that Communists were plotting to overthrow the United States government, so he carried out a series of measures that violated people's civil rights (and were, in fact, patently illegal).

Follow the links within the text to learn more about suspected communists, including Emma Goldman, Alexander Berkman, and Mollie Steimer. There are also brief overviews of International Workers of the World (IWW), Herbert Hoover, the Espionage Act of 1917, and the Sedition Act of 1918.

Senator Joseph McCarthy—A Multimedia Celebration
http://www.webcorp.com/mccarthy/mccarthypage.htm
middle school and up

This site is a terrific place to learn about the McCarthy era—the period during the 1950s when Senator Joe McCarthy hunted down supposed communists from his post as the head of the House Un–American Activities Committee.

What makes this site interesting is that you can listen to audio clips of McCarthy denouncing so-called communists. You will get a sense of how McCarthy manipulated people's fear and prejudices to institute a reign of political persecution now known as McCarthyism. You will find out how communists were imagined in the collective American mind.

After you've listened to several of McCarthy's speeches, don't forget to check out the audio clip of his downfall. The very first audio clip listed on the site is the one delivered by the counsel for the Army before a live national television audience. ("At long last, have you no sense of decency?")

The one major downside to *Senator Joseph McCarthy—A Multimedia Celebration* is that it contains no interpretive articles or essays for you to read. There is also no biographical material about this senator from Wisconsin on the site. Nevertheless, the various audio clips are invaluable in developing an understanding of the history of communism in America.

CONGRESS

Best Search Engine:	http://www.google.com/
Key Search Terms:	Congress
	House of Representatives
	Senate

The Center on Congress
http://congress.indiana.edu/index.htm
middle school and up

Geared toward young people and students, this site was developed by the Center on Congress at Indiana University as a means to better understand the U.S. Congress and encourage civic involvement. The site is very straightforward and runs smoothly. Choose from the links at the top of the page to get started. Go to "Learn About Congress" for another list of options pertaining to congressional functions, makeup, and logistics. Here you can view a simulation of what the average American thinks of Congress and the legislative process. This "Public Criticisms of Congress" presentation will heighten your interest with its integration of sound and video. You can also click on "Congress Today" to access information about House and Senate floor activities and schedules. Or, if you want more in-depth material on Congress, visit the "Links to In-Depth Analysis" link under the "Congress In-Depth" option at the top of the home page. Here you will come across online libraries, reports, and various analyses of the U.S. Congress, including those of the U.S. State Department, Foreign Press Center, and the House Judiciary Committee.

CongressLink
http://www.congresslink.org/
middle school and up

CongressLink provides information about the U.S. Congress, how it works, its members and leaders, and the public policies it produces. The Information Center houses the main guide to Congress, contact information, issues, and legislation. Check out the large amount of legislation related to the September 11, 2001, terrorist attacks. The "Features" section provides historical information and congressional procedures. Classroom Resources include lesson plans, historical materials and classroom aids. "Congress for Kids" addresses younger students, although log-in is required. The site is available in French, German, Spanish, Portuguese, and Italian.

Congress.org
http://www.congress.org/
high school and up

This site is provided by Capital Advantage, an online grassroots activism site dedicated to citizen-to-government communication. The

Congress.org site is the place to go if you are interested in current congressional events. This is the way to learn about contacting your local representative or senator, writing letters to voice your opinion, even the simple task of registering to vote.

In addition to *Congress.org*'s focus on action and involvement, this site also includes all the pertinent information on Congress. You will notice sections like "Elected Officials" where you can find out the names of every elected government official, from the President on down to the local levels. You can also go to "Bills in Congress" to find out about current legislation and votes in both chambers of Congress. For example, click on "religion" here and you will see a list of all recent, current, and upcoming votes taken in both the Senate and the House of Representatives.

CONSTITUTION

Best Search Engine: http://www.google.com/
Key Search Terms: Constitution

Constitution Finder
http://confinder.richmond.edu/
middle school and up

If you are searching for the constitution of a nation other than the United States, try this stellar index site from the University of Richmond. You will find just about every country on the globe with a handy-dandy link to its constitution and other related documents, such as charters and amendments. Nations of the world are listed alphabetically, and each is linked to its constitutional text posted somewhere on the Internet. Point and click to jump from the name to the text. Use the alphabetical-listing search keys for more convenient maneuvering.

The Constitution of the United States
http://www.nara.gov/exhall/charters/constitution/conmain.html
middle school and up

Like *A Roadmap to the U.S. Constitution*, this Web site is comprehensive. However, it goes into a lot more detail, making it a better choice for high school and college students. One bonus feature of this Web site is that you can view digital copies of the Constitution itself.

The Constitution of the United States is organized into several sections, which you can access from the main menu on the home page. Click on "The Founding Fathers" to access biographies of all 55 delegates to the Constitutional Convention. To read the Constitution, select "Transcription" from the home page. As you browse the document you will find links to the biographies of the 39 delegates who signed it. Amended passages are also linked, so you can see how the Constitution has changed over the years since it was first adopted.

For an in-depth view of the Constitutional Convention and the ratification process, check out the long essay in the "More Perfect Union" section. There is also a helpful short essay on George Mason and why he opposed the adoption of the Constitution. For fast and fun facts about the document, click on "Questions and Answers Pertaining to the Constitution." In addition, the site has a transcript of a speech by Dr. Michael Beschloss explaining how the actual document that was drafted in 1787 has been protected and preserved over the years. To feast your eyes on an original copy, simply scroll down the screen until you have the option to download digital copies of the document one page at a time.

James Madison: His Legacy
http://www.jmu.edu/madison/
middle school and up

James Madison is often called the Father of the Constitution because of the important role he played in writing the document and getting it ratified. So you can learn a lot about the political thought, issues, and events surrounding the Constitution by studying his life. This encyclopedic Web site can tell you everything you've ever wanted to know about James Madison—and then some! But don't worry. The site is a snap to navigate, and it's easy to find the information on Madison and the Constitution.

For a basic overview of Madison's life, click on "Biography" from the menu on the home page. If you want to focus your research more specifically on Madison and his relationship to the Constitution, just browse the following sections of the site: "American Confederations," "Constitution," "Federalist Papers," and "Bill of Rights." Of course, if you are interested in Madison's presidency, you can click on the "President James Madison" heading from the main menu.

In *American Confederations*, you can read Madison's notes on the Articles of Confederation, the basis of U.S. central government prior to the Constitution. In these notes, Madison outlines the weaknesses of the Articles and lays out the themes that he would return to in more detail in the *Federalist Papers*. In the "Constitution" section, you can read both Madison's letters about the Constitutional Convention and his notes on the debates there. These letters are particularly helpful if you want to explore the clash between the Federalists and the Anti-

Federalists at the Convention. Clicking on "Federalist Papers" allows you to read the full text of that document. In this section you can also access a letter Madison wrote to Thomas Jefferson about the Constitution. In the "Bill of Rights" section you will find several documents written (at least in part) by Madison, in which he again addresses federalist issues. Remember that the Bill of Rights was a compromise measure incorporated into the Constitution so that Anti-Federalists would accept the document. The Virginia Declaration of Rights was a precursor to the Constitutional Bill of Rights. There's also an "Introduction" to the Bill of Rights and Madison's speech when he proposed the Bill of Rights to the Constitutional Convention.

A Roadmap to the U.S. Constitution
http://library.thinkquest.org/11572/
middle school and up

This fantastic Web site explores the U.S. Constitution from lots of different angles—and it does so in a straightforward style that will make sense to all students. In easy to understand language, *A Roadmap to the U.S. Constitution* discusses the history behind the famous document and gives a detailed look at the creation of the Constitution. The site also presents the Constitution as a "living document." You can read about contemporary constitutional issues and Supreme Court cases that affect everyone.

A Roadmap to the U.S. Constitution is divided into five major sections. To read the Constitution, click on "Constitution" from the main menu on the left side of the home page. You will have the option to "Browse the Constitution," or, if you are in a hurry, you can get an overview of the "Important Sections." If you click on "Origins" from the main menu, you can trace the people, events, and concepts that influenced the Constitution's framers. Within this section, you can select the period that interests you: "When in Rome" (impact of classical thinkers), "English Influences" (such as the Magna Carta), "Colonial Influences" (like the Mayflower Compact), or "Philosophers" (Locke, Montesquieu, and Rousseau).

If you want to learn the nitty-gritty of how the Constitution was hammered out, click on "Creation" from the main menu. In this section, there are several good pieces. Select "Delegate Dossiers" for biographies of some of the Constitutional delegates. "Virginia and New Jersey Plans" talks about the two competing blueprints for the Constitution. "Smoothing Out the Bumps" discusses the many conflicts that arose at the convention and explains how they were resolved. "Federalists and

Anti-Federalists" explores how these conflicts did not end once the document was written.

Are you interested in the Constitution's history once it was down on paper? If so, look at "Issues and Cases" from the main menu. The "Issues" section discusses constitutional issues from the past and the present, such as abortion, affirmative action, capital punishment, judicial review, and slavery. "Cases" provides a brief history of the most important cases of the Supreme Court.

If you already have a sense of what you are looking for, you can skip browsing entirely and just go directly to the site's handy search engine (you will find it at the center of the home page). Those of you with questions and comments will like the site's two online bulletin boards. Click on "Messages" to access these.

This Web site has a lot of information—and it's fun and easy to navigate. However, A Roadmap to the U.S. Constitution doesn't go into a tremendous amount of detail. More advanced students will want to bolster their research with material from sites such as The Constitution of the United States.

CONTINENTAL CONGRESS

Best Search Engine: http://www.google.com/

Key Search Terms: Continental Congress

Continental Congress
http://www.infoplease.com/ce6/history/A0813368.html
middle school and up

The InfoPlease site gives a simple but thorough overview of the Continental Congress, America's system of government prior to the ratification of our Constitution. There is a simple map to follow here, beginning with an introduction to the Continental Congress and followed by sections on the First, Second, and Postwar Continental Congresses. The advantage of the InfoPlease site is the way it simplifies this topic. You can come here first to get a general idea about the Continental Congress and its historical significance, and then pinpoint areas of interest for further research. The other benefit to this site is that it doesn't miss anything important. Throughout the articles, as you come upon names of people who played significant roles during this era, you will find links offering brief biographies. So there's quite a lot of information here, but it is simplified, so you might consider it a first stop.

To Form a More Perfect Union
http://memory.loc.gov/ammem/bdsds/bdexhome.html
high school and up

Here's a great site for researching the Continental Congress, which governed the United States from 1774 to the adoption of the Constitution in 1789. You can learn how the Congress organized the Revolutionary War and inspired citizens to support independence. The site also provides background on the key issues facing the Congress after the war, particularly the problem of incorporating western territories that led to the passage of the Northwest Ordinance of 1787. Finally, you can review the limitations of the Articles of Confederation, the basis of U.S. central government prior to the Constitution, and trace the steps in the creation of the Constitution.

The site is primarily text with links to key players and important documents. To get to the era you want, simply click on the appropriate topic at the opening page. If you just want documents, you can scroll to "Continental Congress and Constitutional Convention Broadsides" at the bottom of the screen. You can then access 274 documents either by keyword or subject. The documents include treaties, laws, congressional reports, resolutions and proclamations as well as the Declaration of Independence and the Constitution. If you just want a flavor of some of the documents, use the links in the text. You will be transferred to broadsides such as one signed "Constitutional Mechanic," addressing criticism of the Congress. "Suffer not yourselves to be misled by partial representation; not to be deluded by the false clamours of designing men: but consult the real interest of the State and the happiness of your country." The language is eighteenth-century, but the thoughts are very contemporary. The site also contains a concise chronology, which you can access through "Continental Congress and Constitutional Convention Broadsides" at the bottom of each screen.

DEATH PENALTY

Best Search Engine: http://www.google.com/
Key Search Terms: Death penalty

Death Penalty Information Center
http://www.deathpenaltyinfo.org/
middle school and up

This extremely well-accredited site is known for its reliable perspectives and its attempt to maintain a level of objectivity in the analysis it presents on the death penalty issue. You will find an audio-video section containing perspectives and presentations on a range of death penalty-related topics. For example click on "Mental Retardation and the Death Penalty" to see a video clip on Earl Washington, who was coerced into confessing that he'd been involved in the rape and murder of a woman in Culpeper, Virginia. Later it was discovered through DNA that he was in fact innocent and he was offered a full pardon. The audio-video section of this site is especially engaging because it involves you on a more personal level.

Another unique feature this site offers you is its "Educational Curriculum" section. Click here and you will find two separate sites: one for teachers and one for students. Go to the student site and you will discover a ton of useful material. It's designed like an outline to a report, with an introduction, then a list of main topics followed by other subtopics, then a link to additional resources at the bottom of the outline. From this "Death Penalty Curricula for High School" page, you can research topics like the arguments for and against the death penalty, history of the death penalty, state-by-state data, and various courtroom cases. This is *the* site to visit if you want to get the full picture of the death-penalty debate.

National Coalition to Abolish the Death Penalty
http://www.ncadp.org/
high school and up

As its name indicates, the National Coalition to Abolish the Death Penalty (NCADP) is an organization dedicated to abolishing the death penalty in America and, ultimately, throughout the world. Remember this as you make your way through its Web site. Some of the information here may seem biased or one-sided. But there is an important benefit to researching the NCADP site, in that you will get a clear picture of the arguments against capital punishment. The key is to make sure to address both sides of this extremely heated and emotional debate, and given the amount of information on the NCADP Web site, you will definitely get the material you will need in considering the anti-death-penalty side of the argument.

Go straight to "About Us" for an overview of the NACDP. Here you will read about this organization's purpose. It is the only fully staffed national organization exclusively devoted to abolishing capital punishment. You will also touch on its focus, which encompasses legislative, media, grassroots, and human-rights advocacy. From the home page you can also go to "Domestic Alerts" or to "International Action" to become informed about the latest news headlines or events pertaining to capital punishment. By going to "Domestic Alerts," you will get information on the "Execution Alert," which is a monthly bulletin that publishes execution updates on a national scale. By scrolling down this page, you will also begin to see, primarily, which states employ capital punishment as a means of sentencing. Here you will also read detailed accounts of situations involving executions. For example, you can click on the name of one of the few females scheduled for execution in Florida. A former prostitute, she confessed to killing six men, although she claims to have done so in self-defense, resisting violent assaults by men while working. This case is one of the many campaigns taken on by the NCADP. Scroll down a bit more and you will see several links to e-mail accounts, addresses, and phone numbers—all of which have been provided in an effort to gain public awareness and support for a re-evaluation of these cases.

Go to "Facts and Stats" for the capital punishment statistics. This chart is divided into years since 1976 and contains the number of executions versus the number of commutations in each year. It then breaks them into jurisdictions, so, again, here you will notice the huge increase in executions since 1976 and which states utilize this form of punishment predominantly.

The NCADP site also offers some useful reference tools. You can go to "Lifelines," a monthly publication of political issues and news related to capital punishment. You might also click on "Affiliate Links" or "Directories" for information on other anti-death-penalty groups. The "Abolitionist Directories" categorize NCADP coalition affiliates by focus, including national activism, state-level activism and religious groups.

DECLARATION OF INDEPENDENCE

Best Search Engine: http://www.google.com/
Key Search Terms: Declaration of Independence

The Declaration of Independence
http://www.ushistory.org/declaration/
middle school and up

This Web page lets you learn all about the Declaration of Independence—why it was written, who was involved with the writing, and what the Declaration accomplished. The page is simple, focused, and easy to use. Simply scroll down the screen to navigate.

The page includes links to follow to get biographical information about the signers of the Declaration of Independence, an excerpt from

Thomas Jefferson's autobiography that talks about the days leading up to the signing of the Declaration, and a copy of the Declaration itself so that you can read for yourself. You can even visit the Graff House, where Jefferson wrote the Declaration.

The excellent though small list of links includes a site from the National Archives and Records Administration that outlines the history of the Declaration from 1776 to the present.

NARA: Exhibit Hall: Declaration of Independence
http://www.archives.gov/exhibit_hall/charters_of_freedom/declaration/
     declaration_history.html
middle school and up

This page is part of the NARA site on the Declaration of Independence. It teaches you about the history leading up to the drafting and signing of the Declaration. It begins by discussing the final push toward independence from the British Crown. Addressed here are such historical markers as the Lee Resolution, the Prohibitory Act, the Privateering Resolution, and Thomas Paine's "Common Sense." Next, this article moves on to describe the Committee of Five, comprised of five men who would collaborate to create the Declaration. You will also read about the different stages involved in the drafting of this document and which drafts have been preserved over the years. You will then learn about the final engrossment (the process of preparing it in a large, clear hand) of the Declaration and about the steps taken to preserve it properly. The page closes with a very in-depth account of the Declaration of Independence's migration from Baltimore to Philadelphia, Washington, The Library of Congress at Fort Knox, and, finally, the National Archives in Washington, D.C., where it resides today.

The NARA site on the Declaration of Independence touches on every imaginable aspect of the document. If you want additional resources or readings, you will find those here as well. This page is just text, so be prepared to read. Because of the detail, it's also lengthy, but the language used is very clear. And you won't have any trouble maintaining an interest here. Reading all about its history is a fun way to get an education about the Declaration.

DEMOCRACY

Best Search Engine: http://www.google.com/
Key Search Terms: Democracy
                       Political systems

The Center for Voting and Democracy
http://www.fairvote.org/
middle school and up

This nonpartisan think tank is devoted to fair elections where every vote counts and all voters are represented. You will find all kinds of information here on the types of issues that are of fundamental importance in a democracy—proportional representation, instant runoff voting, redistricting, voting rights, voter turnout, and more. Each of these topics is a straightforward essay defining the topic and discussing its relevancy in various situations. Within each essay you will find links to other useful sections of this site and to other sites with relevant information on the topic.

Easy to navigate, *The Center for Voting and Democracy* Web site has a search function, an online library, and a simple menu of options on the left side of the page.

Political Systems
http://dspace.dial.pipex.com/town/street/pl38/sect2.htm
middle school and up

Although not an academic site, this one appears to be fairly objective in its treatments of the various political systems of the world, and it's more comprehensive than other similar sites. You will find a good list that is divided into two main categories—the collectivists and the individualists—and then subdivided by specific political system. Systems discussed include autocracy, communism, conservatism, democracy, fascism, imperialism, monarchy, pluralism, plutocracy, socialism, theocracy, anarchism/nihilism, liberalism, libertarianism, objectivism, capitalism, and republics.

Once you've read this overview of the systems, you will probably want to locate further resources on a specific system. Some of the descriptions contain links to pages that discuss the political system in more depth. If you don't see any links to the system you want to explore, simply check out the other sites listed below or do a keyword search at Google.com.

What is Democracy? Defining Democracy
http://usinfo.state.gov/products/pubs/whatsdem/whatdm2.htm
middle school and up

This page, part of an informational government Web site, provides a very clear definition for representative democracy. It begins by defining democracy in general and the element of freedom, an integral component of democracy. Scroll down a bit and you will read about representative democracy, one of the two primary forms of democracy (the other being "direct"). In this section, you will get a full understanding of this concept as well as a good comparison with direct democracy. Further along, you will read about representative democracy today and how it typically works on the local, state, and national levels. This page closes its discussion on representative democracy by addressing the issue of majority versus minority voices in a representative democracy, and how the rights of the minority are still protected by the U.S. Constitution.

DEMOCRATIC PARTY

Best Search Engine: http://www.google.com/

Key Search Terms: Democratic Party

Democratic National Committee
http://www.democrats.org/index.html
middle school and up

As stated in their official Web site, The Democratic National Committee plans the Democratic Party's quadrennial presidential nominating convention, promotes the election of party candidates, and works with national, state, and local party organizations, elected officials, candidates, and constituencies to respond to the needs and views of the Democratic electorate and the nation. This means that their interest lies solely with the Democratic Party.

If you want to know about the Democratic Party and what it stands for, just go to this site, click on "About the DNC," then go to "Democratic Party Platform," "Our Leadership," or "History of the Democratic Party," where you will gain an understanding of the ideologies and beliefs on which the party stands. Click on "Landmark Dates in Democratic History" to view a time line of events pertaining to the party, such as its original formation by Thomas Jefferson in 1792 or the date of the official naming of the Democratic Party in 1840. This time line spans from 1792 to the present, touching on all major events that have affected this political party in America.

DEVOLUTION REVOLUTION

Best Search Engine: http://www.google.com/

Key Search Terms: Devolution Revolution

The Context of the Political Devolution Revolution
http://www.pscinc.com/PSR/Adv/1995/050595.cfm
high school and up

This *Advisor* article, written in 1995, will give you some historical perspective behind the Devolution Revolution theory. It breaks this social and political theory down into a few important subcategories, namely, "From Standardization to Customization," "From Centralization to Automation," and from "Specialization to Integration." These major trends are representative of a current shift in American society, from a more general and standardized need to very individualistic demands. This shift pertains to goods and services, to economics, and to politics and government.

The article here is straightforward. After addressing the issues mentioned earlier, the analyst addresses the "alienation of government" due to its inability to respond well to this shift toward the individual in America. It then proceeds to discuss the difficulty government has in responding, given that its basis and history are contradictory to this kind of mindset.

The article does a good job of defining the Devolution Revolution for students. It does not go into a lot of detail, though, so it should not be used for in-depth analysis.

The Devolution Revolution
http://www.brook.edu/dybdocroot/comm/PolicyBriefs/pb003/pb3.htm
high school and up

This site is the home of a policy brief, published by the Brookings Institution, a Washington, D.C., center researching American economic, political, and social policies. This policy brief, entitled, "Why Congress is Shifting a Lot of Power to the Wrong Levels" addresses the effects of a shift in authoritative power from the federal level to the state and local levels without regard to regional levels, where most problems exist for metropolitan communities. It attacks Congress for this shift in power and the difficulties and inefficiencies associated with it, and then attempts to provide a solution based on withholding federal funds until regional problems are dealt with.

This brief provides an example of America's so-called Devolution Revolution, signifying a political trend in which power is being shifted from the federal government to local, community, neighborhood, and individual levels. Although it reads as an academic report would and may seem a little dry at times, it will give you a clear illustration of this political theory.

DRED SCOTT CASE

Best Search Engine: http://www.google.com/

Key Search Terms: Dred Scott

The Dred Scott Case
http://library.wustl.edu/vlib/dredscott/
high school and up

Dred Scott was an African American slave who, because he had lived for a long period of time in two free territories, filed a lawsuit to be granted his freedom. Eleven years later, this suit ended with a Supreme Court decision declaring that Scott, as a Negro, was not a U.S. citizen, had no legal rights, and was to remain a slave. The *Dred Scott* case was important in that it served to turn back the clock concerning the rights of African Americans, ignoring the fact that black men in five of the original states had been full voting citizens dating back to the Declaration of Independence in 1776.

The Supreme Court decision in the *Dred Scott* case declared that Congress had no power to limit slavery in free territories, and it inflamed sectional conflicts, which contributed to the Civil War. This simple site offers a detailed chronology of events surrounding the case as well as the court records. To access the documents from the trial and appeals courts just click on "Dred Scott Case Exhibit Table of Contents." To read the Supreme Court decision, go to the bottom of the chronology and click on "Scott v. Stanford." And for more information and sites addressing the *Dred Scott* case, click on the links provided at the bottom of the "Dred Scott Chronology" page.

ELECTIONS

Best Search Engine: http://www.google.com/

Key Search Terms: Elections

Electoral process

Administration and Cost of Elections (ACE) Project
http://www.aceproject.org/

The Web site of this group contains an online version of the *International IDEA Handbook of Electoral System Design*, a valuable reference on all aspects of the design and administration of election systems. From the home page, choose the language you wish to read, then use the color-coded menu at the left to pick the topics you wish to explore.

Options include "Electoral Systems," "Legislative Framework," "Electoral Management," "Boundary Delimitation," "Voter Education," "Voter Registration," "Voting Operations," "Parties and Candidates," "Vote Counting," "Media and Elections," "Election Integrity," and "Election and Technology." Once you choose a topic, you may be given a list of subtopics to narrow your focus. This is an excellent source of information—clear, accessible writing that's not overly detailed. The only fault you may find with the material is that it is sometimes rather dry, but persevere because you can count on the accuracy and usefulness of this information if you are researching the election process.

The site also contains a glossary and good links to other information, but we think you will find plenty to answer your research questions here.

Elections Around the World
http://www.electionworld.org/

Here's a wealth of information in what at first may seem like an intimidating format. Don't be scared off by the busyness of the page. *Elections Around the World* packs a lot of information into its very useful site, but it is actually well organized, so just take your time and you will locate the information you need.

If there is a specific country you want to research, use the alphabet at the left side of the page to search for that country. Pick "A" for Argentina, for example, and then scroll down until to you see the link for "Argentina." When the "Argentina" page appears, you will find the executive elected officials, Parliamentary elected officials, description of how elections work in the country, and descriptions of and links to the political parties in Argentina. Plus, there's all kinds of statistical information if you are interested.

Back at the home page, you can link to a calendar of elections around the world; a home page for political parties around the world, with lots of hyperlinks included; a home page for political institutes around the world, also with hyperlinks; a home page for parliaments; links to other election resources on the Web; and more.

Electoral Calendar
http://www.angelfire.com/ma/maxcrc/elections.html
middle school and up

If your research involves international elections, you won't want to miss this comprehensive but simple site. It contains, among other things, an electoral calendar that includes general, presidential, municipal, regional, administrative, and legislative elections and referendums in every country, so you can look up the date when elections occurred or will occur. Click on the year of your choice under "Previous and Next Elections" for a chronological listing of elections. The site is updated weekly, so you can count on the information here being current. If you are looking for information on election results around the world, try the previous site.

Elections: The American Way
http://memory.loc.gov/ammem/ndlpedu/features/election/home.html
middle school and up

This site is clear and straightforward. It is the place to go if you don't know much about America's election process or if you just need a refresher. It is divided into five sections: "Candidates," "Voters," "Party System," "Election Process," and "Issues." Click on "Election Process" to find a step-by-step guide to the presidential election process and information on the evolution of primaries. Here you will also read about contentious issues like campaign finance reform. Or go to "Voters" to get some interesting data on the voting history and women, African Americans, and Native Americans. Proceed to "Women" and you will learn of the women's suffrage movement in America and of several key players in this historical struggle in America. By the way, another feature of this site is its inclusion of detail links along the way, so if you want more information on important names and events, just click on them.

Federal Election Commission
http://www.fec.gov/
high school and up

It is the Federal Elections Commission's responsibility to administer and enforce the Federal Election Campaign Act (FECA)—the statute that governs the financing of federal elections in the U.S. You will have the easiest time viewing the FEC site by first clicking on "Citizen Guide," which is a general route (for students) through the site. Here you will find an assortment of material on the FEC, campaign financing, and elections in general. There is a subcategory focusing on "How Elections Work." Included in this part are topics like "Voter Registration and Voting," "2002 Congressional Primary Dates," "The Electoral College," "Voting Age," and "Federal Elections '98." You can also click on "FEC Functions" to learn all about the roles of this commission and to read a history on it, including that pertaining to the FECA.

ELECTORAL COLLEGE

Best Search Engine: http://www.google.com/

Key Search Terms: Electoral College

U.S. Electoral College
http://www.archives.gov/federal_register/electoral_college/
    electoral_college.html

The Office of the Federal Register coordinates the functions of the Electoral College. Here it has compiled data on past and present presidential elections. You can go to "Past Electoral Results" or to "2000 Presidential Election" to access the popular-vote and the electoral-vote totals. You can also see a list of the Electoral College members here or read about state laws and requirements having to do with the popular vote.

Go to "General Information," then to "Procedural Guide to the Electoral College" to find a wealth of material teaching you about the Electoral College and how it functions. Here you read about the roles of the states versus that of Congress. You can also go to "Role of NARA" to discover that the archivist of the United States (via the Federal Register) is involved in every stage of the elections. Go back a bit and you will see a solid overview of the Electoral College processes, including historical and procedural information.

EMANCIPATION PROCLAMATION

Best Search Engine: http://www.google.com/

Key Search Terms: Emancipation Proclamation

Abraham Lincoln Papers at the Library of Congress
http://memory.loc.gov/ammem/alhtml/malhome.html
middle school and up

This Library of Congress online collection (which is still being completed) offers you insight into what President Abraham Lincoln thought about emancipation, slavery, and his own Emancipation Proclamation. Since the collection is still a work in progress, some material might not yet be available. But the site is a one-of-a-kind resource.

To concentrate on the Emancipation Proclamation, scroll down the home page until you see the heading "Special Presentations." Directly below this is a link called the "Emancipation Proclamation." Click on this, and you will be taken to the "Introduction" of this section, which discusses events leading up to Lincoln's historic issuing of the Emancipation Proclamation. At the bottom of the screen is a menu with other information on the Proclamation: "Timeline" and "Gallery." The time line is a year-by-year chronology of the Lincoln presidency that highlights the various events leading up to the Proclamation. The "Gallery" section allows you to view various drafts of the document, as well as a letter in which Lincoln summed up his thoughts on the matter of emancipation.

The only major downside to *Abraham Lincoln Papers at the Library of Congress* is that it doesn't provide much interpretive help. So once you've found your primary documents, you might want to turn to other sites, such as *The Emancipation Proclamation*, to place them in their historical context.

The Emancipation Proclamation
http://www.nara.gov/exhall/featured-document/eman/emanproc.html
middle school and up

This is a really helpful Web site because it gives you a number of perspectives on the significance of the Emancipation Proclamation. It also lets you read a transcript of the text and view the original document. *The Emancipation Proclamation* is part of the National Archives and Records Administration (NARA) *Online Exhibit Hall.*

To get a quick overview of what the Emancipation Proclamation meant, read the short essay in the middle of the home page. As you work your way down, you can click on the individual pages to get a close-up of the original document in Lincoln's handwriting. If you want to read the entire Emancipation Proclamation, select "Transcript of the Proclamation" from the menu on the left side of the home page.

The Web site also allows you to access a first-rate article about the Emancipation Proclamation, with a discussion of both its triumphs and its shortcomings. Click on "The Emancipation Proclamation: An Act of Justice" from the menu on the home page. The piece was written by historian John Hope Franklin, and initially appeared in *Prologue: Quarterly of the National Archives and Records Administration.* There are even lots of illustrations to make the article more lively. Once you've gotten a sense of how history has judged the Emancipation Proclamation, it's time to learn how the famous document changed—or didn't change— the lives of former slaves. Click on "Audio" from the main menu to check out the audio file of Charlie Smith, a former slave, talking about his life after the Proclamation.

Emancipation Proclamation From the View of a 1903 South Carolina Second-ary School Textbook
http://www.geocities.com/Heartland/Hills/6240/emancipation.html
middle school and up

How did pro-slavery Southerners feel about Lincoln's Emancipation Proclamation? Did they quickly learn to accept their slaves' freedom? This Web site, which is nothing more than an excerpt from a 1903 schoolbook, conveys how little Southerners respected the notion of freed slaves, much less racial equality. This site makes for an interesting (and sad) comparison with the account of the life of the former slave you can find on the NARA (*The Emancipation Proclamation*) site. The Geo-cities site doesn't have any bells or whistles, so all you have to do is scroll down and read. Nevertheless, the perspective it provides could be helpful in your research.

E PLURIBUS UNUM

Best Search Engine: http://www.google.com/
Key Search Terms: E pluribus unum

E Pluribus Unum
http://www.assumption.edu/ahc/
middle school and up

E Pluribus Unum is an online project intended to illustrate the con-cept of *e pluribus unum* (one from many) throughout American history. It is divided into sections corresponding to three different eras: 1770s, 1850s, and 1920s.

Go to 1770s and you will see a multitude of topics that fall under the main heading "The Rhetoric of the Revolution." Included in this exhibit are analyses and images illustrating the communications circuit during America's Revolutionary era, such as pages from books, public an-nouncements, newspapers, songs, and general celebratory practices re-lated to the revolution.

If you are interested in the 1850s, click on the date, then click on "Featured Articles and Books," where you will see an outline of topics addressed in this section, including an essay about the laws and govern-ment in America during this time of transition, and an analysis of public forums and oration in the nineteenth century.

Go to the 1920s and you will read an essay entitled "Wars for Civi-lization" that discusses the most important elements of the early twen-tieth century, like World War I and the postwar years, Prohibition and

America's first rebellious generations, the Ku Klux Klan and racism, and the general shifting of tradition and moral beliefs.

The idea here is to illustrate America's effort to settle into itself. *E pluribus unum*, or one society from many cultures, is the foundation on which this country stands. This project attempts to provide a full spectrum of samples related to American life during these formative years. It does so successfully, although it may appear slightly disorganized in some areas. The format of each time section is not the same, but as long as you are not expecting uniformity, you should be able to extract a ton of great visual information here.

EQUAL EMPLOYMENT OPPORTUNITY COMMISSION

Best Search Engine: http://www.google.com/
Key Search Terms: Equal Employment Opportunity Commission
                        EEOC

U.S. Equal Employment Opportunity Commission
http://www.eeoc.gov/

The Equal Employment Opportunity Commission's Web site is an extensive reference site for employees and employers. It is the mission of the EEOC to ensure that no individual is discriminated against in the workplace. This site is a bit complicated due to the degree of material involved, but by clicking on a few key links, you should be able to find what you want to know.

Go to "About the EEOC" and you will see a list of EEOC practices and responsibilities. Or go to "EEOC Enforcement Activities" to find sections explaining in full detail what the EEOC does for workers and employers, such as handling administrative (discrimination) charges and the maintenance of the EEOC's mediation-based alternative dispute resolution (ADR). The ADR program encourages parties, with the assistance of a neutral mediator, to participate in deliberations to resolve discrimination cases.

You can also go to "Laws, Regulations, and Policy Guidance" to learn about EEOC laws and compliance guidelines. From here, click on "EEOC Regulations," where you will discover a list of anti-discrimination regulations published in the Federal Register.

And, of course, this site also includes the standard helpful links, like "Related Sites," "Statistics," and "News and Press Releases." The complexity of this site can be cumbersome, but if it's specific information on the EEOC that you are searching for, you will find it here.

Monster.com: EEOC Resources
http://equalopportunity.monster.com/eeoc/
middle school and up

Monster.com comes through for students with this site. It is comprised of information related not only to the EEOC, but also to employment discrimination in general. Here you will find a list of topics like sexual harassment, age discrimination, national origin discrimination, and pregnancy discrimination. You can click on any of these key topics to access a synopsis of them. You can read about the Civil Rights Act of 1964 and how it addresses these different issues. You can also read about the specifics pertaining to them, such as what an employer can and cannot legally do and what repercussions exist in cases in which laws are broken. Go to the *Monster.com* site for answers to "what if?" questions concerning job discrimination. There is even a link entitled "ADA: Questions and Answers" if you already have a specific question.

EQUAL RIGHTS AMENDMENT

Best Search Engine: http://www.google.com/
Key Search Terms: Equal Rights Amendment
ERA
Civil rights

Chronology of the Equal Rights Amendment
http://www.now.org/issues/economic/cea/history.html
middle school and up

The National Organization for Women created this site outlining the evolution of the Equal Rights Amendment. It's very straightforward. Just scroll down the page and you will see a list of dates along with the brief telling you what was happening at the time. You will get the full picture here. Also included are the helpful detail links, where you can go for a definition or for more detail if you are unfamiliar with terms along the way. This site spans the years from 1923 to today.

Equal Rights Amendment
http://www.equalrightsamendment.org/
middle school and up

If you visit just one Web site on the Equal Rights Amendment, this should be the one. It has been constructed for the sole purpose of educating and informing people about the historical amendment affirming the equal application of the U.S. Constitution to both females and males. Written in 1923 by Alice Paul, the Equal Rights Amendment (ERA) must be ratified by three more U.S. states before it becomes part of the U.S. Constitution.

The ERA Web site offers a complete online education on everything related to the Amendment. If you are interested in the history of the document, just click on "History" from the home page, and you will discover all kinds of interesting details, as well as historical images dating back to the women's suffrage movement in the early 1900s. This page lays out a comprehensive time line of events. Read about important women involved in the long struggle for voting rights. Learn of the National Woman's Party, a small, militant group that not only lobbied but conducted marches, political boycotts, picketing of the White House, and civil disobedience to gain in the fight for equal rights with men. Maybe you want to understand more about the principles on which this document is based, or about the real need for its ratification today. You can click on "Why" to read an analysis written by the chair of the ERA Taskforce, Ms. Roberta Snow. Snow outlines the realities of sexual inequalities that still dominate American society.

This site's only glitch is that there are some pages that are still being constructed or fine-tuned. So you may happen upon a page that hasn't yet been completed. But the overall quality of the ERA site is excellent.

EXECUTIVE BRANCH (SEE ALSO BRANCHES OF GOVERNMENT, JUDICIAL BRANCH, AND LEGISLATIVE BRANCH)

Best Search Engine: http://www.google.com/

Key Search Terms: Executive branch + government

Congress for Kids
http://www.congressforkids.net/executivebranch.htm
middle school and up

The *Congress for Kids* site explains the executive branch of American government in simple, accessible terms. If you don't know the first thing about it, or if you need a quick refresher course, visit this site. It goes over the legislative process and the President's role in it, the qualifications of a President, and the impeachment process (and impeachment cases in America's history). This site contains limited information. Don't depend on it for detail. Instead, use it for a brief overview of the legislative branch.

Executive Branch
http://www.aboutgovernment.org/executivebranch.htm
middle school and up

This site is set up much the same as the *GovSpot* site. It, too, is broken down into categories relating to the executive system, but this site is simply a reference site. Come here if you need additional sources, sites, or general information about specific executive-branch topics. All of these sites are reliable educational sites and should prove to be very useful. Just click on a category from the homepage and you are on your way.

Gov Spot: Executive Branch
http://www.govspot.com/executive/
middle school and up

This site is organized into four topics: "The White House," "Departments," "Executive Office of the President," and "Reference." By linking into "The White House," the official Web site of the President and the executive branch of the U.S. government, you will get information straight from the horse's mouth. (The White House site contains a wealth of information in itself, so you will want to consider visiting it regardless of where else you go.) Also, if you are interested in the specific departments that fall under the executive title, go to "Departments" from the home page. Here you will see a list of executive departments, such as transportation, interior, education, and labor. Click on any of these departments and you will be transferred to the respective Web site. All of these departments have their own sites, and they are quite well organized and easy to use. Third, if you want to know about the President of the U.S., go to "Executive Office of the President," where you will see another list of offices, like the Office of National AIDS Policy, or the Domestic Policy Council. Finally, if you need additional references and resources, you can get them by clicking on "Reference." You will get three lists of reference sources pertaining to the President, the First Lady, and the Vice President.

FEDERAL RESERVE SYSTEM

Best Search Engine: http://www.google.com/
Key Search Terms: Federal Reserve

Board of Governors of the Federal Reserve System
http://www.federalreserve.gov/
high school and up

Although the Board of Governors site does not incorporate the excitement and fun that its counterpart, *Fed101*, does, it is another very useful and informational site if you are studying the Federal Reserve or personal finances in general. Come here to read "A Beginner's Guide to Securing a Financial Future" or "Federal Reserve Bulletin Articles."

Fed101
http://www.kc.frb.org/fed101/indexflash.cfm
middle school and up

Fed101 is hands down the place to go for educational information about the Federal Reserve. Created by the Federal Reserve itself, this well-designed and organized site is essentially an online, interactive museum that allows you to quickly hone in on particular subjects. Choose from five broad sections: "History," "Structure," "Monetary Policy," "Banking Supervision," and "Financial Services."

Fed101's "History" section offers an excellent time line that is loaded with photos, graphics, maps, and charts that help you truly understand the development of the Federal Reserve System. You can go to "History" to discover historical challenges that the Federal Reserve has encountered over time, like early agrarian-minded Americans feeling uncomfortable with a large and powerful (the country's largest corporation at the time) central bank.

If you just want to learn how the Bank is organized, you can click on "Structure" and you will find an awesome visual aid that will tell you exactly how the Bank is put together and more about the functions of the Bank. You will learn about advisory councils, which are responsible for ensuring that the general public is involved with Federal Reserve activities. More goodies in the "Structure" section include a description of the paradoxes of the Fed, explanations of the roles played by the Board of Directors, Board of Governors, and Federal Open Market Committee, and much more.

The "Monetary Policy" section provides info on the basics of the monetary system, how the Fed creates money, and the significance of economic indicators. Look in the "Banking Supervision" section to get a better understanding of how the Fed supervises financial institutions, read a course textbook, and examine a virtual bank. The "Financial Services" section offers info on currency, checks, and electronic payments. Each of the five large sections also offers an interactive quiz and a selection of annotated links pertinent to the subject.

Federal Reserve Bank of Philadelphia
http://www.phil.frb.org/publicaffairs/fedworks.html
high school and up

As one of the 12 banks within the Federal Reserve System, the Federal Reserve Bank of Philadelphia has developed this insightful Web site. Look in the light blue box in the upper right quadrant of the home page to find links to detailed explanations of each of the responsibilities of the Federal Reserve. These responsibilities include conducting the nation's monetary policy, supervising and regulating financial institutions, performing services for the U.S. Treasury, serving the district's consumers and community groups, and supporting the nation's payment system.

For additional information, click on "Frequently Asked Questions." In this portion of the site, you will find questions and answers grouped under the following headings: "Federal Reserve," "Savings Bond and Treasury Securities," "Direct Payment," "Currency and Coins," "Statistical Information," "Federal Reserve Information Services," and "General Information." You can also visit the "Publications" section of the site to find scores of consumer and educational booklets, research publications, and community-affairs publications.

Federal Reserve Economic Database (FRED)
http://www.stls.frb.org/fred/index.html
high school and up

The Federal Reserve Bank of St. Louis created FRED, a clearinghouse of financial and economic data. The data files are grouped into 12 categories, which include "Interest Rates"; "Business/Fiscal"; "Consumer Price Indexes"; "Monetary Aggregates"; "Commercial Banking"; "Employment and Population"; "Daily/Weekly U.S. Financial Data"; "Gross Domestic Product and Components"; "Producer Price Indexes"; "Exchange Rate, Balance of Payments, and Trade Data"; "Reserves"; and "Regional." Some files are in .zip or compressed format. Remember that while FRED is an excellent source of data, you will need to utilize other resources to put all the data into some context. The Federal Reserve publication "Monetary Trends," which you can access from FRED, is one place to begin making sense of it all.

United States Monetary Policy
http://woodrow.mpls.frb.fed.us/info/policy/

This Federal Reserve Bank of Minneapolis site on monetary policy in the United States also covers the Federal Open Market Committee (FOMC) of the Federal Reserve. It provides an excellent overview and introduction to the topic of monetary policy, while also introducing you to the role of the Federal Open Market Committee, which is the most important monetary policy-making body of the Federal Reserve System.

The site is logically divided into the following seven sections: "What Is Monetary Policy?," "Monetary Policy Indicators," "Monetary Policy Objectives," "More Monetary Policy Links," "Instruments of Monetary Policy," "Federal Open Market Committee," and "Resources for Teachers." Under each of these sections, you will find numerous annotated links on related topics.

To acquaint yourself with the Federal Open Market Committee, go directly to the section of that name. You will find basic introductory resources for the novice, such as a definition and overview of the committee's function, as well as minutes of FOMC meetings, and access to the Beige Book, which is a summary of commentary on current economic conditions prepared before each FOMC meeting.

FEDERALISM

Best Search Engine: http://www.google.com/
Key Search Terms: Federalism

                        Federalist Papers

Constitution Basics: Federalism
http://www.constitutioncenter.org/sections/basics/basic_1c.asp
middle school and up

Here's a definition to get you started—the concept of federalism in one quick paragraph. Although you won't walk away an authority on the subject, you will be able to define federalism and its place in American history.

The Gilder Lehrman Institute: History Online
http://www.hfac.uh.edu/gl/contents.htm
middle school and up

Although you will find a complete history of America from the Revolution up to the end of the Civil War, this is a good place to get a quick introduction to the Federalist era, the period in American history generally defined as 1787 to 1801, from the writing of the Constitution through the presidency of John Adams. Just scroll down to the first link, "Critical Issues in American History." When you get to that page, scroll down to the section called "The First New Nation" and begin reading there. You will see links to short essays on "The Formative Decade,"

"The Birth of Political Parties," "The Presidency of John Adams," and much more.

Return to the home page for an "Interactive Timeline of the American Revolution" or a "Glossary of American History." There's also a list of succinct essays on major historical controversies and several online quizzes you can take to test your command of this period in U.S. History.

FEDERALIST PAPERS

Best Search Engine: http://www.google.com/
Key Search Terms: Federalist Papers

The Anti-Federalist Papers
http://odur.let.rug.nl/~usa/D/1776-1880/federalist/antixx.htm
high school and up

In 1778 the states debated the merits of the proposed Constitution. Those who supported the Constitution defended it in *The Federalist Papers,* which became a classic of American political thought. Those who opposed ratification also presented their position in papers, leaflets, and discussions in the Continental Congress. Because their arguments never appeared in one body of work, it's hard to find a good collection of Anti-Federalist thought. If you are studying these views, go to this simple site. Here you will find almost fifty documents that present Anti-Federalist concerns on issues such as states' rights, direct elections, suffrage, and slavery.

The Anti-Federalist Papers site is very simple and easy to use. Documents are organized chronologically under two main heads, "The Federal Convention of 1787" and "Ratification of the Constitution." Just click on the document you need.

The Federalist Papers
http://www.vote-smart.org/reference/histdocs/fedlist/
high school and up

Alexander Hamilton, John Jay, and James Madison wrote the *Federalist Papers* in 1787 to gain support for the ratification of the recently drafted Constitution. This Web sites allows you to read the *Federalist Papers* in their entirety.

The Federalist Papers is a bare-bones site, simply providing links to each of the 85 individual entries that comprise the *Papers.* Simply click on an individual paper you want to read from the index on the home page (you can browse, but it'll be a whole lot easier if you already know what you are looking for). As you read these famous documents, you will learn about the problems the young republic had went through under the Articles of Confederation. For example, since the Articles gave the federal government only very limited powers, the United States struggled to repay its war debts and fund its budget. The themes outlined in the *Federalist Papers* were the same ones that motivated federalist politicians during the Federalist era.

While this is a good site if you are already somewhat familiar with the period, or are just looking for primary source material, remember that this site has no background information. You will be able to read the *Federalist Papers,* but there's nothing to help you interpret the document. Use the *Gilder Lehrman Institute: History Online* Web site, found under the Federalism entry, to place the *Papers* in their historical and political context.

FEUDALISM

Best Search Engine:　http://www.google.com/
Key Search Terms:　Feudalism

Feudalism
http://mars.wnec.edu/~grempel/courses/wc1/lectures/19feudalism.html
middle school and up

This one-page site is another online lecture identifying the predominant features of ancient feudal societies. It provides a useful definition and overview of feudal society and concentrates on slightly different aspects of feudalism than the University of Kansas lecture site.

Here you will read about the historical rise of this form of government and how it was a result of the Fall of the Roman Empire. You will learn where feudalism is thought to have originated in northern Europe and gain insight into the hierarchy of authority and power in feudal societies. There's information on land rights, feudal contracts, and the exchange of land rights for military services.

Although condensed and to the point, this site is actually packed with quite a bit of good information. If you visit both these sites, you will also get a solid introduction to the origins of kingdoms, a slightly different form of government that actually survived through the ages and still flourishes in many parts of the world.

University of Kansas: The Rise of Feudalism
http://www.ku.edu/kansas/medieval/108/lectures/feudalism.html
middle school and up

The *Rise of Feudalism* site offers a discussion about the origins of feudal societies in the medieval world. The interesting feature of this site is the way it illustrates features of feudalism. Geared toward students, it makes sense of this age-old form of government by providing contemporary analogies along the way. You will see black text, which defines particular aspects of feudal societies in their early context, and red text, which gives examples of the same feudal characteristics, but in the context of the modern America that we're all familiar with.

Just scroll down to read about elements of feudalism, such as economic structures, people's rights, military powers, the division of classes, and political organization. Remember to refer to the red text if you need an example that you can actually identify with.

FIRST LADY

Best Search Engine: http://www.google.com/
Key Search Terms: First Lady
                            Presidents' wives

First Lady
http://www.whitehouse.gov/firstlady/
middle school and up

The White House site's section about the First Lady is designed to do two things. First, if you want to know about the current First Lady—her biography, her political involvement, projects, and speeches—you will find it all here. You can click on the titles of any of her recent speeches to find out about issues in which she's involved. You can also go to the biography link, which will tell you of the First Lady's background, her professional history, and interests. The other half of this site is dedicated to former First Ladies. Entitled "The First Ladies Gallery," it contains information on every First Lady in American history. Just click on the names to read whatever information researchers have been able to collect on these women over the years.

FISCAL POLICY

Best Search Engine: http://www.google.com/
Key Search Terms: Fiscal policy

Cato Institute: Fiscal Policy Studies
http://www.cato.org/research/fiscal.html
high school and up

The Cato Institute's Fiscal Policy Studies Program makes its position loud and clear. As the Cato Institute is a proponent of a free market and smaller government, the *Fiscal Policy Studies* site is largely a critique of the tax and spending policies of both major political parties. If this sounds like an interesting or provocative viewpoint that could aid your research, then continue on.

Click on "Fiscal Policy Facts and Figures" to see a gallery of charts illustrating the latest trends in government taxation and spending. You can also investigate *Fiscal Policy Studies* by the following topics: tax policy, budget policy, corporate welfare, or state and local issues. On the main page, you will also find lists of relevant press releases, commentaries, briefing papers, and staff-written articles that appeared in the mainstream media.

Center on Budget and Policy Priorities
http://www.cbpp.org/
high school and up

The Center on Budget and Policy Priorities is a nonpartisan think tank that researches and analyzes government policy programs, with an emphasis on those that affect low- and moderate-income populations.

You will find a wealth of information here specifically about state fiscal policies. Click on "State Fiscal Policy" to find a special report series on the state fiscal crisis, as well as a special report series on federal budget proposals.

Fiscal Policy
http://www.finpipe.com/fiscpol.htm
high school and up

Written for the *Financial Pipeline* Web site, this page provides a discussion of the term "fiscal policy," which it defines as "the expenditure a government undertakes to provide goods and services and to the way in which the government finances these expenditures."

You will learn about how taxation and borrowing offer two methods of financing. The page also delves into the two organizational systems for democratic government—a unitary system and a federal system—and shows how these systems influence fiscal policies. The text goes on to provide examples of government expenditures, taxation, and borrowing, describing real-life scenarios from Canada, Brazil, the United States, and other countries. You will appreciate the site's conversational—yet informative—tone. The hyperlinked text to related articles on monetary policy, interest rates, and bonds also come in handy.

FOREIGN POLICY

Best Search Engine: http://www.google.com/

Key Search Terms: Foreign policy

The American Foreign Policy Council
http://www.afpc.org/
high school and up

Founded in 1982, the American Foreign Policy Council (AFPC) is a nonprofit organization dedicated to disseminating foreign-policy information not only to the public, but also to political leaders both in the United States and abroad. It is this organization's objective to assist in policy building. One of the most unique and distinguishing characteristics of the AFPC is its involvement with Russia and its struggle to build a solid and stable democracy.

Visit this site if you are interested in learning about the policy side of foreign policy. In other words, this organization and its Web site will teach you about the actual process of forming international political policies. It does this by focusing on three primary geographical regions: China, Russia, and Eurasia (the Middle East and Central Asia). From the home page, click on "Programs." Here you will find another option to choose one of the three regions. Click on one of these and you will link to a separate page that provides an overview of the program and its particular focus points. For example, go to "China Program" and you will read about their weekly publication, called the *China Reform Monitor*, which is used to publish political updates pertaining to China's slow transition into democracy. You can also visit the home pages of the "Russia Program" and the "Eurasia Program."

Also, you can read about recent AFPC publications, including articles and editorials that have been featured in a variety of newspapers and journals worldwide. Just click on the "Publications" link from the home page to visit them. This will give you an awareness about the AFPC's mission and their objectives.

The AFPC's Web site is very straightforward, as is the focus of this organization. The site does not contain an overwhelming amount of material, which makes it reasonably simple to get through. But don't expect any additional information. You will read about foreign policy related to China, Russia, and regions of the Middle East. This material is very valuable, given the AFPC's authority on these areas. But you won't find anything else. The AFPC sticks to what it knows best here.

The Brookings Institute: Foreign Policy Studies
http://www.brook.edu/dybdocroot/fp/fp_hp.htm
high school and up

The Brookings Institute scholars present views and analysis on foreign-policy issues to the public through written pieces, broadcast appearances, and testimony before Congress. The material that has been compiled on this Web site contains the Institute's most important and pressing studies. It is a fantastic source of research data. The Brookings Institute division on foreign policy has become one of the best-respected and most renowned authorities on the subject. Just wander through the headlines and study titles on the home page to take advantage of this site.

Go to the bottom of the page and you will see a list of featured centers and projects. This section includes study programs on the Middle East, France, northeast Asia, globalization, internally displaced persons, and the National Security Council Project. All of these topics are separate study centers within the Brookings Institute. Just click on any of them to launch the home page, where you will get a full description of the program, the initial need for it, and a layout of all the most recent publications, speeches, and reports that have been generated on the topic. Go to "Internally Displaced Persons" and you will gain access to a report on Sri Lanka, a press release on Turkey, a congressional testimony on Sudan, and many more fascinating publications.

From the home page, you can also access information on upcoming forums and events pertaining to foreign policy, usually organized by the Institute itself. Past events have included a Newsmaker's Forum at which former Vice President Al Gore spoke about America's economic policy. You might also take a look at the Institute's recently published books. These contain a wealth of material for students interested in foreign policy. Most importantly, though, on the home page, you will see a list of policy issues on the right side of the page. This is where the Brookings Institute introduces the most central and vital topics.

The Brookings Institute Web site is a wonderful place to visit for foreign policy studies. The information is thorough and useful to students.

The Institute for Policy Studies
http://www.fpa.org/
high school and up

The Foreign Policy Association (FPA) is a national, nonprofit, non-partisan, nongovernmental educational organization founded in 1918 to educate Americans about the significant international issues that influence their lives. The FPA's site is intended to promote public awareness and involvement in foreign-policy issues. The site is well designed and user-friendly. The topics covered here are wide-ranging, so it is a good idea to narrow your foreign-policy research down so you know what to look for when you visit the FPA site.

First, if you want to know about the FPA's history and how it was formed, you will want to click on "About FPA" from the home page. Here you will get a general overview about the organization's mission, focus, and objectives. You can also find out about the FPA's education program, called Great Decisions, which is the core of their outreach agenda. Great Decisions promotes discussion and designs educational forums that take place at various locations, such as local Ys, libraries, rotaries, etc. You can also get a more detailed account of the FPA's history by clicking on it from the "About FPA" page.

Back at the home page, if you are interested in learning about what's going on with America's foreign policy—a kind of in-a-nutshell news brief department, look to the right side of the home page for several of the most important headlines. This is the best way to get up to speed. Click on the topic for an in-depth analysis. Also, maybe you want to find out about FPA partners, affiliates, or other groups involved in the foreign-policy forum. Click on "Global Forums" and you will have access to discussion boards that have been categorized by region and country. Go to these discussion rooms to get some perspective on these issues and to see what people think about different policy issues.

The FPA site is intended to promote public awareness. It does a good job of offering students and researchers a diversity of information routes. For example, there is a definite push to become a member of the FPA, there are books and publications offered to you (for a fee), and there is a lot of upcoming-event promotion. These features serve the purpose of getting viewers involved, but the major downfall is that there is not an overwhelming amount of data on this site. There are many ways to find research material via this site, but there aren't many ways to research *at* this site. But the FPA is definitely on top of its game, so you should visit their site if, for no other reason, to learn about the major issues related to foreign policy today.

FOREIGN SERVICE

Best Search Engine: http://www.google.com/
Key Search Terms: Government + foreign service
U.S. State Department

U.S. State Department
http://www.state.gov/
high school and up

Counterpart to the State Department site for kids, the official site of the U.S. State Department has information on every aspect of Foreign Service. Use this site instead of the kids' site if you are looking for more in-depth information than what you can find at the kids' site. You will find sections here devoted to "Press and Public Affairs," "Traveling and Living Abroad," "Countries and Regions," "International Issues," "History, Education, and Culture," "Business Center," "Other Services," and "Employment."

Use the index at the left side of the home page to see the subtopics under each of these sections. Each one is a link, so navigating this fairly deep site is simple.

U.S. State Department for Kids
http://www.state.gov/kids/
middle school and up

The student version of the State Department Web site is the best way to begin your research. It simplifies subjects a bit more than the official site does, making it easier to pinpoint areas of interest for young people. Start by going to "Learn About the State Department," where you will find out about the SD's history and what it does for the U.S. government. You can also study up on the Secretary of State and what his or her responsibilities are, including overseeing 5,000 employees worldwide in order to carry out the President's foreign-relations policies. Or click on "Social Studies" to access more material on international topics. Here you can choose from a list of issues related to foreign policy and diplomacy. For example, go to "Web Sites of U.S. Embassies and Other Diplomatic Missions," and you will see a site directory. From here, visit an international embassy site to learn what's happening in the world around you.

The *State Department for Kids* is an accessible source of information. You should be able to find anything you want here, but if you feel you need a bit more, just click over to the official site.

FOUNDING FATHERS

Best Search Engine: http://www.google.com/
Key Search Terms: Founding fathers
          Constitution framers

National Archives and Records Administration: Founding Fathers
http://www.archives.gov/exhibit_hall/charters_of_freedom/constitution/
    founding_fathers.html
middle school and up

The NARA site on the Founding Fathers, who were delegates to the Constitutional Convention and were key players in the creation of the U.S. Constitution, is a solid, reliable source of information. It gives a little history of the Convention, provides a few photos, and offers a summary of the event. Scroll down a bit and you will see "Biographical Index of America's Founding Fathers," which contains a list of name links where you can go to get more individual details on these 55 men. You can also access information on the Constitution and the Bill of Rights from here.

FREE TRADE

Best Search Engine: http://www.google.com/
Key Search Terms: Free trade
                     NAFTA

*The Benefits of Free Trade: A Guide for Policymakers (Heritage
    Foundation)*
http://www.heritage.org/library/backgrounder/bg1391es.html
high school and up

This lengthy "backgrounder" by the Heritage Foundation offers the flip side to the debate presented by *Foreign Policy in Focus* (see below). Written in August 2000, the article drives homes four specific strengths of the United State's free-trade policy and is spiced up by charts and tables from various sources. Both HTML and PDF versions are available.

Economic Policy Institute Briefing Paper: NAFTA at Seven
http://www.epinet.org/briefingpapers/nafta01/index.html
high school and up

This Economic Policy Institute (EPI) briefing paper, "NAFTA at Seven," offers an interesting analysis of NAFTA's successes and failures since its implementation in 1994. The introduction to the Web site notes that officials in Canada, Mexico, and the United States have regularly declared the agreement to be "win-win-win" for all three countries. It points out, however, that for most working-class North Americans, the agreement is a failure because it excludes any protections for working people in the form of labor standards, worker rights, and the maintenance of social investments.

The EPI Web site provides you not only with an articulate and thought-provoking introduction, but also with three separate essays—from the United States, Canada, and Mexico—that analyze various aspects of NAFTA. For the United States essay, economist Robert Scott describes how NAFTA has eliminated job opportunities for U.S. workers in manufacturing. Mexican economist Carlos Salas points out that while production jobs did move to Mexico, they primarily moved to an isolated area just across the border and did not contribute to the development of Mexican industry. Bruce Campbell of the Canadian Centre for Policy Alternatives reports that NAFTA has resulted in an upward redistribution of income to the richest Canadians, a decline in stable full-time employment, and an erosion of Canada's social safety net.

Free Trade Area of the Americas
http://www.ftaa-alca.org/alca_e.asp
high school and up

Like so many official sites, this one for the Free Trade Area of the Americas may first strike you as bureaucratic and tough to navigate. However, with some guidance, you will find indispensable resources here for your research on the subject. The site houses hundreds of documents dating back to when the FTAA process began at the 1994 Summit of the Americas, with the goal of integrating the economies of the Western Hemisphere into a single free-trade arrangement. Most of these documents can be found in the section labeled "Publications and Databases."

You can also click on "Information by Country" to learn about specific initiatives on a country-by-country basis. Look under "Negotiating Groups" to read about specific FTAA objectives and mandates, such as market access, investments, government procurements, smaller economies, and intellectual-property rights.

Foreign Policy in Focus: Trade
http://www.foreignpolicy-infocus.org/indices/topics/trade.html
high school and up

If you are looking for opinions—and not necessarily hard facts—on American trade policies, this is an interesting site. Foreign Policy in Focus (FPIF), a collaborative project of the Interhemispheric Resource Center and the Institute for Policy Studies, is a "think tank without walls" seeking to make the United States a more responsible global leader and global partner. Its international network of more than 650 policy analysts and advocates are committed to advancing a citizen-based foreign-policy agenda.

The site's index includes "Trade" as one of the key topics. In this portion of the Web site, you will find a collection of relevant "Special Reports," "Policy Briefs," "Progressive Responses," and "Commentaries" that have been written for FPIF. Headlines you will see here include "Democratizing the Trade Debate," "International Trade Overview," and "Have Faith in Free Trade—The Greatest Story Over Sold."

Global Exchange: Free Trade Area of the Americas
http://www.globalexchange.org/ftaa/
high school

Make no mistake about it—*Global Exchange* thinks the Free Trade Area of the Americas has got to go. Despite the apparent bias, this site about the FTAA offers several useful sections, including "Background," "News Updates," "Frequently Asked Questions," and "Links."

In the "Background" section, you will find information on how the FTAA affects individuals, 10 reasons to oppose it, and links to alternative fair-trade agreements proposed by progressive groups. The "News Updates" section is an excellent place to find media coverage of the issue; *Global Exchange* collects headlines and articles from the progressive, conservative, and mainstream media alike. In another section called "Fast Track," you will find information opposing the Bush administration's Fast Track proposal, which would prevent Congress from changing or debating any trade agreement negotiated by the President.

Research Guide: NAFTA
http://www.iisd.org/trade/nafta.htm
high school and up

The International Institute for Sustainable Development (IISD) created this site on the North American Free Trade Agreement (NAFTA). It contains a wide array of information pertinent to your research into NAFTA. You will want to begin with the overview section, then continue reading to learn about the elements of NAFTA that are relevant to sustainable development, such as investment, standards, International Environment Agreements, and dispute resolution.

The site's print- and electronic-resource sections contain references and annotations of print literature on NAFTA and of Web sites, including one with the full text of the agreement. You can also click on "IISD Trade Home" to access IISD's larger collection of material on trade issues, including information and analysis on the World Trade Organization, the China Council, the Americas Project, and Qatar, as well as IISD's general statements on trade and sustainable development.

FREEDOM OF SPEECH

Best Search Engine: http://www.google.com/
Key Search Terms: Freedom of speech
                        First Amendment

The Center for Democracy and Technology: Freedom of Speech
http://www.cdt.org/speech/
high school and up

This section of the Center for Democracy and Technology's Web site focuses on freedom of speech, particularly that related to the Internet. This page is divided into eight sections. Click on "Free Speech Online Basics" and you will get a very solid overview of the Communications Decency Act, a landmark 1997 decision in which the Supreme Court ruled that the Internet is a unique medium entitled to the highest protection under the free-speech protections of the First Amendment to the U.S. Constitution. Click on the "Child Online Protection Act" (COPA) link if you want to know more about this legislation. Here you will read about the most significant constitutional issues raised as a result of the COPA. Also, if you want to learn more about the background on freedom of speech on the Internet debate and how it relates to campaign laws, go to "Political Speech/FEC." Here you can read about campaign laws and their conflicts with the current trend of expressing political opinions online. You can also get the latest legislative news on the Federal Election Commission by scrolling down this page a bit. Also, click on "Resources" to get a list of relevant links pertaining to freedom of expression. This is divided into four sections: "Organizations," "Publications," "Tools," and "User-Empowerment." Go to any of these for access to some more informative sites.

The Center for Democracy and Technology has done a stellar job of disseminating data on the freedom of speech on the Internet debate. Here you will learn about the main issues surrounding this debate, who's involved, and why.

Citizen's Internet Empowerment Coalition
http://www.ciec.org/
high school and up

The Citizens Internet Empowerment Coalition came together to oppose Congress's first attempt to regulate content on the Internet, the Communications Decency Act (CDA), which the U.S. Supreme Court found unconstitutional on June 26, 1997. Now their site is being preserved as a resource on the landmark CDA case. It contains virtually everything you could hope for relating to the CDA lawsuit. Visit this site to read about specific details, background information, and to hear some important opinions regarding the CDA.

The site is very straightforward. Just scroll down to see what's available. On the left, you can click on the red text to access all you need to know about the CDA, including background on the lawsuit, Supreme Court appeals documents, and general information on the Internet free-speech issue. Scroll down and you can read about the details of the case. If you are interested in reading the published views and comments of certain political leaders, you will find this at the bottom of the page. Entitled "Reactions and Press Releases," there are several opinions centered on the CDA by individuals like former President Bill Clinton, senators, and members of Congress.

Peacefire
http://www.peacefire.org/
middle school and up

Peacefire is an organization dedicated to providing the general public with information related to online censorship and freedom of speech on the Internet. Peacefire's main contribution to this cause is to provide facts and research material, which is then used by larger organizations that are equipped to campaign, lobby, and deal with the legal aspects of this issue.

Peacefire's Web site contains a ton of news reports and updates related to the online censorship debate. Students will want to come here for the latest headlines, blocking software reports, information on current or recent censorship legislation, and for a general awareness about how Internet censorship even works. For example, one of the most controversial aspects of this site is a section on the home page that lays out instructions for disabling blocking software, which is used to eliminate access to sites that are deemed inappropriate (for young viewers, etc.). For this, Peacefire has been attacked by various blocking programs, such as CYBERsitter and CyberPatrol.

As stated in the "About Peacefire" link, this site is intended to provide viewers with facts. What you will find here is just that. You can read about everything from the "Blocked Site of the Day," to what the ACLU is currently doing to promote freedom of speech on the Internet. Peacefire is an access point for people interested in knowing what's happening with the online censorship debate.

GAY RIGHTS

Best Search Engine: http://www.google.com/
Key Search Terms: Gay rights
                       Lesbian rights
                       Civil rights

American Civil Liberties Union: Gay and Lesbian Rights
http://www.aclu.org/issues/gay/hmgl.html
middle school and up

The ACLU's site for gay and lesbian rights is superbly organized. Look around at the different sections. You will see one called "Highlights," in which there are many news stories and reports involving the ACLU's involvement in gay and lesbian rights issues. Further down the page, you will find discussion about anti-gay initiatives, civil-rights laws, criminal law, domestic partnerships, job discrimination, and many more topics. Visit these topics (they are all highlighted in red text) and take a look at some of these in-depth reports and articles. Maybe you want to know what's happening in America's schools. Scroll down to the bottom of the page where there is a section called "Youth, Students, and Schools." Here you can access a report on a settlement reached in Washington state with a school district over a gay-harassment incident there. You might also want to read about transgender rights. Click on any of these ACLU news items to learn about current and recent events pertaining to the transgender-rights issue, such as social-security benefits for a transsexual spouse, child-custody battles, or employment benefits for transgender individuals. Or maybe you'd like to visit the "Parenting" section, in which the ACLU describes topics like adoption, parenting legislation, and family relationships in general.

In addition to these several highlighted topic sections, the ACLU has also included a great list of publications related to gay and lesbian rights. Here you will find educational resources, parenting resources, and ACLU progress reports and project dockets. Just click on any of these titles to access the PDF-formatted text version. Also, you will find other resources here as well. There are several links to ACLU projects, background on various legislation, and specially featured Web sites that have been designed for more specific issues. For example, you will find a link to a site called "ShameOnWinnDixie.org," which was created to support an ACLU lawsuit that was filed recently against the WinnDixie stores on behalf of a married Louisiana trucker.

You will also have access to the most important or pressing gay and lesbian rights issues, all displayed at the top of the site. Or, if you are interested in becoming more involved with the ACLU and its causes, you can click on "Take Action" or "Keep Current." The ACLU Web site is very comprehensive and simple to navigate. It is all in the form of an outline. Just pay attention to the issue that interests you the most and see what the ACLU has to say about it.

Human Rights Campaign
http://www.hrc.org/
high school and up

As mentioned above, the Human Rights Campaign focuses on gay, lesbian, bisexual, and transgender rights. This is another activism site that contains a lot of resources for people interested in gay rights. Primarily, the Human Rights Campaign site is designed to offer ways of getting involved in this issue. There are links to local chapters, "Tool Kits" for beginner advocates, and links to write letters to members of Congress. You can also register to vote and get up-to-date details on current campaigns and candidates.

However, the Human Rights Campaign site is also an important source of research material concerning gay rights. You can come here to read about today's controversies, news stories, and political updates. To the left of the site, you will find buttons like "Issues and Legislation," "Grassroots Advocacy," "Campaign 2002," "Volunteering," and "Press Room." Also, at the top of the HRC site, you will find additional tabs that will link you to other useful material. Go to "Coming Out" to read a firsthand account of what it was like to become open about one's sexual preference. Here you will also read about National Coming Out Day, both on a national and local scale. Here you will also learn about the HRC's National Coming Out Project, which is intended to promote honesty and openness about being gay, lesbian, bisexual, or transgender on campus, in the workplace and in the community. Another helpful section in the HRC site is called "Family Net" and addresses issues like parenting, marriage, relationships, and joint property ownership. Or go to "Work Net" if you are looking for research material on the gay-rights issues as they relate to the workplace and employment. Here, you will even find specific information hailing certain companies for their treatment of gay and lesbian employees and their partners.

Also, in each of these sections within the HRC Web site, you will also find additional information throughout the page such as how to approach certain challenging situations, and general support information. In this way, HRC really comes through as one of the most helpful, informative, and supportive resources available online. You can learn how to contact an attorney, how to find diversity trainers for your business, and how to find additional literature and studies for research. This site is truly a gold mine for students and should not be missed.

SpeakOut.com: Gay Rights
http://www.speakout.com/activism/gayrights/
high school and up

SpeakOut is an opinion-forum Web site. It addresses various activism issues such as gun control, education, religion, politics, animal rights, and the death penalty. This particular page is dedicated to gay and lesbian rights. The most unique aspect about *SpeakOut* is that it offers viewers real opinions from real individuals who feel strongly about gay and lesbian rights. By visiting this site, students will be able to enhance their understanding of the gay-rights issue by reading what many different people have to say about it and by seeing it from a more direct perspective. As opposed to simply reading about current legislation, you can come here and see the impact of this legislation on people's lives. In addition to being a home base for activism and being heard, *SpeakOut* is also a home base for reliable research material and activism information.

The site is pretty straightforward. Just notice that the center and the left are dedicated to gay-rights issues, while the left side is for general SpeakOut topics. Go there if you are interested in learning more about SpeakOut and its origins and many other projects. Stick to the other parts if you want to focus on gay and lesbian rights. Scroll down the center of the page to read some important news stories regarding gay rights. Click on the bold headline for an in-depth look at the story. To the left, notice different SpeakOut campaigns and petitions. Or go to the "Learn More" section to read about gays in the military, antidiscrimination laws, hate crimes, and gay marriage. Also, down a bit further, you will find access to some very useful links. These sites all deal with gay and lesbian rights. Included in this list are sites like "Human Rights Campaign," another important advocate for gay rights and equality, and "Gay and Lesbian Alliance Against Defamation," an organization dedicated to changing the way gays and lesbians are portrayed in the media.

GOVERNORS

Best Search Engine:	http://www.google.com/
Key Search Terms:	Governors
	United States governors

National Governors Association
http://www.nga.org/
middle school and up

The National Governors Association (NGA) Web site is the place to learn about the roles and responsibilities of U.S. governors in general. The NGA is a kind of governors' guild. Any position or opinion stated here is a unified one. For example, if you are interested in learning what America's governors (i.e., the NGA) think about the Clean Water Act, you will find it here. If you want information on individual governors, you can get that as well, just not the same kind of material. For example, click on "Governors" to get a list of governors' names and their respective states. You will find background information, such as educational and professional histories, as well as their biographical information and photos. You will generally *not* find their political positions related to individual state issues. For this kind of information, you will need to visit their independent Web sites, which you can also access here.

The NGA site is helpful if you want to get an idea of how the nation's governors are involved in national issues and policy-making. But it can be a little discouraging because it's difficult to find solid, specific information. Because it would be nearly impossible to address the current politics of all 50 states in one Web site, most views are generalized for the sake of the group, or the NGA.

GRANDFATHER CLAUSE

Best Search Engine: http://www.google.com/
Key Search Terms: Grandfather clause
 Civil rights

Reading the Fine Print: The Grandfather Clause in Louisiana
http://historymatters.gmu.edu/d/5352/
high school and up

This site is part of a collaborative project involving George Mason University and the City University of New York. Here you will learn about the post-Reconstruction era in the South and the way Southern states attempted to disempower African Americans and maintain Democratic Party dominance. The grandfather clause allowed men to register to vote only if they could have voted in 1867 (before African Americans were allowed to vote in the South) or were descended from an 1867 voter.

In addition to outlining the grandfather clause and its place in American history, this site also displays a few of its sections for you. One absurdity in the document—another attempt at eliminating the votes of African Americans—is a stipulation stating that individuals must be able to read and write in order to vote. Of course, African Americans were prohibited from attending school, so most did not learn to read and write.

GREAT COMPROMISE OF 1787

Best Search Engine: http://www.google.com/
Key Search Terms: Great Compromise + 1787

U.S. Senate Historical Minutes: A Great Compromise
http://www.senate.gov/learning/min_1bb.html
middle school and up

Here, the U.S. Senate site offers a segment on the Great Compromise of 1787. This agreement, reached during the fragile stages of the creation of the U.S. Constitution, provided a dual system of congressional representation. In the House of Representatives each state would be assigned a number of seats in proportion to its population, while in the Senate all states would have the same number of seats.

As straightforward as the Great Compromise seems today, so is this Web page. It is a simple recap of the historical events surrounding the disagreement. Just read along to get a sense of the politics at the time the Constitution was being framed.

GREAT DEPRESSION

Best Search Engine: http://www.google.com/
Key Search Terms: Great Depression
         Stock market crash + 1929

Looking Back at the Crash of '29
http://www.nytimes.com/library/financial/index-1929-crash.html
middle school and up

This *New York Times* online special feature does a good job of explaining the stock-market crash of 1929. It covers the causes of the crash, as well as the long-term consequences. There are some interesting photographs, and you can even check out articles about the crash that the *New York Times* ran in 1929.

For those of you interested in reading an interpretive article about the crash, check out the main article on the home page by Floyd Norris. The bulk of historical material is in the second part of the essay. You will need to click on "More" at the bottom of the home page to access it. There are lots of photographs mixed in with the text.

When you are ready for some primary source material on the crash, turn to the original *Times* articles. The site lets you read *every* article printed in the *Times* from the week of October 28, 1929, as well as the front pages. This material will help you understand how people viewed the stock-market collapse as it happened. The articles will also reveal something about the tenor of the times. For instance, one article declares, "Women Traders Going Back to Bridge Games; Say They are Through Forever." To view these articles simply click on the titles from the menu on the right side of the home page (look under the heading "A Bad Week").

Slouching Towards Utopia? The Economic History of the Twentieth Century
http://econ161.berkeley.edu/TCEH/Slouch_Crash14.html
high school and up

You won't find a better place on the Internet to learn about the economic history of the Crash of 1929 and the Great Depression than this terrific site by J. Bradford DeLong, an economics professor at the University of California at Berkeley. Don't use *Slouching Towards Utopia* to research the social and political history of the Great Depression, though. This site's focus is on the economic events of the period and why they happened. *Slouching Towards Utopia* is clearly written, easy to understand, and chock-full of graphs and charts to help make sense of the material.

To navigate the site, simply scroll down the screen as though you are reading a book chapter. When you reach the end, you have the option to go to the next chapter. De Long does an excellent job looking at the consequences of the Great Depression in this chapter, though, so don't feel obligated to read more.

Voices from the Thirties: Life Histories from the Federal Writers' Project
http://www.memory.loc.gov/ammem/wpaintro/exhome.html
middle school and up

After exploring *Slouching Towards Utopia* and *Looking Back at the Crash of '29*, you probably have a good sense of the causes and the consequences of the stock-market crash and the Great Depression. But what was life like during the Depression for everyday folks? This wonderful Web site, which is part of the Library of Congress's *American Memory Project,* will help you find out.

In the late 1930s, when one out of every four Americans was out of work, President Franklin Roosevelt launched the Works Project Administration (WPA), which employed people to use their skills for public good. Unemployed authors were placed into the Federal Writers Project (FWP) and assigned the task of recording the life stories of Americans. Before the project was discontinued in the mid-1940s, the FWP had conducted interviews with more than ten thousand men and women from all different regions, occupations, and ethnic groups. This Web site makes their stories available to you.

If you want to read an overview of the FWP, click on the "Introduction" from the menu on the right side of the home page. To save yourself from having to sort through more than ten thousand documents, you probably will want to start your research by first looking at the excerpted interviews. Click on "Excerpts from Sample Interviews" from the home-page menu. The sample interviews are divided by occupational type: "All in a Day's Work: Industrial Lore"; "Rank and File"; "Hard Times in the City"; "Testifying"; and "Making Do: Women and Work." There are several excerpts under each of these categories. The interviews include the subjects' occupations and wages, to help you better understand their economic status during the Depression.

If you don't find the material you want in these samples, you can dive into the main collection. Remember that the FWP collection contains interviews recorded up to 1940 (when the Depression had technically ended). To access the main collection, click on "WPA Life Histories Home Page" from the bottom of the *Voices from the Thirties* home page. You can then either search for documents by keyword or by state. If you choose to search by state, you can conduct keyword searches of the documents in that state, or you can browse all the documents from that state.

GUN CONTROL

Best Search Engine: http://www.google.com/

Key Search Terms: Gun control

                           Gun control legislation

Guncite: Gun Control and Second Amendment Issues
http://www.guncite.com/
middle school and up

This is the end-all, beat-all Web site for students researching the full gun-control controversy. *Guncite* is an online resource dedicated to disseminating information on gun control. Its coverage includes related statistics and perspectives, Second Amendment analysis, breaking news, an extensive online "reading room," and many links to other sites related to gun control. The only problem you may face is a lack of time to get through all the material and perspectives concerning the gun-control debate you will find here. It's not that it lacks organization and clarity, just that it is chock-full of material.

A good way to start working your way through is to take a look around to get a full view before you decide which of the many issues you want to explore. Consider the Second Amendment. Under this heading alone, there are more than twenty-five articles available to you that address the amendment's relevance in the gun-control debate. If you are interested in the views of political leaders on gun control, you will find it here. Or, if you want to research children's access to guns, click on "The Gun Control Reading Room" near the bottom of the site. Maybe you want to know about the Brady Bill, passed in 1998, which requires a licensed importer, manufacturer, or dealer to contact the national instant criminal background check (NICS) before transferring any firearm to an unlicensed individual.

No matter what angle you are researching, you are sure to find some helpful information here at *Guncite*. The best part of the site is that you will also find views representing both sides of the debate, which is crucial for a complete understanding of the issue.

Gun Laws, Gun Control and Gun Rights
http://www.jurist.law.pitt.edu/gunlaw.htm
high school and up

This site is all about the legal end of the gun-control debate in America. It is presented by *Jurist*, an online legal-education network. The information here, again, is intended for individuals on all sides of this ongoing debate. The difference between this *Jurist* site and the *Guncite* site is that this one deals almost exclusively with the legal and political aspects of the gun-control controversy. There is little opinion and few personal views here. It's more about the factual and legal nuts and bolts that surround the issue. You will read about gun-control cases, legislation, political positions, leading cases on gun law, relevant statutes, the opinions of legal scholars, and statistical reports. *Jurist* is an essential stop for those of you interested in gun-control legislation.

HATCH ACT

Best Search Engine: http://www.google.com/

Key Search Terms: Hatch Act

Federal Hatch Act: Federal Mediation and Conciliation Service
http://www.fmcs.gov/agency/ogc/federal_hatch_act.htm
middle school and up

This one-page Web site on the Hatch Act of 1939 (amended in 1993) is brief but direct. Here you will read a synopsis of the act that originally restricted federal (and certain state and local) government employees in their ability to participate in political activities. This site is simple and to the point. It lays out the general idea behind the Federal Hatch Act, lists the dos and don'ts specified by the act, then proceeds to address the most commonly asked questions related to it. A good place to begin your research, this site contains all the basics on the Federal Hatch Act.

Hatch Act for Federal Employees
http://www.osc.gov/hatch_a.htm
high school and up

This site, part of the Office of Special Counsel (OSC) lays out the Federal Hatch Act for you in more detail than the FMCS site does. Here you will find everything related to this legislation. There's even a list of letters written by the Hatch Act Unit to various federal employees, called advisories, which answer specific questions related to the Hatch Act. There is also a PowerPoint presentation on the act's stipulations if you are interested in taking the virtual route to understanding this legislation. You won't have any trouble getting in-depth material here. And if you have a specific question concerning the Hatch Act, there will most likely already be an answer at the bottom of this site, under the "Frequently Asked Questions" section.

HATE CRIMES

Best Search Engine: http://www.google.com/

Key Search Terms: Hate crimes

Civil Rights Organization
http://www.civilrights.org/issues/hate/
middle school and up

This site has a wealth of information pertaining to hate crimes in America. The *Civil Rights Organization* is dedicated to informing online viewers about hate crimes as well as a gamut of other civil rights issues.

This particular page on hate crimes is simple and coherent. It is divided into two sections, one that addresses general hate-crime details, including links for "Overview," "History," "Resources," "Stories," and "Update." You will even see a "Toolkit" link, where you will find information on how to organize, lobby, and contact your elected officials about hate crimes. If you scroll down a bit, you will see another section comprised of news stories, press releases, and hate-crime alerts. For example, if you want to find out about the wave of attacks against Arab-Americans and Muslims following the attacks of September 11, 2001, you can click on one of several articles addressing this issue under "Press Releases." Or if you are more interested in the legislation of hate-crime laws, such as the Local Law Enforcement Enhancement Act, you can get up-to-date information like this by clicking on "Alerts."

Hate Crimes
http://www.infoplease.com/spot/hatecrimes.html
middle school and up

A hate crime is characterized by motivations of hostility toward the victim as a member of a group. Crimes against persons of different ethnic, religious, and sexual orientations have always been present in American society, but the disturbing fact is that statistics show them to be increasing in frequency.

This *InfoPlease* site contains an article, published in August 1999, entitled "Defining Hate Crimes: No Longer a Black and White Issue." The article does a thorough job of touching on all of the important aspects of hate crimes. It includes sections on the evolution of these crimes, on current and controversial legislation, even on understanding the perpetrators and victims of hate crimes. It is a valuable starting point if you are interested in studying this topic. You will also find links to other important sites that carry on the fight against hate crimes.

Southern Poverty Law Center
http://www.splcenter.org/
middle school and up

The Southern Poverty Law Center (SPLC) is a nonprofit organization that combats hate, intolerance, and discrimination through education and litigation. In doing so, the SPLC takes on special projects and programs including the Intelligence Project and Teaching Tolerance. Their Web site is a very valuable resource for students interested in hate crimes. It focuses on each of their primary programs, including the ones listed above, and on educating its viewers about each of them. Here you will see how the SPLC attempts to address several of the most important issues surrounding hate crimes and civil-rights abuses.

Click on "Wall of Tolerance" to read about this public tribute that is dedicated to thousands of Center supporters and others who have advanced the cause of tolerance. The Wall will be the focus of a new Southern Poverty Law Center exposition in Montgomery, Alabama, which has historically been deeply entrenched in the battle for equality and tolerance. Also, go to "Teaching Tolerance" and you will learn about this SPLC project aimed at fostering equity, respect, and understanding in the classroom. "Teaching Tolerance" is designed to assist teachers and educators around the nation. This project includes hands-on classroom resources, activities, grant information, and general material to assist in fighting hate in the classroom. Also, click on "Legal Action" if you want to know more about the SPLC's involvement in the legislative side of battling hate. Here you will read about anti-hate litigation, landmark cases, information and instructions on requesting litigation assistance, and even a Prisoner Rights Manual, which is a guide designed to help inmates protect their health and safety. Finally, read about the SPLC's "Intelligence Project." This is one of the most important features of the SPLC site. Here you can access current information on hate groups, patriot groups (of which there were 158 identified in 2001 by SPLC monitors; these groups typically advocate or adhere to extreme antigovernment doctrines). These groups are identified on this page by state and name.

The SPLC is a serious organization and is dedicated to combating hate. Their site is well designed and clear. Simply by researching each of these anti-hate and anti-intolerance projects, students will learn a lot about discrimination in America. It is important to pay attention to the scope of groups like the SPLC. By doing this, you can discover what areas (education, monitoring hate groups, legislation, etc.) are the most problematic and which ones deserve the most attention. The SPLC Web site will teach you this.

HOUSE OF REPRESENTATIVES

Best Search Engine: http://www.google.com/
Key Search Terms: US House of Representatives

Office of Clerk: U.S. House of Representatives
http://www.clerk.house.gov/
high school and up

The Office of Clerk Web site is a kind of online information and document headquarters for the House of Representatives. Here you will find historical data and archives related to the House and its members. This site is very smooth and easy to use. There are useful tabs to the left like "Educational Resources," "Historical Highlights," and "Legislative Activities." If you want to find out about the Congressional profile—for example, the proportion of Democrats to Republicans in the House—you can find it by clicking on "Membership Information." The Clerk site also includes all the crucial general updates, such as news stories, House floor proceedings, contact information for representatives, and elections.

This site is a goldmine if you are studying the House of Representatives. Again, you will find it very easy to use, so you shouldn't have a bit of trouble extracting the information you want.

United States House of Representatives
http://www.house.gov/
middle school and up

The House of Representatives is the larger of the two chambers comprising the U.S. Congress. Along with the Senate, the House is responsible for the legislative process, including the debate on, and the ultimate acceptance or rejection of, proposed legislation. The House of Representatives Web site is an important source of information related to its functions. You can start by clicking on "Search House Sites" if you know what particular area of the House you are interested in, such as committees or individual member names. This is essentially a search engine for the House site. You can also go to "House Operations," where you will find several links to operational topics, like rules of conduct and codes, related to the legislative process. On the right side of the home page, you will see a list of House office links, which will take you to the committee, leadership, and member offices. If you want to get some specific information about the Committee on International Relations, for example, you can do it by clicking on "Committee Offices."

The rest of the site will link you to current House schedules, news items, employment opportunities, and general material on the legislative process. This is where you will find the bulk of your information, as it addresses the more general function-related issues. Maybe you want to know about the actual process of voting on a legislative proposal once the president has passed it on to Congress. This is where you will find it. There's even a link to the Thomas site, which is the authority on legislative-process education.

The House site's biggest flaw is its lack of organization and smoothness. It can be difficult to navigate. When you click on a link expecting to find some useful material, you will often just find another list of links. And when you do get to the sought-after information, it's not easy to sort through. It's not a very well designed, user-friendly Web site. But the information is there, and it is the official Web site for the House of Representatives.

IMPEACHMENT

Best Search Engine: http://www.google.com/
Key Search Terms: Impeachment

Encyclopedia Americana: Impeachment
http://www.gi.grolier.com/presidents/ea/side/impeach.html
middle school and up

Here's a good definition to get you started. This one-page site is extremely straightforward. It gives you a clear definition of the term "impeachment," describes how the impeachment process in the United States works, and touches on specific impeachment cases throughout history, including those of former presidents Andrew Johnson, Richard Nixon, and Bill Clinton.

In addition to getting the facts on their impeachment trials, you can learn all sorts of background history that made these men vulnerable to impeachment. You will learn that President Johnson, a Southerner, was more sympathetic toward the defeated Confederacy than was his Republican-majority Congress, which resulted in political animosity almost from the beginning of his presidency. You can also read about the Watergate scandal surrounding Nixon's investigation and about his involvement in its cover-up. Finally, you will learn about former President Clinton's brush with impeachment, including his questionable Whitewater real-estate venture as governor of Arkansas, and the incriminating testimonies of Paula Jones and Monica Lewinsky.

This site will give you a general understanding about impeachment in the United States. It does have a shortcoming, though, in that none of its information is very detailed. So although you can get the main idea behind impeachment and its place in American history, you will want to begin, not end, your search here.

Finding Precedent: The Impeachment of Andrew Johnson
http://www.impeach-andrewjohnson.com/
high school and up

This is a "must visit" site if you are researching the impeachment of Andrew Johnson. It's easy to use and a great blend of primary and secondary material. Here you will find information on the political background of the impeachment; the arguments for and against impeachment; the articles and rules of impeachment; and a who's who of 28 important figures in the impeachment drama. You can also get an overview of Johnson's presidency with links to appropriate articles in *Harper's Weekly*, the most important periodical of the time.

The arguments surrounding impeachment come from *Harper's Weekly*, which gives you the contemporary flavor of the debate. The biographical section is particularly helpful because it covers a wide variety of individuals from Johnson and his major opponents and defenders to prominent journalists who covered the trial.

The site is extremely simple to navigate. Just click on the appropriate topic from the home page. The link from "Impeachment Arguments" brings you to a topical list of entries. This is a good outline of the kinds of arguments presented in the case. Clicking on an individual entry will get you to the *Harper's* editorial in which it is discussed.

Online NewsHour: the Impeachment Trial
http://www.pbs.org/newshour/impeachment/
middle school and up

If you are researching former president Bill Clinton's impeachment trial, this Public Broadcasting Service (PBS) site is a gold mine. It contains their online coverage of the events surrounding the trial, as well as the U.S. poet laureate's reflections on what impression the trial may leave on the country; the transcript of four senators discussing the trial; and Clinton's reaction to the Senate's vote to acquit him of both articles of impeachment, in addition to other useful documents.

IMPERIALISM

Best Search Engine: http://www.google.com/
Key Search Terms: Imperialism

The Age of Imperialism
http://www.smplanet.com/imperialism/toc.html
middle school and up

Think of this Web site as one-stop shopping for information about U.S. overseas expansion. You will find material on a range of topics, including photographs, maps, notes on key figures, and time lines. You name it, and this Web site will have it!

The Age of Imperialism is organized into five main sections: "Expansion in the Pacific"; "Spanish-American War"; "Boxer Rebellion"; "Panama Canal"; and "U.S. Intervention in Latin America." Click on any of these topics from the home page to enter a world of interactive history. Each section gives you the pertinent historical information along with an easy-to-understand analysis of the events. You will not only get the "who, what, when, and where" of each topic, but also the "why."

The other fantastic aspect of this Web site is its links, which put a wealth of information at your fingertips. You can click to access biographies of various American presidents, texts of treaties between the U.S. and other nations, detailed maps of areas, and time lines. For example, in the section on the Boxer Rebellion, you can link to the "Background of Ching China," "A Concise Political History of China," "John Hay's Open Door Notes," and various maps. Check out the links to outside resources, too. Click on "Bibliography" from the home page for links to supplemental resources.

The Birth of U.S. Imperialism
http://www.geocities.com/Athens/Ithaca/9852/usimp.htm
high school and up

This Web site has loads of good information on U.S. expansion in the nineteenth century. However, it is much less comprehensive than *The Age of Imperialism*, and it is definitely written for an older audience. Expect more complicated writing. Definitely check out *Age of Imperialism* first, and then use this Web site to fill in any gaps you might have. It's also blander than *The Age of Imperialism*, so don't expect pictures or maps to help you with your research.

This Web site is arranged according to several key terms that are related to the history of U.S. imperialism, such as the Monroe Doctrine and Dollar Diplomacy. After a brief discussion of the concepts, the site gives links to other sources. Click on these for good primary source material. For instance, if you click on the "Avalon Project" link under the "Monroe Doctrine," you can read the text of the Monroe Doctrine.

The Web site also includes an essay on the history of U.S. imperialism. This provides some good background, but parts of it are way too advanced for younger students. Click on "Bibliography" if you need to find books on the topic.

An Outline of American History
http://odur.let.rug.nl/~usa/H/1990/ch6_p8.htm
middle school and up

Are you looking for a basic Web site that can answer quick questions on U.S. imperialism? If so, this no-frills Web site is for you, but don't expect photographs or much supplementary material. It hits the major points, but not much more.

An Outline of American History provides a brief explanation of the key events of this era—the Spanish-American War, Theodore Roosevelt's "Rough Riders," and American involvement in China. Click on the links for additional information. For example, you can access Mark Twain's thoughts on U.S. intervention in the Philippines, read John Hay's first "Open Door Note," or take a look at the biographies of some U.S. presidents. Some of the links take you back to *The Age of Imperialism* site, though, so don't hope for too much new material here.

INDEPENDENT PARTIES

Best Search Engine: http://www.google.com/

Key Search Terms: Independent political parties

                      Independent parties

Independent Parties
http://www.directory.google.com/Top/Regional/North_America/
    United_States/Society_and_Culture/Politics/Parties/

At this index page, you will find Google's compilation of various independent political parties in America. This site is simply a directory of independent-party Web sites. Browse the list first, then just click on the name of the party to go to the official site if you want firsthand information on its beliefs and structure.

Because the Internet is the most effective and efficient means of networking with fellow party members, most of these independent parties have a current, functioning Web site. Going right to the source here is a fun way to research these parties, as they generally include lots of information about specific causes and political missions.

INTEREST GROUPS

Best Search Engine: http://scout.cs.wisc.edu/index.html
Key Search Terms: Special interest groups
                      Interest groups
                      Advocacy groups

Political Advocacy Groups
http://www.reinert.creighton.edu/advocacy/
high school and up

Created by a political-science librarian at California State University in Chico, the *Political Advocacy Groups* Web site offers an excellent online directory of U.S. political pressure groups, interest groups, and lobbyists. The list is composed of organizations that personally contact, pressure, or educate representatives; conduct and disseminate policy-oriented research; organize grassroots citizen activism; and/or provide financial resources to congressional candidates. *Political Advocacy Groups* is the ideal place to go if you need to understand the ideology or actions of an organization, politician, or editorialist.

The directory compiles complete contact information and brief organizational descriptions of more than two hundred groups, spanning the political spectrum. You can browse the subject categories (which include "Tax Reform," "Immigration," "Political Parties," etc.) or use the alphabetical list of organizations. An interesting feature of the site is its "Newspaper Citations" ranking, which rates the relative power of a group by tabulating the number of times major newspapers mentioned, cited, or quoted it.

Voter Information Services: Congressional Report Cards
http://www.vis.org/
high school and up

Voter Information Services (VIS) is a nonpartisan organization devoted to providing voters with the latest information on congressional voting. Its "Congressional Report Cards" section contains data on congressional votes from 1991 to the present.

Although the site is a little tricky to figure out at first, it's worth the effort. In the report cards, you will sink your teeth into information about more than fifty advocacy groups and their positions on congressional voting. This means that you can search the report cards to find out how senators and representatives vote in relation to the views of special-interest groups. Here's the catch: it's going to cost you a fee. Recently, *VIS* implemented an annual fee of $3.65 (a penny a day) to access the reports.

INTERNAL REVENUE SERVICE

Best Search Engine: http://www.google.com/

Key Search Terms: Internal revenue service

Internal Revenue Service
http://www.infoplease.com/
middle school and up

InfoPlease is the online spin-off of a company that has produced almanac publications and reference databases for more than sixty years. This colorful site lets you tap into a massive collection of almanacs on almost every imaginable topic—chock-full of millions of authoritative factoids. For information on the Internal Revenue Service, it's particularly handy.

Click on the subject area "Taxes," and look for "History of the Income Tax in the United States," "Internal Revenue Service," "Federal Corporation Taxes," "State Taxes on Individuals," and more. If you follow the link for the "Internal Revenue Service," you will find a clear explanation of how the IRS operates that addresses the organization and levels of tax offices in the United States. You will also read about the important transition from filing taxes by hand to the new improved world of electronic tax filing. If you want to learn how much tax money has been collected over the last thirty years and how it is broken down into different categories, such as employment taxes and individual taxes, just click on "IRS Statistics" for that and many other fun facts. You will even learn about filing appeals with the IRS should you choose to dispute your tax liabilities.

Internal Revenue Service: The Digital Daily
http://www.irs.gov/irs/display/0,,i1 = 46&genericId = 23092,00.html
high school and up

The Internal Revenue Service, a branch of the Department of Treasury, is responsible for collecting the nation's taxes according to the Internal Revenue Code enacted by Congress. The IRS's official Web site can be very useful for finding detailed information about its operations, though it can get a little complicated at times due to the volume of information related to such a large government agency.

Fortunately, the site is clearly organized with areas of interest along the top of the page and a table of contents and search engine along the left side. You can click on "About IRS" to get a synopsis of what the IRS does, including its history and bureaucratic structure. You can also study the way the IRS works with the various types of corporations, nonprofits, and individual taxpayers. The site explains how the appropriate type of taxation process varies depending upon the taxpayer. The IRS Web site is pretty clear and easy to follow as long as you know where you want to go. It is definitely the easiest way to access information about taxation processes and rules in America.

Internal Revenue Service Tax Interactive
http://www.irs.gov/individuals/display/0,,i1 = 1&genericId =
    15548,00.html
middle school and up

This site educates teenagers about the U.S. tax system, the effect of taxes on their day-to-day lives, and new electronic ways to file tax returns. You will find sections on "Farmers," "Foreign Nationals," "Household Employers," "Innocent Spouses," "Overseas Taxpayers," "Retirees/ Senior Citizens," "Students," and "Self-Employed." You can learn how to file taxes electronically, study up on the history of taxes in the United States, access numerous special topics, learn key tax terms, or read the "Frequently Asked Questions."

The site is not quite as cool as some other government sites for kids, but it will answer your basic questions without making you wade through a lot of heavy-duty tax talk. However, if it's the heavy-duty stuff you are looking for, try the *Digital Daily* site above. You will find more history of the IRS and our particular system of taxation there.

JIM CROW LAWS (SEE ALSO BLACK CODES)

Best Search Engine: http://www.google.com/
Key Search Terms: Jim Crow laws
                                   Black codes
                                   Poll tax + Jim Crow

Jim Crow
http://www.africana.com/tt_026.htm
middle school and up

This Web page, which is part of the *Africana.com* site, isn't flashy, but it is an excellent history of the Jim Crow era in the American South. So if you want a quick lesson about Jim Crow laws, start here. The essay briefly covers a wide range of topics including the origin of the term "Jim Crow," the post-Civil War black codes, the U.S. Supreme Court decision *Plessy v. Ferguson* (which enshrined the doctrine of separate-but-equal in U.S. law), types of Jim Crow laws, and the reasons for the breakdown of the Jim Crow system. To navigate, simply scroll down the home page. Click on "Next" at the bottom of the screen to continue reading.

Jim Crow Laws
http://www.nps.gov/malu/documents/jim_crow_laws.htm
middle school and up

This site provides a quick overview of Jim Crow laws. The best part is that it lets you read samplings of Jim Crow laws from states all across the nation. Although it just gives you a taste of the primary source material related to the topic, this site is perfect for younger students who aren't ready to plow through entire documents such as those on the *Race and Place* Web site. To navigate the site, simply scroll down the home page.

Race and Place: An African American Community in the Jim Crow South
http://www.vcdh.virginia.edu/afam/cvilleenter.html
high school and up

This excellent Web site focuses on the community of Charlottesville, Virginia, during the era of Jim Crow laws. It tells the story of an African American community fighting to claim its right to vote that was guaranteed by the 15th Amendment but denied under Jim Crow. It is a tale of oppression and also of heroic resistance.

Once you've entered the site from the home page (click on "Enter"), you can easily access its three main sections. If you want to get a sense of the composition of the African American community in Charlottesville during this period of oppression, you can explore the city's 1910 census of families with at least one African American member. Just click on "Census" under the heading "Explore Our Databases." The site has a sophisticated search engine that lets you search the census by a person's name, gender, occupation, race, marital status, or position in the family. You can also explore Charlottesville's city directory and directory of African American businesses in a similar way. You will see the links right below the one for the census.

The site has another wonderful section that lets you look at primary documents that are related to voting rights during the Jim Crow era. Click on "Disenfranchisement and African-American Resistance in Charlottesville: 1900–1925" (under the heading "Read About African American Life During the Era of Jim Crow"). There are also some fantastic interpretive articles in this section. Check out the "Timeline of State and Local Politics" for an overview. "Virginia Suffrage Legislation" lets you read the documents that disenfranchised African Americans—

the state's 1902 Constitution (you can see the passage requiring voters to pay a poll tax) and the Walton Act (stipulating that voters must pass a literacy test). The primary source documents can be accessed by clicking on "Broadsides, News Clippings, and Political Correspondence." You will find digital copies of flyers, newspaper articles, and letters.

For those of you who are more visually oriented, check out the site's tremendous photograph collection of the Charlottesville African American community. Click on "Holsinger Studio Collection" from the home page, followed by "Search the Digital Image Database" and "African American Photographs." You can then scroll through an index of all the photos, which include portraits of people and homes.

JUDICIAL BRANCH (SEE ALSO BRANCHES OF GOVERNMENT, EXECUTIVE BRANCH, AND LEGISLATIVE BRANCH)

Best Search Engine: http://www.google.com/
Key Search Terms: Judicial branch + government

Department of Justice Web Page for Kids
http://www.usdoj.gov/kidspage
middle school

The *Department of Justice Web Page for Kids* will teach you everything you need to know about legal and civil rights, federal court procedures, drug abuse prevention, and ways to get involved in community action to help prevent crime.

Try "Inside the Courtroom" if you are interested in the federal criminal court process. Perhaps you are participating in a project that involves setting up a student courtroom. If so, this section of the site will prove quite useful for that as well. "Get It Straight" links you to the Drug Enforcement Administration site and contains quite a bit of good information on drug abuse prevention. Go to "Hateful Acts Hurt Kids" if you are researching racism or prejudice.

The site also links to the *FBI Kids & Youth* Web site and the Ten Most Wanted list in case your research leads you in the direction of the villains.

Famous American Trials
http://www.law.umkc.edu/faculty/projects/ftrials/ftrials.htm
middle school and up

If you are interested in specific trials that have shaped the American government and judicial system, try this excellent site. It provides an in-depth look at a number of landmark legal battles you have probably already encountered in your studies. For each case reviewed, you will find a wealth of diverse information, such as an overview of events, a time line, photographs, audio clips, transcripts of testimony, biographies of participants, and much more.

You will find trials from as far back as the Salem witch hunts of 1692 and the *Amistad* case of 1839. Most of the cases included, however, are from the twentieth century. They involve civil-rights issues, Vietnam War crimes, the Chicago Seven, and the McCarthy era.

Federal Judicial Center
http://www.fjc.gov/
middle school and up

The Federal Judicial Center (FJC) is the research and education source for the federal courts. The FJC Web site is a simple one. You have three options here. You can go to "Publications" to access reports, manuals, and other materials related to the judicial system. The alphabetized publications catalogue can then be found to the left, so if you know which topic you want to research, this is the way to go. For example, click on "Class Action Litigation" to find "A Study of Class Actions in Four Federal District Courts" which you can then download in Adobe format.

The second option you have back at the FJC home page is to click on "Federal Judicial History." Here you will be able to access biographies of federal judges since 1789, the histories of individual courts, and landmark cases. This is a fun way to track the evolution of America's judicial system, such as how its moral and ethical standpoint has changed with time. Finally, you can click on "Current FJC Activities" to read about today's judicial hot topics.

Because this site is straightforward and simple, you will find it's a snap to quickly locate information on your research topic. Aside from the standard list of relevant links on the left, you really only have a few ways to access information, but there's no shortage of material. The FJC just eliminated the frivolous stuff.

The Federal Judiciary
http://www.uscourts.gov/
middle school and up

This site is a gold mine for students researching U.S. federal courts. It contains all the fundamentals plus a lot of extra perks, like its own judicial library of publications and statistical reports. From the library you can click on "Understanding the Federal Courts" to jump to a page containing everything you might want to know about the court system, like the jurisdiction of federal courts, U.S. judges, legal terminology, and general FAQs. Back at the home page, you can also study the U.S. court system by clicking on "Supreme Court," "Court of Appeals," "District Courts," or "Bankruptcy Courts." This helps to eliminate some of the confusion associated with such a complex government system. Another one of this site's touches is its "What's New" button. Here you will find a bulletin board containing not just current news items, but also recent changes that have occurred within the federal judicial system, like judge-ship vacancy announcements or changes in the Codes of Conduct for U.S. judges.

JURY SYSTEM

Best Search Engine: http://www.google.com/
Key Search Terms: Jury system

The American Jury
http://www.crfc.org/americanjury/index.html
middle school and up

This online resource guide to the American jury system is packed with useful information and links. You can study everything from the origins of the American jury, to jury damage awards, to jury reform. Just click on any of these subtopics to the left of the page. You can also choose from the buttons to the right, which include "Lessons and Activities," "Web Resources," and "Print Resources." Here you will be directed to all kinds of multimedia sources. You can see portraits of the prosecution and defense attorneys who argued in historically famous jury trials. You can also view other historical documents, like a 1933 headline from a Montgomery, Alabama newspaper discussing opinions and details of the Scottsboro murder case. Although this Web site gears a lot of its material toward teachers and classroom activities, it can also be very educational to the student viewer.

LAME DUCK

Best Search Engine: http://www.google.com/
Key Search Terms: Lame-Duck Amendment

C-SPAN's Capital Questions
http://www.c-span.org/questions/week170.asp
middle school and up

This is a fun page to read. You will find out about the origins of the term "lame duck" and its evolution in American politics. It touches on the constitutional amendment, called the Lame-Duck Amendment, ratified in 1933, which moved the date on which a new Congress regularly convened from the first Monday in December—thirteen months from the previous November elections—to January 3, just two months after the elections. By reading this page you will understand the logic of the Lame-Duck Amendment and the purpose it has served. It's a rather interesting term and has a history that can be traced as far back as the 1700s in England.

LEGISLATION

Best Search Engine: http://www.google.com/

Key Search Terms: Legislation + government

How a Bill Becomes a Law
http://www.infoplease.com/ipa/A0101183.html
middle school and up

Start here for a basic diagram of the legislation process. This *InfoPlease* site tells you exactly how a bill becomes law. If it's the process that you find confusing, you won't want to miss this concise one-page explanation. It uses simple terms and lays it out step by step, covering the roles of the Senate, the House of Representatives, and the President.

Legal Information Institute: Cornell University
http://www.law.cornell.edu/topics/legislation.html
high school and up

If you want a more in-depth look at the legislative process in the United States, this is the site to visit. Here you will find a more detailed explanation of how laws are passed than what you will find at the *InfoPlease* site.

The best part about this site is its source menu to the right of the page. You will see links for both federal issue sites and for state issue sites. You can click on "State Statutes by Topic" to find a list of all kinds of statute topics, like adoption, poverty, or marriage. Then click on any of these to find out the statutes on a state-by-state basis. There are plenty of links that will help you in your legislative research here, whether it concerns the federal government or state governments.

LEGISLATIVE BRANCH (SEE ALSO BRANCHES OF GOVERNMENT)

Best Search Engine: http://www.google.com/

Key Search Terms: Legislative branch

The U.S. Legislative Branch
http://www.thomas.loc.gov/home/legbranch/legbranch.html
middle school and up

The *Thomas* Web site is the authority on the legislative arm of American politics. It is the official home of Congress, comprised of the Senate and the House of Representatives. The site is pretty clear. The home page is divided into three sections. The first deals with congressional topics. It includes links to the Senate and to the House, which will take you to their separate home pages, or to the individual sites of senators and representatives. The next section is entitled "Legislative Agencies and Commissions." Here you will find links to the Library of Congress, the Medical Payment Advisory Commission, and the General Accounting Office, to name a few. Or go to the "Office of Technology Assessment" to discover who's responsible for the maintenance and preservation of the United States Capitol Complex, including the Capitol, the congressional office buildings, the Library of Congress buildings, and the Supreme Court. The third section of the *Thomas* site offers links to different information sources pertaining to the legislative branch. You can click on "Educational Resources" to get a list of more links to independent sites dedicated to educational topics. For example, click on the "Congress Q & A" link to jump to a University of Indiana Web site, which answers general questions concerning Congress and the legislative process in general.

Overall, this site contains all the necessary information. You should be able to either get the answers you need here or find the appropriate link to the answers you are looking for. However, the *Thomas* site is a little underdeveloped and skimpy.

LIBERTARIANS

Best Search Engine: http://www.google.com/

Key Search Terms: Libertarians

Home Page for Libertarianism
http://www.libertarian.org/
middle school and up

The *Libertarian.org* site is dedicated to the theory and thought upon which this political third party is founded. Here you will find a lot of theory material. It is not the Libertarian Party's Web site, but the Web site for libertarianism, the concept. So instead of pages that keep you up-to-date on current legislation and news events, you will find sections like "History," "Theory," "Policy," and "Movement," which explain why the party was created in the first place and what beliefs it espouses.

First, the site contains an essay touching on the major characteristics of the libertarian party. Then at the bottom of the page you will find the above-mentioned sections. Click on "Policy" and you will get a very clear explanation of libertarian policy. This section even includes a diagram illustrating libertarianism's position on the ideological spectrum in relation to other political parties. You can also refer to "History" if you are interested in the roots of libertarianism. Here you will learn that Thomas Jefferson, James Madison, John Adams, Patrick Henry, Thomas Paine, and George Washington are considered to have been great libertarian heroes of their time.

This site is informative and well organized. The political verbiage is virtually nonexistent, and the details are very easy to follow. This site would be helpful to all levels of students.

Libertarian Party: Home Page
http://www.lp.org/
high school and up

This Web site encompasses the policy/action side of the Libertarian Party's online domain. Here you will read about current news and legislation pertaining to the Libertarian Party. It contains all direct-involvement material that goes hand in hand with its theory site.

Again, the site is well organized and simple to access. At the top of the home page you will find all the sub-pages. Click on "Campaigns" to get up to speed on Libertarian candidates in today's elections. Here you will discover that over three hundred Libertarians hold elective office, which is more than twice as many as all other third parties combined. Or go to "Get Involved" to learn of ways in which you can offer your support to the Libertarian cause. You can also click on "LP News and Events" to read about today's Libertarian political headlines. Here you can also link to "Your State's LP" to find out about the Libertarian Party's influence on a state-by-state basis.

LIBRARY OF CONGRESS

Best Search Engine: http://www.google.com/
Key Search Terms: Library of Congress

Library of Congress
http://www.loc.gov/
middle school and up

Go straight to the source here. The best Web site to visit if you want information on the Library of Congress (LOC) is its official site. This is the world's largest library, with more than 120 million items on approximately 530 miles of bookshelves! It is there to serve the research end of Congress. With such an immense amount of material, the best part about the LOC Web site is the way it is organized. It's extremely simple to navigate here. You can go straight to a search by clicking on one of several options found under the "Find It" tab. Here you can do an advanced search, or click on "Ask a Librarian." You might want to refer to the "Index A-Z," or just look at the site map to see where you want to go.

The next helpful tab on the LOC home page is called "Especially For . . ." Here you can find material designated specifically for teachers, publishers, researchers, etc. This makes it easier to customize your search.

Next you will see "Information and Services," under which all general LOC information can be found, like contact numbers, copyright information, and employment/fellowship opportunities.

To the far right there is a section on current news and events that is updated regularly to keep viewers up to speed. Finally, at the top of the home page you will see links to a few popular online collections, including the *Thomas* legislative Web site, a site for families and kids, and "Exhibits," where you will find online galleries containing a ton of multimedia accompaniments.

That's it in a nutshell. Despite an almost immeasurable amount of information, the LOC gets high marks for organization. You shouldn't have any trouble finding what you want here.

Library of Congress Learning Page
http://lcWeb2.loc.gov/ammem/ndlpedu

This is the Library of Congress's *Learning Page* for its immense *American Memory* historical collections. If you are looking for some sort of historical primary source material, such as documents, photographs, or sound recordings you will want to check out *American Memory*.

The collections generally include, but are not limited to, the following: photos from particular time periods, documents from special projects, portraits of a particular group, motion pictures from certain locations, recordings of speeches, pamphlets, books, and memorabilia of specific events.

Each area of information is organized to make selecting materials as easy as possible. In addition, a search engine is available to organize a search. The Web site includes a section for educators as well.

LINE-ITEM VETO (SEE ALSO VETO)

Best Search Engine: http://www.google.com/

Key Search Terms: Line Item Veto

Thomas: Line Item Veto
http://rs9.loc.gov/home/line_item_veto.html
middle school and up

The *Thomas* government Web site takes the complicated line-item-veto issue and breaks it into fundamental terms in this one-page site. It's not a very complex topic, but since the mid-1990s it has been quite a point of political contention in the United States. This has made it very difficult to locate a basic Web site that clearly defines the line-item veto and gives you an outline of its recent course in American politics.

This page is divided into two sections: "Brief Description" and "Background." It's as basic as it sounds. You will get a definition of the veto law, which went into effect January 1, 1997, and was swiftly struck down by the Supreme Court a year and a half later. You will then read about the background on the line-item-veto law, the way this function worked, and the complicated process involved in using it.

This page does not address the heated debate that has surrounded the line-item veto since Bill Clinton put it into effect in 1997. It does not explain why Congress subsequently struck it down. It does not present the pros and cons of the veto law. What this site does give you is a clear and simple description of the line-item veto. Here you will gain a sense of why the law raised questions and controversy in the first place.

MAGNA CARTA

Best Search Engine: http://www.google.com/

Key Search Terms: Magna Carta

NARA: *Magna Carta*
http://www.nara.gov/exhall/charters/magnacarta/magmain.html
middle school and up

The National Archives and Records Administration (NARA) presents a very useful page on the Magna Carta. This 800-year-old document was initially created to protect the rights and wealth of English nobility, but has evolved over time to be interpreted as a charter for the greater freedoms of all mankind. Its influence was so far-reaching that certain aspects of the document were incorporated into the U.S. Constitution nearly 600 years following its initial drafting.

This site will give you a solid understanding of the Magna Carta. The main page includes an in-depth look at the historical document. Here you will read about its original content and the impetus behind its creation in 1215. You will also see how, over time, it was repeatedly reinterpreted for political purposes. You can follow the influence of the Magna Carta from England to America as British colonists ventured west in search of new lives and freedom from the throne. Finally, you will see how aspects of the political charter were included in our constitution.

You can click on links to the right to get more detail on the Magna Carta, like an in-depth look at its history and the influence it had on American constitutionalism. You can also see a full translation of the 1297 Magna Carta.

MARBURY V. MADISON

Best Search Engine: http://www.google.com/
Key Search Terms: Marbury v. Madison

Marbury v. Madison (1803)
http://www.jmu.edu/madison/marbury/index.htm
middle school and up

There is no provision in the Constitution that gives the U.S. Supreme Court the power to declare laws unconstitutional. So how did the court get it? This Web site will tell you.

The Supreme Court established what is known as its "doctrine of judicial review" in 1803, when it heard the landmark case of *Marbury v. Madison*. This site will tell you all about this historic case. To get an overview of the case, click on "Explanation and Background" from the menu on the home page. For a more detailed look at William Marbury (and why he was suing James Madison, the secretary of state), read

"Marbury's Travail." (Click on the title from the home page to access it). If you'd like to read a detailed perspective on John Marshall and the impact of this case, select "John Marshall—Definer of a Nation" from the home page. For biographies of the key people in this case, click on their names under "Note on the Players" on the home page.

MARSHALL PLAN

Best Search Engine: http://www.google.com/
Key Search Terms: Marshall Plan

For European Recovery: The Fiftieth Anniversary of the Marshall Plan
http://lcweb.loc.gov/exhibits/marshall/marsintr.html
middle school and up

This Library of Congress Web page focuses on the implementation and consequences of the Marshall Plan. Formulated by Secretary of State George Marshall, the Marshall Plan was a U.S.-sponsored program to stabilize the economies of 17 European countries to prevent them from turning to Communism in response to the poverty, unemployment, and upheaval of the post-World War II period. The Marshall Plan was the centerpiece of the American Cold War strategy in Europe during the late 1940s and early 1950s.

For European Recovery is an excellent Web site. You will find an easy-to-follow timeline, a blow-by-blow description of the Marshall Plan, and lots of primary source documents. For a quick overview of the Marshall Plan, click on "Introduction" from the table of contents on the home page. For a detailed chronology of the events taking place in Europe and the United States, select "Key Dates" from the table of contents.

The bulk of this Web site is devoted to describing the Marshall Plan. You will find a number of subject headings under "Key Dates" in the table of contents. You can either click on the specific topics that interest you or read them all to get the big picture. After clicking on a heading, you will be brought to a brief essay that gives you the rundown on what happened. Almost every one of these essays contains links for you to access primary source material. For instance, under the first heading, "Marshall Announces His Plan," you can read a digital copy of the 1947 *Washington Post* article that outlined Marshall's program right after he first formulated it.

You will find other interesting primary source documents as well. For example, you can view digital copies of books published about the Marshall Plan. Click on their titles ("The Marshall Plan and the Future of

U.S.-European Relations," "How to Do Business Under the Marshall Plan" or "The Marshall Plan and You") from the table of contents on the home page. If it's photographs that you are after, click on "Album: The Marshall Plan at the Midmark" from the table of contents. Just click on the photograph title that interests you.

The one major downside to *For European Recovery* is that it has no search function. This means that you will have to pick through the individual subject essays to find the documents you need.

The Marshall Foundation: The Marshall Plan
http://www.marshallfoundation.org/about_gcm/marshall_plan.htm
middle school and up

Soldier and statesman George C. Marshall was named secretary of state in 1947 and won the Nobel Peace Prize for the Marshall Plan, a financial assistance program offered to countries devastated by the effects of World War II. This site is reserved for information on the Marshall Plan itself. It's a comprehensive page that should not be missed by any student interested in the effects of World War II.

The page is divided into several sections, including a summary of the Marshall Plan and its expenditures. It will walk you through the preliminary stages of the drafting process, the strategies and disadvantages of the proposed plan, and the several important announcement speeches in which Marshall sought support and funding for his European-aid plan.

This page has some comprehensive material on the process involved in the formulation of the Marshall Plan. If you are interested in the early stages of the plan and its authorization, visit this site. However, one major downfall here is that it doesn't address the actual effects of the plan. Beyond the plan's intentions to boost financial development in its recipient countries, the site does not present any specific cases illustrating the far-reaching impact of the Marshall Plan in Europe and, ultimately, in the entire Western world.

MARXISM

Best Search Engine: http://www.google.com/
Key Search Terms: Marxism

Marxists Internet Archive: Student Section
http://www.marxists.org/subject/students/
middle school and up

This section of the Marxist Internet Archive is provided for newcomers to Marxist thought and ideas. It is divided into five parts. The first is an overview of the foundations of Marxism. This section will walk you through the political theory step by step, via concept links. The section itself contains minimal information, but that's the point here. You are supposed to click on terms for definitions as you come upon them.

The other sections on this site are comprised of selected readings from various political discourses dealing with Marxism. This is where you will want to pay attention to the writers' names and the titles of their essays and books, because these individuals are well-respected theorists. In order to understand Marxist thought, you have to understand its historical context, which can be detected in these discussions. Just click on any title or term along the way for more detail or for a link to the complete document. You will also find synopses of Marxist perspectives on other forms of government like capitalism, communism, and socialism.

The important thing to remember about this site is that it is there to offer you a link to more specific details. It's a directory of sorts, which has compiled material and names thought to be crucial for a complete understanding of Marxism. Excerpts from, and links to, these written works are provided at this site. So most of the work has already been done. All you have to do is read what's there.

What is Marxism? A Bird's Eye View
http://www.pipeline.com/~rgibson/whatismarxism.html
middle school and up

This site, created by New York University professor Bertell Olmann, is your first stop in your studies of Marxism. The language used here is clear and straightforward. It contains only text. You might treat it as you would a chapter in a textbook. It is divided into six sections. The first is called "Origins" and talks about the origins of Marxism being linked to German philosophy, English political economy, and French utopian socialism. The second section is called "Marxist Philosophy." This essay, addressing the fundamentals of Marxism, may seem a little perplexing to some students as the theory and language is quite advanced. The third and fourth sections discuss Marx's system of labor, worker alienation, and value theories. This is where you will find the essence of Marxism. The fifth essay addresses the history and evolution of capitalism and capitalist society, which is in direct opposition to Marxist thought. And if you are interested in the role that Marxism plays in today's society, Olmann discusses it in the sixth section of this site, entitled "Marxism Today."

Although Olmann's site is a bit tedious at times, it does a good job of condensing Marxist thought into something beginning students can digest. Read it to get the main idea without being bogged down with a lot of frustrating terminology.

MAYFLOWER COMPACT

Best Search Engine: http://www.aolsearch.aol.com/
Key Search Terms: Mayflower Compact

The Mayflower Web Pages
http://www.members.aol.com/calebj/mayflower.html
middle school and up

If you are only planning to visit one Web site about this topic, make sure this is it! This site has just about everything you will need, including the text of the Mayflower Compact. Better still, it's a snap to navigate. Some big Web sites are disorganized and make you constantly click back and forth between screens. Not this one. All you have to do is scroll down the table of contents on the left side of the screen. The pages you select will pop up on the right side. You won't have to spend a lot of time hunting around, either, because the table of contents is detailed enough that you know what you will be getting when you select an item.

Do you need passenger lists of the people aboard the *Mayflower*? No problem, this Web site has them, along with photo scans of William Bradford's original passenger list and genealogical charts of every person on this ship. Maybe you are looking for information about the *Mayflower* ship itself? Again, this site has got you covered. You will find a history of the vessel, an essay on its crew, and a description of the voyage to America. What about primary source material? You got it! This site has the Internet's largest collection of original documents on this subject. There's the Mayflower Compact and the peace treaty with the Massasoit. There's a complete library of full-text versions of Pilgrim writings, including *Mourt's Relation: A Journal of the Pilgrims at Plymouth, Of Plymouth Plantation* (William Bradford's history of the colony), copies of the colonists' letters, and contemporary accounts of Plymouth written by the Pilgrims.

With all this primary material, does the site overlook general historical background? No way. Just look in the "Historical Information" section for essays on all sorts of topics, such as the Pilgrims' religious beliefs, common *Mayflower* myths, and Native Americans in the region. There's even a section of lists that contains a ton of quirky details (like a list of all the passengers who died in the first winter, or a list of Revolutionary War soldiers who were descendants of *Mayflower* families).

MAYOR

Best Search Engine: http://www.google.com/

Key Search Terms: Local government + U.S. mayor

The U.S. Conference of Mayors Web site
http://www.usmayors.org/USCM/home.asp

If you want to know what a mayor in the United States does with his or her time, this is the site to view. Here you will read about current events and news stories involving U.S. mayors. You will notice all the different levels at which mayors are involved. Or if you want to find information on any of the thousands of mayors holding office in the United States, you can find that here too by typing in a city name on the top left side of the page. You can also click on mayoral elections to find out about the mayoral election process or about current election events.

McCARTHYISM

Best Search Engine: http://www.google.com/

Key Search Terms: Joseph McCarthy + U.S. history

House Un-American Activities + McCarthy

McCarthyism
http://www.spartacus.schoolnet.co.uk/USAmccarthyism.htm
middle school and up

If you want a solid overview of the McCarthy era with a lot of links to other resources, look no further. This Web site does a terrific job of explaining the McCarthy era. It begins its coverage in 1940 when Congress passed the Alien Registration Act and concludes with McCarthy's public downfall in 1954. In between, it provides a thorough history of McCarthyism with links to just about every conceivable related topic. Although this site conveys a lot of complex material, it does so in a clear and concise style.

It's also easy to navigate the site—all you have to do is scroll down the home page. As you go, you will see numerous links to follow to learn more about people, organizations, and events that were connected somehow with McCarthyism. There are links to J. Parnell Thomas, the Hollywood Ten, the Rosenbergs, and the American Communist Party, to name just a few.

Senator Joseph McCarthy—A Multimedia Celebration
http://www.webcorp.com/mccarthy/mccarthypage.htm
middle school and up

This site is a terrific place to learn about the McCarthy era—the period during the 1950s when Senator Joe McCarthy hunted down supposed Communists from his post as the head of the House Un–American Activities Committee.

What makes this site interesting is that you can listen to audio clips of McCarthy denouncing so-called communists. You will get a sense of how McCarthy manipulated people's fear and prejudices to institute a reign of political persecution now known as McCarthyism. You will find out how communists were imagined in the collective American mind.

After you've listened to several of McCarthy's speeches, don't forget to check out this audio clip of his downfall. The very first audio clip listed on the site is the one delivered by the counsel for the Army before a live national television audience. ("At long last, have you no sense of decency?")

The one major downside to *Senator Joseph McCarthy—A Multimedia Celebration* is that it contains no interpretive articles or essays for you to read. There is also no biographical material about this senator from Wisconsin on the site. Nevertheless, the various audio clips are invaluable in developing an understanding of the history of communism in America.

MINORITY LEADER

Best Search Engine: http://www.looksmart.com/
Key Search Terms: Minority leader

Office of the House Democratic Leader: Front Page
http://www.democraticleader.house.gov/
middle school and up

This is the home page of the minority leader of the House of Representatives. You will find "Leader's Corner," "Issues and Answers," "Media Center," and the option to read everything in Spanish if you prefer. Latest headlines and newsworthy tidbits related to the minority leader can be found on the home page as well.

Use "Leaders Corner" if you would like to access any of the House Democratic Party Web sites, such as the sites of various committees or other House members. "Issues and Answers" is where you can delve into the issues being debated in the House—homeland security, social security, corporate accountability, and other topics.

United States Senate
http://www.senate.gov/learning/brief_9.html
middle school and up

This is a better site to visit if you want an overview of the minority leader's job. The Senate's official homepage will give you a breakdown of power in the Senate. Here you will learn who the current minority leader is, how a person is elected to fill this office, and even a brief history of the position. You will read about the duties of the Senate minority leader, like keeping legislation moving and protecting the rights and interests of fellow party members. You will also learn that the minority leader works closely with the majority leader to ensure smoothness and efficiency during Senate proceedings. If you don't know much about the framework of the U.S. Senate, this is an informative site. If you are interested in the history behind the minority leader position, there is a fun link at the bottom of the page that will take you to a list of people who have filled this position since its inception in 1920.

MONARCHY

Best Search Engine: http://www.looksmart.com/
Key Search Terms: Monarchy

Encarta Encyclopedia: Monarchy
http://www.encarta.msn.com/find/Concise.asp?z = 1&pg = 2&ti =
    761576548

This encyclopedia page on monarchy is a good place to start if you want a basic definition of the term. It is a one-page site and provides only the essential elements, but you can extend your search by clicking on "Comparisons with Other Political Systems," under "Related Articles." Here you will find several more articles on monarchies, such as historical monarchies, constitutional monarchies, and modern monarchies. By combining the information you find throughout these subpages, you will walk away an authority on one of the oldest forms of government and one that has existed in every corner of the globe.

Links to Pages About Monarchy
http://www.users.wineasy.se/dg/mlinks.htm

This is a directory site that you will want to refer to if you are looking for specific information on monarchy. It is divided into several sections: "Official Pages," "Unofficial Pages," "Supporters of Monarchy," "Pages Concerning Monarchy," and "Fan Pages." You can link to the *Official*

Royal Homepage of Thailand from here, or to the Imperial Family of Japan. You can jump to the Monarchist League of Canada, a group dedicated to the continued support of Canada's constitutional monarchy. You can also scroll down and click on "Fantasy Monarchy" if you are interested in learning about usurpers and imposters throughout history who've taken illegal claims to the throne. Just jump around this monarchy directory to learn about this widespread and ancient form of government.

MONROE DOCTRINE

Best Search Engine: http://www.google.com/
Key Search Terms:

The Monroe Doctrine (1823)
http://www.usinfo.state.gov/usa/infousa/facts/democrac/50.htm
high school and up

Use this Web site, part of the large site maintained by the U.S. State Department, to read the text of the Monroe Doctrine as well as an article putting it in historical context. It also includes some suggestions for further reading. The site is very simple—just scroll through the text of the document.

The Roosevelt Corollary to the Monroe Doctrine
http://www.uiowa.edu/~c030162/Common/Handouts/POTUS/
    TRoos.html
high school and up

In 1902, President Theodore Roosevelt announced an official broadening of U.S. policy in Latin America. This Web page allows you to read his modification of the Monroe Doctrine, which is known as the Roosevelt Corollary to the Monroe Doctrine. The site provides some background on the Roosevelt Corollary. To read the primary document, scroll down the home page.

MONTGOMERY BUS BOYCOTT

Best Search Engine: http://www.google.com/
Key Search Terms:

The Montgomery Bus Boycott
http://www.watson.org/~lisa/blackhistory/civilrights-55-65/montbus.html

The *Montgomery Bus Boycott* site is part of the Civil Rights movement portion of an African American history project. The all-text site is very basic, but it offers a very good overview of the boycott. There are no links to sidetrack you, so take your time absorbing the details. The essay here provides a backdrop to the boycott, touching on important historical figures Rosa Parks, Jo Ann Robinson, and Claudette Colvin. It then goes into the details surrounding the boycott, such as the effect it had on local whites and the business community.

You can use this site to get the full picture of the Montgomery bus boycott, but it's not recommended if you are seeking many reference links or multimedia accompaniments.

The Montgomery Bus Boycott Page
http://www.socsci.colorado.edu/%7Ejonesem/montgomery.html
middle school and up

If you are studying the Montgomery bus boycott, you will love this site! *The Montgomery Bus Boycott Page* is a clearinghouse of information on the boycott. All you have to do is click on the links to access the best of the Internet on this topic.

Scroll down the home page to view the index of links available. There are links to several detailed articles about the boycott, an essay that focuses on Rosa Parks, a ready-to-use lesson plan on the subject (with photographs and other material), and an online exhibit about the boycott from the National Civil Rights Museum.

NATIONAL ARCHIVES AND RECORDS ADMINISTRATION

Best Search Engine: http://www.google.com/
Key Search Terms: NARA

National Archives and Records Administration
http://www.archives.gov/
middle school and up

Where can you go to better learn about the National Archives and Records Administration than at the official NARA site? Just click on "About Us" and you will find the "Vision, Mission, Values" page, which will describe NARA fundamental qualities like its dedication to the access of evidence that documents the rights of American citizens, the actions of federal officials, and the "national experience." Or you can take the interactive route to understanding NARA by clicking on "Take a Virtual Tour." See how NARA manages national archives and how it determines what to include in its collection.

The NARA site is extensive. In the "About Us" page alone, there are more than fifteen subtopics. Learn about the "Vision, Mission, and Values" that drive NARA. Or if you want to look at a calendar of events, you can find that in "About Us" as well. Back to NARA's home page, maybe you are interested in looking at the current online exhibits. Click on "Exhibit Hall" to be transported to a four-page directory of exhibits that will give you a brief description and provide a link if you decide you want to take a look. Some of the exhibits included here are "The Declaration of Independence," "American Women," "John H. White: A Portrait of Black Chicago," and "Through the Eyes of a Child."

NATIONAL ASSOCIATION FOR THE ADVANCEMENT OF COLORED PEOPLE (NAACP)

Best Search Engine: http://www.google.com/
Key Search Terms:

The National Association for the Advancement of Colored People
http://www.naacp.org/
middle school and up

The National Association for the Advancement of Colored People is the nation's biggest civil-rights organization. Founded in 1905, the NAACP was formed in response to the African American fight for civil and political liberties. Since then, this organization has grown to include in its mission civil-rights issues relating to all people. This official Web site will tell you all you want to know about the NAACP, its goals and agendas, its history, and ways to get more involved. From the main page, click on "NAACP at Work." Here you will see a list of projects in which the NAACP is involved. For example, go to "Education" and read about a mission to prevent racial discrimination in educational programs and services, advance educational excellence, and promote an Equal Opportunity Education agenda. Also from the home page, you can view a time line of the NAACP's evolution. Notice important historical events like the Supreme Court case *Brown v. Board of Education*, the passing of the Civil Rights Act, and a Louisiana voter campaign defeating avowed racist and former Ku Klux Klan leader David Duke in his Senate race.

The NAACP site is an interesting way to piece together not only the historical fight for equality among African Americans, but also the evolution of America's moral and ethical mindset in terms of racial diversity. Also, as the NAACP deals with civil-rights issues regardless of the race involved, you will also gain an understanding about what issues in American society are currently considered to be problematic.

NATIONAL ENDOWMENT FOR THE ARTS (NEA) (CONTROVERSY OVER GOVERNMENT INVOLVEMENT IN ARTS)

Best Search Engine: http://www.google.com/
Key Search Terms:

National Endowment for the Arts
http://www.arts.gov/index.shtml
middle school and up

Congress formed the National Endowment for the Arts in 1965 as an independent government agency to recognize and fund "significant projects of artistic excellence" in America. This category encompasses everything from educational projects, community-involvement campaigns, and mass-scale arts exhibits such as the Vietnam Veterans' Memorial and PBS's *Great Performances*. The NEA is a very strong presence in all areas related to arts in America.

The NEA Web site is straightforward and easy to use. From the home page, click on "Learn About the NEA," then on "Guide to the NEA." Here you will see several areas of NEA involvement. If you want to know about state or regional arts agencies, you can access a directory of organizations nationwide. Or, from the home page, go to "Endowment News" to see what's going on today in the NEA. Here you will find a time line of events, and if any of it interests you, just hit "Read It" to get the details. If you are an artistic student with interest in scholarships and other educational opportunities through the NEA, you can go to "Applications and Grants Forms" to find out about the process involved in applying.

Finally, the NEA site has included some galleries of work on the home page. Go to "Explore" and you will be walking through a virtual art exhibit. Just choose a topic, like "Artifacts: Kids Respond to a World in Crisis" or "Closing the Gap on Tap."

NATIONAL BUDGET

Best Search Engine: http://www.google.com/
Key Search Terms: National budget

National Budget Simulation
http://www.budgetsim.org/NBS/
High school and up

Here's a fun way to figure out all the math, economics, and government involved in balancing the national budget. It's a game, so there's nothing too serious here, but you will run across the same types of issues faced by government leaders and have to make real-life kinds of budgeting decisions. Short descriptions of each area of the budget acquaint you with the complexity of the task.

Look Who's Footing the Bill!
http://www.kn.pacbell.com/wired/democracy/
middle school and up

Want an interactive exercise to help you explore the significance of the national debt? *Look Who's Footing the Bill!* uses the national-debt controversy to inspire students toward taking democratic action. After exploring the issue from four perspectives, you will have the opportunity to answer the question, "What is so big about a $5 trillion debt?" You can then use the interactive "Thesis Maker and Online Outliner" to begin the persuasive essay you will ultimately send to your congressional representatives.

The site is self-directed so that you can easily move through a series of links to explore the issues, look up definitions, and write your response to the all-important question.

U.S. National Debt Clock
http://www.brillig.com/debt_clock/
high school and up

Just watching this site's National Debt Clock as it ticks upwards gives you a tangible sense of our country's debt. What the rest of the site does is to help you *understand* it. In the "FAQ" section, you will learn the difference between debt and deficit, see a pie chart depicting the makeup of the debt, and read about how it has grown over time.

In the site's "In the News" section, you will find links to media coverage of the national debt, from sources like CNN, the BBC, and ABC News. There's also a section of annotated links to other Web sites concerning the national debt, including the Concord Coalition, the Independent Budget Office, and the U.S. Department of Treasury.

NATIONAL SECURITY

Best Search Engine: http://www.google.com/
Key Search Terms: United States + Security
                     National Security Council

The National Security Archive
http://www.gwu.edu/~nsarchiv/
high school and up

This George Washington University site is the home of documents related to national security in the U.S. Here you will be able to access publications, archives, transcripts, and files containing national-security information on everything from the Cuban Missile Crisis to September 11, 2001, to President Nixon's efforts to influence presidential elections in Uruguay in 1972. This is a sophisticated and extensive collection of resources.

National Security Council: Foreign Policy Studies: Brookings
http://www.brook.edu/dybdocroot/fp/projects/nsc.htm
high school and up

This site contains a very comprehensive study of the National Security Council (NSC). The Brookings Institution is known for its attention to detail and its thorough studies. The NSC site is essentially a one-pager, though you will not be wanting for information. If you are interested in learning about today's NSC, click on "A New NSC for a New Administration," where you will read a policy brief about recent and current changes happening within the NSC. Here you will also read about the history and evolution of this organization. There are also oral-history transcripts available here if you want to hear, firsthand, about important events in the history of American security. Just click on the title of the transcript to listen. Towards the bottom of the page, you will see "NSC Projects in the News." Click on headlines to read about current NSC news, although some of the articles are not so up-to-date. Of course, this site also includes a "Related Sites" area where you can go if you want more material. Or go to the "Roundtable" to read about NSC and security priorities.

NATURAL RIGHTS

Best Search Engine: http://www.google.com/
Key Search Terms: Natural rights

FactMonster: Natural Rights
http://www.factmonster.com/ce6/history/A0835002.html
middle school and up

If you are having trouble defining the term "natural rights," the *FactMonster* site will be helpful to you. It's very brief, but it does a good job of explaining this political theory. Just scroll down and read along. If you come upon terminology that you can't quite place, there are also definitional links throughout this page, where you can go for a little more information. Just click on the underlined terms.

Jeffersonian Perspective: Natural Rights
http://www.geocities.com/CapitolHill/7970/jefpco08.htm
middle school and up

This site is called "Jeffersonian Perspectives" and it's the home of analysis of present-day political issues as they relate to the historical writings of Thomas Jefferson. This commentary, concerning the theory of natural rights, is simple and straightforward. Although it may be a bit advanced for younger students (as is the theory itself), it does a good job of placing the natural-rights theory in a contemporary perspective. This essay alternates, with each paragraph, between stating a bit of Jeffersonian perspective and offering a modern interpretation of that perspective. For example, one paragraph of Jefferson's writing states, "A free people [claim] their rights as derived from the laws of nature, and not as the gift of their chief magistrate." This is followed with a bit of analysis—an attempt to identify exactly what Jefferson was talking about and an attempt to clarify some of the complex language. This will help students to gain a solid understanding of the theory of natural rights.

NATURALIZATION

Best Search Engine: http://www.clearinghouse.net/
Key Search Terms: Naturalization

                        Immigration

Immigration and Naturalization Service (INS)
http://www.ins.usdoj.gov/
high school and up

Although the INS Web site appears less conducive to student research than some other government agencies, there's still plenty to be found here. In fact, if you are searching for statistics on immigration (or confirming numbers from another Web source), you'd be downright fool-hardy to overlook this site.

To tap into INS statistics from the home page, simply click on "Statistical Reports." (You will go to http://www.ins.usdoj.gov/graphics/aboutins/statistics/index.htm.) You will find monthly statistical reports; fiscal-year-end statistical reports; and fact sheets, reports, and definitions of immigrants, refugees, asylum-seekers, parolees, naturalizations, illegal immigrants, and more. From the INS home page, you can also delve into a section called "Teacher and Student Resources." Here, you will find an offering of historical and sociological resources on immigration and the INS.

Immigration Index
http://www.immigrationindex.org/
high school and up

This site's motto—"the immigration resource directory on the net"—sums it up pretty well. The *Immigration Index* contains an incredible collection of news and information about immigration worldwide.

You will save yourself a good deal of Web searching by using this collection of annotated and categorized links. The resources are organized into the following categories: asylum, conflict, country data, deportation, detention, discrimination, e-mail lists, funding, gender, government, human rights, trafficking, legal, migration, news, and studies.

Center for Immigration Studies
http://www.cis.org/
high school and up

The Center for Immigration Studies (CIS) is an independent, non-partisan, nonprofit research organization devoted to research and policy analysis of the economic, social, demographic, fiscal, and other impacts of immigration on the United States. You will find CIS's well-designed Web site easy to use for your research.

On the home page, headlines from current news and articles are compiled on a toolbar—just click on the headline to go directly to a full article. Another toolbar provides a list of common topics in immigration studies, such as assimilation and citizenship, refugee resettlement and asylum, guest workers, current numbers, and more. Click on a topic to read about it, access relevant reports prepared by CIS, and find links to other useful Web sites.

NEW DEAL

Best Search Engine: http://www.google.com/
Key Search Terms: New Deal

New Deal
http://www.gi.grolier.com/presidents/ea/side/newdeal.html
middle school and up

If you need a quick overview of the New Deal, this Web site is for you. As part of the Grolier Encyclopedia's excellent online series *The American Presidency*, the page also offers easy access to a summary of New Deal policies and program.

To read about the New Deal, just scroll down the page. The essay covers the two phases of the New Deal, the various relief and recovery programs that comprised the New Deal, and an analysis of the opposition to Roosevelt's proposals. It concludes with an evaluation of the New Deal's legacy.

There are very few links in the essay, but the one to "Franklin D. Roosevelt" leads you to a biography that puts the New Deal in the context of Roosevelt's political life. The links to the Democratic Party and Congress lead you to general overviews. They do not focus on the role of these institutions in the New Deal.

New Deal Network: A Guide to the Great Depression
http://www.newdeal.feri.org/
middle school and up

This site is a fantastic place to find documents and photographs related to the New Deal. The *New Deal Network* also does a great job covering various aspects of the Great Depression and the New Deal. Its only drawback is that it doesn't have a basic overview of the history of the New Deal. So *don't* use this Web site if you are only looking for secondary source material describing what the New Deal was. Visit an encyclopedia site like the Grolier site (above) first, and then use the *New Deal Network* to get a fuller picture of the era. That said, this site does have a time line about New Deal and Depression events.

The site is organized into two main categories—"Research and Study" and "Features"—both of which you can access from the same main menu on the home page. The "Research and Study" section allows you to look for specific documents and photographs in the *New Deal Network's* gigantic online collections. If you need primary texts, select "Documents" from the main menu. You will then have at your fingertips more than seven hundred newspaper and magazine articles, speeches, letters, and other texts. You can search the collection by subject, date, author, or publisher/collection. So, if you are looking for President Roosevelt's speeches, search by author, find his name in the author index, and select the one(s) you want to read. The "Photo Gallery" works similarly. Select it from the main menu, and then click on a subject heading from an index (you can only search the photographs by subject).

The "Features" section has online exhibits of Depression and New Deal-era topics. They contain documents, photographs and essays written by historians. Because they are about fairly narrow subjects, the "Features" probably won't be the most helpful part of this site if you are trying to find material on a specific subject (unless you are lucky enough to have picked a topic that's the same as a feature!). Nevertheless, the "Features" are interesting, and they'll help you get a feel for the New Deal. Some of the topics are "Student Activism in the 1930s," "African-Americans in the Civilian Conservation Corps," and "Dear Mrs. Roosevelt" (letters to the first lady from poor children requesting assistance of some kind).

And there's more! The "Classroom" section (in the main menu) provides "Lesson Plans," a "Discovery Guide," a "Student Showcase" of online New Deal history projects by students, and "Additional Resources." Don't overlook the "Timeline" that covers 1933 and 1934. It conveys the important political, economic, and social events that took place then. Some of the entries in the "Timeline" have links to follow to learn more about a particular event. You can access the "Timeline" in the menu at the very top of the page once you select "Classroom."

NEW DEMOCRATS

Best Search Engine: http://www.google.com/
Key Search Terms: New Democrats

New Democrats Online
http://www.ndol.org/
high school and up

You will find this Web site very helpful if you want to learn about the Democratic Party of the late twentieth and early twenty-first century, particularly about the Democrats during the administration of Bill Clinton. At the heart of the New Democrat movement was the Democratic Leadership Council (DLC), an organization founded by Al From and once chaired by Clinton. Many of the programs and policies Clinton pursued while in office—such as welfare reform and balancing the federal budget—had been promoted by the DLC as a way to help Democrats get credit for things that previously been thought of as Republican issues. *New Democrats Online* explains these positions. For an overview of the New Democrat position, click on "The Third Way" from the menu on the left side of the home page. To read about New Democrats in the news, click on "Press Center" in the same menu. Further down the home page, you will find a discussion of New Democrat policies on an issue-by-issue basis. Click on the one that interests you, ranging from "Technology and the New Economy" to "Trade and Global Markets" to "Health Care."

NEW JERSEY PLAN

Best Search Engine: http://www.google.com/
Key Search Terms: New Jersey Plan

The Great Compromise
http://www.cyberlearning-world.com/nhhs/amrev/begin.htm
middle school and up

This simple site will tell you about the New Jersey Plan and, more importantly, how it fits into the Great Compromise puzzle. You will read about both the New Jersey Plan and the Virginia Plan, including which states supported which plan, and then you will read about the eventual compromise, known as the Great Compromise, which finally solved the problem of state representation. This site reads like a news brief, giving you the main idea.

Federal v. Consolidated Government: New Jersey Plan
http://www.press-pubs.uchicago.edu/founders/documents/v1ch8s9.html
middle school and up

This site does not read like a simple news brief. It actually contains the original text of the New Jersey Plan for you to read. Section by section, all the specific details are here if you are interested. But that's all there is here. If you are in search of any analysis of the New Jersey Plan, you will not find it here, but if you want to take a look at the original document, this is the place.

NORTH ATLANTIC TREATY ORGANIZATION

Best Search Engine: http://www.google.com/
Key Search Terms: NATO

CNN: NATO at 50
http://www.cnn.com/SPECIALS/1999/nato/
high school and up

This CNN In-Depth Special looks into NATO's past and at how the organization's mission is evolving for the future. The site contains an interactive map, interactive time line (not as good as the one at http://www.nato.int), and brief biographies of secretaries-general of NATO. You will also find three meaty articles focusing on NATO's "midlife crisis," its shifting role in the world, and on the reasons some countries are currently seeking NATO membership.

North Atlantic Treaty Organization
http://www.nato.int/home.htm
high school and up

Naturally, if you are researching the North Atlantic Treaty Organization (NATO), you will want to visit the organization's own Web site. The "Welcome" section offers an excellent overview of NATO itself and how it has evolved; you will find background here on the original treaty, current member countries, and the fundamental role of NATO.

The section called "NATO Update" is an amazingly rich resource; it presents a complete chronology (1945 to the present) of all past and upcoming NATO-related events and activities, including links to information relevant to events in any given year. The "Issues" section is another gold mine, offering extensive background information, documents, multimedia, and fact sheets about issues on NATO's current agenda. Also, look in the site's "Document and Publications" section for basic texts, fact sheets, press archives, speeches, the NATO Handbook, and more.

NOW (NATIONAL ORGANIZATION FOR WOMEN)

Best Search Engine: http://www.google.com/
Key Search Terms: National Organization for Women

National Organization for Women
http://www.now.org/
middle school and up

The National Organization for Women is the largest organization of feminist activists in the U.S. There are 550 chapters in all 50 states. NOW's goal is to bring about equality for all women, and its priorities include winning economic equality and equal rights for women; reproductive freedom and other women's health issues; fighting discrimination against lesbians and gays; and ending violence against women.

NOW's official Web site is very straightforward. Click on "About NOW" for an unconventional approach to defining the organization. There are no long essays here, just illustrative examples of the issues that concern NOW. You will see real faces of real women who have found support with NOW. You will read about their circumstances and needs, and you will get a clear picture of the work NOW does. Or, if you are interested in NOW's evolution and why it was created in 1966, go to "History." You will read a sort of time line of campaigns. Here you will learn which issues NOW finds most pressing. And if you want more detail about any of them along the way, just hit the link and you will get an explanation. Click on "Nuts and Bolts of NOW" if you want to know where the local, state, or regional chapters are located.

If you want to know more about the specific campaigns and projects NOW is currently working on, scroll down a bit and you will see "Action Alerts." Here you can click on any of these concerns to read a summary of what's going on, how NOW is addressing it, and what the general population can do to help. These campaigns do not only concern the U.S. NOW also fights for the fair treatment of women on an international scale.

National Organization for Women: Political Action Committee
http://www.nowpacs.org/
middle school and up

The NOW *Political Action Committees* site is a branch of their main site, *NOW.org*. However, this site is dedicated specifically to politics. Here you will read about campaigns to support women in office and women running for office. You will get up-to-date election coverage and news on NOW-supported candidates. There's even a voter's guide that will set you in a NOW-conscious direction with your vote. Just click on the headlines that interest you. You will not only get more details, you will also discover ways to get involved in campaigns and political issues that concern you.

PARDON

Best Search Engine:	http://www.google.com/
Key Search Terms:	Pardon + government
	Presidential pardon

Presidential Pardons
http://www.jurist.law.pitt.edu/pardons.htm
high school and up

For this Web site, *Jurist*, a legal-education network, has compiled information on Presidential pardons and clemency topics. This site includes definitions, the history and origins behind the pardon, and instances in which the pardon has come into play in American politics, and much more related material. "The Quality of Mercy Strained: Wresting the Pardoning Power from the King" is an article addressing the history and philosophy behind the pardon. According to this article, the notion of clemency lies as far back as Judeo-Christian theology. Another interesting feature of this site is the section entitled "Constitutional Basis," which defines the source of pardon power as it is stated in the Constitution. Or go to "News," "Cases," or "Committee Hearings," where you will be able to get current information on what's going on in U.S. politics in relation to pardons and clemency issues. There is also a "Glossary of Terms" for those complicated legal and political terms.

This page has a lot to offer students looking into the elements of pardon power and clemency. *Jurist* has done a great job of covering all aspects in one single site. There doesn't seem to be anything missing here; it's definitely a one-stop site on pardon issues.

PEACE CORPS

Best Search Engine: http://www.google.com/
Key Search Terms: Peace Corps

Peace Corps
http://www.peacecorps.gov/indexf.cfm
middle school and up

The official Web site of the Peace Corps will tell you anything you want to know about the organization. Here you can do everything from finding out what countries the Peace Corps is involved in, to reading feedback from returned volunteers, to learning about the application process and what the Peace Corps seeks in its volunteers. Go to "Assignments" to learn about the major areas of need that are addressed by this international organization. Learn about projects such as clean water, sustainable farming, education, business, and health. Or click on "Countries" to access a long list of countries in which the Peace Corps has been active. Read about how the Peace Corps was formed, in 1961, as a result of President Kennedy's initiative. Also in the "History" section, you can take a look at the time line, where you will get a sense of the increased growth and interest in the Peace Corps since its inception. If you want to know how to apply and what the guidelines, prerequisites, and educational requirements are, just click on "Applicant Toolkit" or "Apply Now" to get an overview.

PENTAGON

Best Search Engine: http://www.google.com/
Key Search Terms: Pentagon
                        U.S. Department of Defense

The Pentagon: Headquarters for the United States Department of Defense
http://www.defenselink.mil/pubs/pentagon/
middle school and up

The Pentagon Web site was designed to give viewers an education on the actual Pentagon building. Although this is no way to learn about the Department of Defense, which is housed inside the Pentagon, it is still a neat way for students to become more familiar with the extent of this building's operations. So although this site does not address the actual defense activities that occur inside the Pentagon, it does a thorough job of addressing all the operational and administrative elements behind the smoothness of the Pentagon's functions. You can go directly to "About the Pentagon" for an overview. Here you will read about its location, the massiveness of its operations, and general building features. Go to "Related Information" and then to "Welcome to the Pentagon." This is a virtual tour guide for visitors to the Pentagon, and it offers a fun way to grasp its size and complexity.

PLESSY V. FERGUSON

Best Search Engine: http://www.google.com/
Key Search Terms: Plessy v. Ferguson

Plessy v. Ferguson
http://www.africana.com/Articles/tt_325.htm
middle school and up

Use this Web site to learn about the 1896 U.S. Supreme Court decision *Plessy v. Ferguson*. This landmark decision essentially allowed states to continue to enforce Jim Crow laws in the South, holding that so long as services of "equal" quality were available to both races, there was no constitutional problem with enforced segregation. The site offers a basic essay on the case from *Encarta Africana*. There are no bells and whistles or links to other articles here, but the essay really helps you put the landmark case in historical context.

Plessy v. Ferguson
http://www.watson.org/~lisa/blackhistory/post-civilwar/plessy.html
middle school and up

If you want to read portions of Supreme Court opinions in the case go to this site. It gives you excerpts from the majority's opinion and Justice John Marshall Harlan's eloquent dissent, in which he wrote "Our Constitution is color blind." Here you also have access to links relating to issues of racial inequality in the south, like *Brown v. Board of Education* and the *Dred Scott Case*. By considering these as well in your analysis, you will be better able to place the context in which the *Plessy v. Ferguson* case took place.

POLITICAL ACTION COMMITTEE

Best Search Engine: http://www.google.com/
Key Search Terms: Political action committees

Grolier Multimedia Encyclopedia: Political Action Committees
http://www.gi.grolier.com/presidents/aae/side/pac.html

The *Grolier Encyclopedia* page on political action committees (PACs) is a great starting point for students who lack a clear understanding of this concept. This page offers a solid explanation and proceeds to address elements like the Federal Campaign Act barring corporations from forming PACs, and early 1990s proposals to eliminate PACs altogether. This page will give you the essentials, but not much more.

POLITICAL CAMPAIGNS

Best Search Engine: http://www.google.com/
Key Search Terms: Political campaigns

Politics and Political Campaigns
http://library.thinkquest.org/12587/?tqskip1 = 1&tqtime = 0607
middle school and up

Created by high school students, this *Thinkquest* site may sometimes read a little rough, but the content offers a terrific exploration of the history of political campaigns. If you want to explore historical political parties or campaigns and elections from the distant past, this is a great set of resources. You will find a time line of the American government's history, links to specific campaigns, personalities, and parties throughout history, an interactive gallery where students can test their knowledge of the topic, and a chat room where you can discuss politics if you are so inclined.

POLITICAL CULTURE

Best Search Engine: http://www.google.com/
Key Search Terms: Political culture

Political Culture in America
http://www.socialstudieshelp.com/APGOV_Political%20Culture.htm
high school and up

This article, from Thomas Dye's book *Politics in America*, is a great introduction to the general idea of political culture, as well as the specifics of political culture in America. It begins by explaining the idea of political culture as a set of commonly shared ideas about government and then goes on to identify the most prevalent themes in American political culture, including an extensive discussion of political liberalism and conservatism.

This Nation
http://www.thisnation.com/socialization.html
middle school and up

Which political subculture do you belong to? This page on political socialization at *This Nation* offers a brief but excellent introduction to political culture in America that will help you define the term and inspire you to think about your own beliefs—how you came to hold them and what they really mean.

Also, don't miss the links to other sites that explore America's political culture.

POLITICAL PARTY

Best Search Engine: http://www.google.com/
Key Search Terms: Political parties

Directory of U.S. Political Parties
http://www.politics1.com/parties.htm

Here's a superb directory of U.S. political parties, complete with descriptive introductions and links to related groups for each party. The page starts with the two major parties—Democratic and Republican—including links to their various committees and subgroups associated with them. Following that is a section on third parties. You will find everyone from the America First Party to the Pansexual Peace Party to the World Socialist Party here, and each link comes with an overview of the party and other associated resources.

PoliSci.com
http://www.polisci.com/almanac/nations.htm
middle school and up

If your research into political parties and political history has an international scope, try this *PoliSci.com* site. It's a great place to go for facts and figures and quick overviews. It's an almanac of international political information, with sections devoted to "Executive," "Legislative," "Judicial," "State/Local," "Parties," "Nations," "Organizations," "Documents," and "Economics."

POLITICAL SYSTEMS

Best Search Engine: http://www.google.com/
Key Search Terms: Political systems

FactMonster: History of Fascism
http://www.factmonster.com/ce6/history/A0858080.html
middle school and up

FactMonster has an excellent article that addresses the history of fascism. It's part of a larger fascism article, which has sections on "Characteristics of Fascist Philosophy" and "The Fascist State," as well as a "Bibliography," all of which might interest you, too, depending on your particular area of research. See the links at the bottom of the "History" page if you'd like to read more.

In any case, start with the "History" section, which contains the following: "Origins of Fascism," "Emergence after World War I," and "Fascism Since World War II." This overview will go a long way toward helping you understand the rise of fascism in Europe, how it managed to win followers, and how its popularity was shaped by other events and movements of the time.

History and Theories of Capitalism
http://www.hsb.baylor.edu/html/gardner/CESCH03.HTM
middle school and up

This gateway site from Professor Stephen Gardner at Baylor University was designed as a companion to his book *Comparative Economic Systems*, but you don't need the book to make good use of the site.

The list of links is divided into four sections: "Precapitalist Economic Systems," "Early Views of Capitalism," "Contemporary Views of Capitalism," and "Global Capitalism." If you are researching the history of capitalism, you will probably be most interested in the links that fall under the "Early Views" section. "Classics of Economics," for example, will take you to a McMaster University archive site that has collected a large number of significant texts in the history of economic thought. It's an ongoing project, but already you can find a wide array of primary source material here, all organized by name of historical economist.

The Labour Movement
http://www.spartacus.schoolnet.co.uk/socialism.htm
middle school and up

This encyclopedic site from Britain's *Spartacus Encyclopaedia* won't give you a historical overview in one brief article, but it will provide you with links to excellent resources on many of the people, organizations, movements, and events at the core of Socialism's history. Scroll down the home page and you will see the following sections: "Pre-Socialist Radicals," "Socialist Writers and Philosophers," "Political Organisations," Labour Journals and Newspapers," "Christian Socialist Movement," "Fabian Society," "Social Democratic Federation," "Independent Labour Party," "The Labour Party 1906–1950," and "The Zinoviev Letter."

The biographies of key socialists at this site are quite in-depth and contain links to related topics also found in the encyclopedia, so your explorations might proceed from Mary Wollstonecraft's biography to the hyperlink on the "Unitarian Society" to "factory reform."

Political Systems
http://www.dspace.dial.pipex.com/town/street/pl38/sect2.htm
middle school and up

Although not an academic site, this one appears to be fairly objective in its treatments of the various political systems of the world, and it's more comprehensive than similar sites. You will find a good list that is divided into two main categories—the collectivists and the individualists—and then subdivided by specific political system. Systems discussed include autocracy, communism, conservatism, democracy, fascism, imperialism, monarchy, pluralism, plutocracy, socialism, theocracy, anarchism/nihilism, liberalism, libertarianism, objectivism, capitalism, and republics.

Once you've read this overview of the systems, you will probably want to locate further resources on a specific system. Some of the descriptions contain links to pages that discuss the political system in more depth. If you don't see any links to the system you want to explore, simply check out the other sites listed below or do a keyword search at Google.com.

PRESIDENT OF THE UNITED STATES

Best Search Engine: http://www.google.com/

Key Search Terms: President

The Presidents
http://www.pbs.org/wgbh/amex/presidents/
middle school and up

This is a truly wonderful, easily navigable site based on the PBS series *The Presidents*. Here you will find very detailed biographies of each of the presidents from George Washington to Bill Clinton as well as links to other Web resources; essays by historians, journalists and teachers; primary documents; and a glossary. To access the material just scroll down the home page.

To find a particular biography just click on "Presidential Biographies" and then select the specific president. All the biographies have a similar structure, making it easy to compare and contrast presidents and trace historical themes. Biographical sections include "Life before the Presidency," "Campaigns and Elections," "Domestic Affairs," "Foreign Affairs," "Impact and Legacy," and a lot more. There are also quotes that reveal the presidential character as well as links to Web sites on the particular president. If you need a quick summary of a president's life, just click on "Brief Biography." There you will find a table giving facts such as birth and death dates, political party, domestic- and foreign-policy highlights as well as a not-so-brief overview of his life. You can also compare presidents by clicking on a biographical section, such as "Domestic Affairs," and then choosing the presidents you want to investigate.

One minor flaw in the site is that on very rare occasions some of the presidents are missing some of the biographical sections. For example, there is no "Impact and Legacy" for Thomas Jefferson! Nevertheless this is a really great site.

Presidents of the United States
http://www.ipl.org/ref/POTUS
middle school and up

If you just need a quick fact about a president, try this site. It doesn't have detailed biographies but it gives you a great *Who's Who*-type entry on each president. Here you can look down a list and find out what other government positions he held, who was his vice president, who was in his cabinet, and even his presidential salary. Each entry also has a bulleted list of notable events of his administration, but you will have to go to the PBS site for details. This site has an impressive list of Internet biographies for each president, as well as a list of other Internet resources, including historical documents associated with the president. There is also a fun "Points of Interest" section of interesting facts, such as that President James Polk hosted the first annual Thanksgiving dinner at the White House.

PRIMARY (SEE ELECTIONS)

PUBLIC POLICY

Best Search Engine: http://www.google.com/

Key Search Terms: Public policy

Annenberg Public Policy Center
http://www.appcpenn.org/
high school and up

The Annenberg Public Policy Center site is an online bulletin that addresses public-policy issues at the local, state, and federal levels. Come here to take a look at the latest issues in the news and in the public eye. With any of the news topics, you will have the option to either view the press release or the full report, both of which are available in PDF format. The other public-policy issues are grouped into categories along the top of the page. Topics include "Political Discourse," "The Internet," "Media in the Home," "Health Communications," and "Women in Leadership." Just click on any of these to read APPC's comprehensive reports or to take a look at their current projects related to these topics.

Global Policy Forum
http://www.globalpolicy.org/
high school and up

If you are interested in international policy, check out this useful site. The Global Policy Forum (GPF) was founded in 1993 to monitor global policy-making at the United Nations. Its goal is to promote a more open, accountable, and democratic policy process at the global level and to make the UN more responsive to citizen concerns. The site's main sections provide analysis and links to key documents concerning the following areas or issues: "UN Financial Crisis," "Security Council," "Social/Economic Policy," "Nations and States," "Non-Governmental Organizations (NGOs)," and "UN Reform."

In addition to the main sections described above, you will like the site's "Resources" section. It houses general Web links, tables and charts, GPF publications, and historical UN documents. To find specific information, you can also use the site's A–Z index or its internal search engine.

RED SCARE (SEE McCARTHYISM)

REPRESENTATIVE DEMOCRACY (SEE DEMOCRACY)

REPUBLICAN PARTY

Best Search Engine: http://www.google.com/
Key Search Terms: Republican Party

Republican National Committee
http://www.rnc.org/
middle school and up

The Republican National Committee's Web site is the best way to learn about the Republican Party online. The easiest way to do this is to click on "About Our Party" to the left. Here you can select from several different topics, like the party's history, its platform, and its rules. Go to "Origin of the Elephant" for a fun way to see how far back in history this party goes. Also, go to the "Republican Oath." This will pinpoint the main ideas behind this political party for you. Back at the home page, you can get a lot of other information about the Republican Party by looking around. Just scroll down to consider the various Republican Party projects, such as the Corporation for National and Community Service or America's Fund for Afghan Children.

RIGHT-TO-DIE MOVEMENT (SEE CIVIL LIBERTIES)

SCOPES TRIAL

Best Search Engine: http://www.google.com/
Key Search Terms: Scopes trial

Famous Trials in US History: Tennessee vs. John Scopes
http://www.law.umkc.edu/faculty/projects/ftrials/scopes/scopes.htm
middle school and up

Whatever info you need about the Scopes "monkey" trial and its participants, this site is absolutely *the* best place to find it. The introductory text alone—well written and comprehensive as it is—suffices to give a clear and detailed view of the events. But you can get a lot more in-depth information than just that here.

Your choices are listed in the boxes running down the left of the page. Why not start at the beginning, with the link to the text of the Tennessee statute that set the whole historic trial in motion? Then you can have a look at the biographies of the trial participants (the biography of defense attorney Clarence Darrow is particularly worth reading in this section), many of whom were as high profile as the case itself. In addition to actual excerpts from the trial, you can also follow the "Observer's Account" link to read the impressions of one woman who was present as the trial took place. The controversy over teaching evolution in schools didn't end when the trial did, so if you want to find out what's happened with it since then—all the way up through the Kansas school-board fight in 1999—follow the "Evolution Controversy" link to that text.

And just in case you don't find everything you need right here, this site is even kind enough to present you with a link to . . . other related links! You will find that option toward the bottom of the front page.

The Scopes 'Monkey Trial': July 10–25, 1925
http://www.dimensional.com/~randl/scopes.htm
middle school and up

This site might not have the most information, but it definitely has the best presentation. Pictures of the trial participants (yes, even including a monkey) are interspersed with images of actual newspaper clippings from the 1925 coverage of the trial. As you scroll down the page, be sure to read the transcript of the interchange between the two lawyers, Clarence Darrow and William Jennings Bryan, when Darrow called on Bryan to take the stand. The substance of the exchange deals with whether the teachings of the Bible should be interpreted literally. Further down, you can get a glimpse of what European nations thought of the United States' famous "monkey trial."

William Jennings Bryan, the Scopes Trial, and Inherit the Wind
http://www.bryan.edu/scopes/inherit.htm
middle school and up

It's not flashy, but this site is a very good place to get a sense of one of the main figures in the trial, prosecution attorney William Jennings Bryan. You will find a lot more information here than a simple rundown on Bryan's role as an attorney at the Scopes trial, though. This site gives a concise overview of his life, and the strongly held convictions that led him to take up the cause of creationism in the courtroom. As you scroll down the page, you will see paragraphs on Bryan's personal life, the political offices he held, his religious beliefs, his lasting accomplishments, and of course, Bryan's role in the Scopes trial. If you get nearly all the way down the site, you will notice a numbered list. Check this out to read corrections of misconceptions that have sprung up surrounding Bryan and the trial. Here's a particularly interesting one: Bryan wasn't, in fact, opposed to the teaching of evolution in schools. He simply wished it to be taught as a theory, alongside other theories, like creationism.

SENATE

Best Search Engine: http://www.google.com/
Key Search Terms: Senate

MSN Learning and Research: Senate, United States
http://www.encarta.msn.com/encnet/refpages/RefArticle.aspx?refid=
    761586759

The MSN site on the U.S. Senate will give you a great overview of this legislative body, its constitutional origins, its membership, committees, and the rules and procedures involved in the legislative process. Just scroll through the article to read it. You will find several definitional links along the way that will explain terms in more detail if you click on them. The site concludes with a history of the Senate, from its conception through today.

MSN articles are reliable sources of online research material. This site addresses all the nuts and bolts of the Senate very thoroughly. Although you will have to refer to the official Senate site (listed below) if you need information on current bills and proposals or want to know what's going on in the Senate today, if it's the actual function of the Senate that interests you, this MSN site will tell you what you want to know.

United States Senate History
http://www.senate.gov/learning/learn_history.html
middle school and up

This page, part of the U.S. Senate Web site, is chock-full of material related to the Senate: its history, its function, and its organization. Start by clicking on "Senate Chronology," where you will be able to view a time line of important Senate events dating as far back as 1787. Many of these dates are accompanied with links if you want more detail. Also, go to "Historical Photos" for a fun way to visually explore the history of the Senate. The biggest collection of research material will be found along the right side of the page. It is divided into five sections: "General Information," "Institutional Development," "Powers and Procedures," "Leadership," and "Officers and Staff." Under "General Information" alone, you could really burn some time. There is a lot of information here, with topics ranging from "Chronological List of Senators" to "Constitutional Qualifications for a Senator" to "Facts and Milestones." If you want to know more about the hierarchy of power within the Senate and how it's organized, just go to "Leadership" where you will read about the Vice President (who is the president of the Senate), the floor leaders, majority and minority leaders, and party whips.

SEPARATION OF CHURCH AND STATE

Best Search Engine: http://www.google.com/
Key Search Terms: Separation of church and state

Americans United for Separation of Church and State
http://www.au.org/
high school and up

Americans United (AU) is an organization that works to protect the constitutional principle of church-state separation. Since its inception in 1947, AU has been promoting this cause through litigation, education, advocacy, and media communication. Its comprehensive Web site lays the debate out in full form for you.

Although AU openly stands for continued separation of church and state and the protection of the Constitution (the First Amendment), you won't feel as though you are being sabotaged with political propaganda. The tone can be strong, but the material is solid. You will read about many different events surrounding this debate. Click on "Church and State," an AU news publication, to read news releases, legal updates, and opinion columns supporting continued separation of church and state. If you want to know more about the legislative process, like what bills are currently being proposed relating to the church-and-state issue, click on "Legislative Updates." Here you can even find your local senator and representative and write them a letter if you want to voice your opinion. Also, there is a section called "Religious Outreach" where you can access a list of religious groups who support church-state separation and religious freedoms. Here you can read the opinions of these religious groups and get a different perspective on the debate. Also, don't forget to scroll down the home page to look at all of AU's "Top Stories."

Separation of Church and State Home Page
http://www.members.tripod.com/~candst/tnppage/tnpidx.htm
middle school and up

This site considers itself to be the home page for the issue of the separation of church and state. Some features that are unique to this site are a section that responds to the major arguments expressed by religious groups, an overview of the debate telling you who's who in the arguments, and an overview of the perspectives of the Founding Fathers and their beliefs about church-state separation.

Start with the part addressing the concerns of the religious right. Here you will see a list of 14 commonly stated arguments, such as the fact that federal officials take their oaths upon a Bible, the Supreme Court's declaration that the U.S. is a Christian nation, and the possibility that the First Amendment is misinterpreted. All of these arguments have been repeatedly made in protest of the separation of church and state. It is important that in your research of this issue, you are able to understand and articulate both sides of the debate.

Another useful feature here is the "Who's Who" section. Here you will round out your perception of this debate by learning what the different factions stand for and why. Read about separationists versus accommodationists and what each side believes. Notice how both sides interpret the Constitution and the Bill of Rights. Another important aspect of this site is an assessment about what the Founding Fathers believed about the separation during the time the Constitution was being written. Here, an effort is made to determine who made the most important contributions to the founding of America. There is also a look at what the most important founders wrote or said about separation of church and state. Finally, this section considers some quotations cited by accommodationists to argue against separation.

The *Separation of Church and State Home Page* is definitely the online authority on church-state separation. Again, the most important element of this site is the consistent inclusion of both sides of debate throughout the study.

SEPARATION OF POWERS

Best Search Engine: http://www.google.com/
Key Search Terms: Separation of powers

Constitutional Topic: Separation of Powers
http://www.usconstitution.net/consttop_sepp.html
high school and up

Although this site does not include any multimedia perks, it will offer you an essential education on the issue of the separation of powers in the U.S. government. This page is in the format of an article, so all you have to do is read along to understand the rationale behind making sure all three branches of government are separate.

Begin by noticing the links to the constitutional amendments that address this separation. There are links provided in the beginning of this article should you want to take a look at the actual text of these amendments.

Next, this page moves into a discussion about the concept of checks and balances. Here you will get to the heart of the matter—that the judicial, legislative, and executive branches were created to limit each other's powers, which ensures that one group doesn't usurp power and become more dominant than the others.

The article then compares and contrasts the U.S. political system with that of other countries in an effort to better explain the American system. Here, you should be able to formulate your own opinion on the separation of powers within the government and whether our system is most efficient and effective, as the constitutional framers deemed it to be.

U.S. National Archives and Records Administration (NARA)
http://www.archives.gov/digital_classroom/lessons/separation_of_powers/
    separation_of_powers.html
middle school and up

As part of its digital classroom, this NARA site is intended for students and is an easy way to get research material. Here you will find an example of the necessity of the separation of powers illustrated in the context of President Roosevelt and his New Deal politics. This is a fun and historical way to develop an understanding about the balance of power among the three branches of government.

The article begins with Roosevelt's plan in 1937 to increase the number of justices in the Supreme Court, which would have had the effect of strengthening judicial power, perhaps to an inequitable level. This is followed by a description of the political climate of the time, the expansion of the role of the judicial branch through the establishment of judicial review (a result of *Marbury v. Madison*), and the New Deal politics that were dominating America following the Great Depression. You will read about Roosevelt's quandary in how to address his conflict with the Court (a result of his New Deal programs continually being struck down by the Court) and how he ultimately proposed an increase in the number of justices. The article closes with a discussion on the different aspects of such a proposal, including the expansion of executive authority, the increase of judicial authority, and the protection of the balance of powers as provided by the Constitution.

SHAYS' REBELLION

Best Search Engine: http://www.google.com/
Key Search Terms: Shays' Rebellion

Shays' Rebellion
http://www.sjchs-history.org/Shays.html
middle school and up

The Supreme Judicial Court Historical Society developed this site for students and researchers of Shays' Rebellion. It is a very straightforward page, consisting of text and some historical photos and sketches. This site is easy to use. Just scroll down to read its content. Here you will learn all about the six-month armed uprising that took place immediately following the American Revolution. Read about the economic depression of the time, about the plight of farmers (especially those in western Massachusetts), and about Captain Daniel Shays, who led the rebellion to petition the government for paper currency, lower taxes, and judicial reform.

Calliope Film Resources, Inc.: Shays' Rebellion
http://www.calliope.org/shays/shays2.html
high school and up

In addition to a thorough recap of Shays' Rebellion, this educational film Web site also offers some very useful analyses on why the rebellion was so significant. Read about the results of the rebellion and how it wound down in 1787 with the election of a more popular governor, an economic upswing, and the creation of the Constitution of the United States in Philadelphia.

The site also offers a lengthy historical synopsis following the introduction. Here you will read important quotes by folks like Samuel Adams and Thomas Jefferson. The text is also broken up a bit with accompanying photos, portraits, and other visual aids, which always serves to lighten up study time a bit. The most important feature, however, is the in-depth look at the plight that led to Shays' Rebellion in the first place, including the deficiencies that existed within this newly formed republic and its government. Click on "What was it really like to be a farmer in debt?" to read from a novel portraying the life of a poor farmer during this time. This excerpt will give you a good idea of the hardships endured following the Revolution.

The historical-synopsis section of this site, the meat of it all, is very detailed. It addresses all aspects of the rebellion in detail, and should not be missed. There really aren't any drawbacks here. You probably won't find a more useful site on Shays' Rebellion.

Shays' Rebellion and Related History
http://www.umass.edu/history/institute_dir/rebel/srebell.html
high school and up

One more site for students to consider when researching Shays' Rebellion, this is a great source for additional material. Consider it a directory. It is divided into a few primary source sections and covers not just Shays' Rebellion, but also other, related rebellions in American history, like Bacon's Rebellion and the Whiskey Insurrection. There is even a map collection here. Just click on it to take a look at exploration and settlement maps as well as territorial maps, many of which pertain to the era of Shays' Rebellion. Finally, you can find nineteenth-century references to Shays' Rebellion here, including memoirs, speeches, and general magazine chitchat.

SOCIALISM

| Best Search Engine: | http://www.google.com/ |
| Key Search Terms: | Socialism |

The Labour Movement
http://www.spartacus.schoolnet.co.uk/socialism.htm
middle school and up

This encyclopedic site from Britain's *Spartacus Encyclopaedia* won't give you a historical overview in one brief article, but it will provide you with links to excellent resources on many of the people, organizations, movements, and events at the core of socialism's history. Scroll down the home page and you will see the following sections: "Pre-Socialist Radicals," "Socialist Writers and Philosophers," "Political Organisations," "Labour Journals and Newspapers," "Christian Socialist Movement," "Fabian Society," "Social Democratic Federation," "Independent Labour Party," "The Labour Party 1906–1950," and "The Zinoviev Letter."

The biographies of key socialists at this site are quite in-depth and contain links to related topics also found in the encyclopedia, so your explorations might proceed from Mary Wollstonecraft's biography to the hyperlink on the "Unitarian Society" to "factory reform."

Draper: The Two Souls of Socialism
http://www.sd-il.com/tss/tss.htm

This site reads like a book. It's lengthy and detailed. It requires time and attention to get through. However, this site is one of the best there is with regard to material on the theories, practice, and history of socialism. You can begin by taking a look at the table of contents in the beginning. Here you will see that the site is divided into 10 sections. These are all the most important elements of socialism. You will read about topics like socialist "ancestors," Karl Marx, anarchism and libertarianism, Ferdinand Lassalle, and the Fabian model. Then either begin scrolling down or choose a topic from the table of contents and go straight to it.

This site is mostly text, but the key here is material on virtually every topic related to socialism. And socialism sites that have an educational tone, as opposed to a propagandistic tone, are few in number. Besides, the theory of socialism is not easy and simple. We should expect nothing else from the sites that attempt to define it for us.

SOCIAL SECURITY ADMINISTRATION

Best Search Engine: http://www.google.com/
Key Search Terms: Social Security Administration

Social Security Online
http://www.ssa.gov/
high school and up

The Social Security Administration (SSA) oversees the Social Security system, which was enacted into law in 1935 by President Franklin
D. Roosevelt. Explore the history and future challenges for this program
at the SSA site, or just look up benefits information. Everything from
supplemental income information to Medicare and Medicaid to disability and survivor benefits is covered here.

For historical information, click on "Understanding Social Security,"
found under the "Quick Start" tab. From here you can click on "Award-
Winning History Pages." The history section of this site truly is amazing.
Here you can choose from many topics. You have the option of reading
a brief historical overview or going to "In-Depth Research" for more
detail. Under "Special Collections," you have access to oral histories,
presidential tapes, a photo gallery, and the "sights and sounds of history,"
which contains a 1935 radio debate on social security and remarks of
President Reagan at the signing of the Social Security Amendments of
1983.

If it's more hard data that you are looking for, head back to the home
page and then just scroll down to "Research and Data" on the bottom
of the left side. From here you can go to "Policy, Research, and Statistics" or "Freedom of Information." The former contains SSA publications and announcements. You can read "Fast Facts and Figures about
Social Security," which gives you just that. In PDF format, this 42-page
report is dedicated to the statistics and figures associated with Social
Security payouts. There are many helpful charts and tables included in
this report as well.

If you are looking at the agency from a bureaucratic perspective, take
a look at "About SSA," where you will get the organizational information, like who's who in the administration and a copy of the agency's
strategic plan. Finally, there are all sorts of bells and whistles along the
way here. There's a multi-language page, a women's page, and, of course,
a great search engine that should be able to get you where you want
to go.

Social Security Reform Center
http://www.socialsecurityreform.org/index.cfm
middle school and up

The Social Security Reform Center is dedicated to disseminating information concerning the debate over social security in America. Here
you can skim through the current news stories, which are found all over

the home page. Go to "Fast Facts" for an overview of the problem, from the creation of the Social Security fund to the "pay-as-you-go" system used by Congress, which, it is estimated, will create a deficit by 2014. Take a look at a detailed time line of events surrounding the history of social security. Beginning back in 1935 when Roosevelt signed the Social Security Act and ending with an in-depth look at today's system, you can begin to see some of the problems and inefficiencies associated with this program. Also included in this section is "Coverage," which discusses who is and who is not covered, payroll taxes, trust funds, payment levels, and eligibility.

This site does a good job of addressing the problems associated with social security without sounding preachy and overly biased. It just lays out all the information. This site is an excellent place to get the full picture of the plight of social security; students should not miss it.

SOVEREIGNTY

Best Search Engine: http://www.google.com

Key Search Terms: Sovereignty + government

Jefferson on Politics and Government: the Sovereignty of the People
http://www.etext.lib.virginia.edu/jefferson/quotations/jeff0300.htm
middle school and up

The notion of sovereignty is integral to America's constitutional history and political evolution. Read through this site, comprised of quotes from Thomas Jefferson, to better understand the philosophy and ideas on which the American government is founded. Although much of Jefferson's language here is formal and slightly complex, there are many references to sovereignty that explicate the political context during the time the U.S. Constitution was created.

Navigation is straightforward. Just scroll down the page and read along as Jefferson discusses issues of federal and state sovereignty, legislation, the idea of power being received from the people, resistance, and even rebellion.

Sovereignty: In the Context of "Indian Law"
http://www.umass.edu/legal/derrico/sovereignty.html
high school and up

The University of Massachusetts addresses the issue of sovereignty as it relates to Indian law in the United States. The article begins by explaining the traditional definition of sovereignty, then addresses the concept of tribal sovereignty. Here you will learn about the colonial era in America, when settlers believed they possessed a divine right to assert sovereignty over Native American tribes. Next, the article goes into an analysis of tribal laws and rights and the evolution of these rights. Read about Justice McLean's decision in 1886, in *United States v. Kagama*, which had the effect of severely reducing indigenous sovereignty. Also read about the Indian Reorganization Act, which provided for the formation of tribal governments under federal authority as vehicles for Indian self-government.

This site will give you an understanding of not just tribal sovereignty (although this is perhaps the most important sovereignty issue currently faced in the U.S.), but it will also explain, within the context of tribal sovereignty, the general definition of sovereignty.

SPEAKER OF THE HOUSE

Best Search Engine: http://www.google.com/

Key Search Terms: Speaker of the House

Office of the Speaker
http://www.speaker.house.gov/
high school and up

Here is the home page of the Speaker of the House of Representatives. A simple menu offers links to "Newsroom," "Issues," "Features," "Documents," "Links," "Search," "Subscribe," and "E-mail." Top news stories can be found in the center of the home page, and the current Speaker's daily schedule of legislation to discuss is available on the right side of the home page, so you can keep abreast of legislation as it is being debated.

For some history and background information on the role of the Speaker of the House, click on "Features" and then on "Role/History" on the drop-down menu that appears. You will find articles at this link on the selection of the Speaker, his role as leader of the House, his role as leader of his party, and his role as a member of the House. The final article you can access at the bottom of the page will give you historical data on all previous Speakers, from 1789 to 1999.

STAMP ACT

Best Search Engine: http://cybersleuth-kids.com

Key Search Terms: Stamp Act + American Revolution

Sugar Act and Stamp Act
http://www.stjohnsprep.org/htdocs/sjp_tec/projects/internet/sact.htm
middle school and up

This straightforward Web site explains the basic significance of the Stamp Act in simple terms. Younger students will particularly appreciate this site. Just scroll down the screen to read the overview. As you go, you will notice that key terms, events, and people are in hypertext. Follow these links to learn more about the topics, which include a quick look at the French and Indian War, a biography of British Prime Minister George Grenville, an essay about the Stamp Act Congress, and a piece on the Townshend Duties (which were passed at the same time that the Stamp Act was repealed).

Older students will probably need more detail than this site gives, although *Sugar Act and Stamp Act* makes a good starting point. The site could definitely use a makeover, though. There are no graphics, pictures, maps, or illustrations to supplement the text.

Declaration of Rights of the Stamp Act Congress
http://www.constitution.org/bcp/dor_sac.htm
high school and up

Would you like to know how the American colonists felt about the Stamp Act—in their own words? *Declaration of Rights of the Stamp Act Congress* is the place! As its name indicates, this site reproduces the Declaration of Rights issued by the Stamp Act Congress—a 1765 meeting of representatives from 9 of the original 13 colonies—in response to the Stamp Act. Not only did the Stamp Act Congress help engineer the repeal of the hated Stamp Acts, but it also helped lay the foundation for the American Revolution.

To read the Stamp Act Congress's resolution, simply scroll down the page. This site contains *only* the primary text (not even a picture), so use another resource, such as *Sugar Act and Stamp Act* for background information about the Stamp Act.

SUPREME COURT

Best Search Engine: http://www.google.com/
Key Search Terms: Supreme Court

Supreme Court of the United States
http://www.supremecourtus.gov/

The government Web site of the U.S. Supreme Court is a good way to begin your research. The best way to start is to click on "About the

Supreme Court." Here you will find a list of subtopics relating to the function, organization, and traditions of the Court. All of these sections are in PDF format, so just click on any of them and wait for a file to open. Go to "A Brief Overview of the Supreme Court" to read about the members of the Court, its constitutional origins, and other organizational details. Or, if you want to know more about the actual processes involved in the Supreme Court, click on "The Court and Its Procedures." Here you will learn about the sitting and recess schedule, the time allotment for cases, and general logistical details. Also found under "About the Supreme Court" you can take a look at biographies of current justices as well as access a list of justices that dates back to the foundation of the Supreme Court. You can even look at the current assignments of today's justices.

If you have any interest in knowing exactly what occurs inside the doors of the Supreme Court, click on "Rules of the Supreme Court" from the home page. You will find a literal book (it's 80 pages!) of information telling you precisely how things work. Although this material may seem very dry, looking through it will give you an understanding about what these justices do with their time, *all of their time,* and about the very specific rules and regulations that must be adhered to for smooth functioning. This file (also PDF) addresses things like guidelines for attorneys and counselors, writ of certiorari, oral arguments, and disposition of cases.

This site has all the details students will need for a thorough study of the U.S. Supreme Court. Just decide where you want to go and what you need to know, and you will find it here.

Supreme Court Hallmarks
http://library.thinkquest.org/11572/cc/index.html
high school and up

If you need a quick, layperson's summary of some of the most important Supreme Court decisions in history, this is the site for you. Here you can find thumbnail descriptions and short summaries of 21 decisions, from *Marbury v. Madison* in 1803 to the *Bakke* decision in 1978. It has no links to other information, and it does have some downsides: it only goes to 1978, and the cases are arranged chronologically, so if you don't know the approximate date of the case you want, you will have to scroll.

Selected Historic Decisions of the U.S. Supreme Court
http://www.supct.law.cornell.edu/supct/cases/historic.html
high school and up

Sponsored by the Legal Information Institute and Cornell University, this Web site gives you access to more than six hundred of the Court's most important decisions, from the inception of the Court to the present. You can access cases from the main page either by clicking on "Topic" or on "Party Name," that is, the name of the case. If you use "Party Name," the site also will connect you to a list of recent U.S. Court of Appeals decisions and Supreme Court opinions citing the case in which you are interested.

The site also enables you to research the opinions of individual justices. Just click on "Opinion Author" and you will get a list of all Supreme Court justices. Clicking on a linked name retrieves all opinions by that justice (including dissenting and concurring opinions) involving cases included in the collection. The list of justices also includes links to brief biographies.

This site is not just historical. Go to the home page and you will be able to view the Court's most recent decisions as well.

TAXES

Best Search Engine: http://www.google.com/
Key Search Terms: Taxes

U.S. Treasury: Fact Sheets on Taxes
http://www.ustreas.gov/education/fact-sheets/taxes/index.html

This part of the United States Department of Treasury's education section is dedicated to teaching students about taxes in the U.S. Here you will find a list of five subtopics related to taxes. All of the articles found in this site are very comprehensive and educational. Choose the "Economics of Taxation" for a summary of why we need to tax. This section addresses government services (and the necessity of taxes), taxes on income, consumption, taxes on property and wealth, and the federal income tax. If you want to know more about the history end of taxes, click on "The History of the U.S. Tax System." Here you will discover how taxation practices have evolved since the colonial era. Also discussed here is taxation during the post-revolutionary era, the Civil War, World War I and II, and during the Reagan years. This section also talks about the evolution of Social Security and Medicare.

MSN Learning and Research: Taxation
http://www.encarta.msn.com/encnet/refpages/RefArticle.aspx?refid=
761573037

This MSN site covers a lot of ground here; you should find that it addresses all of the most relevant aspects of taxation. There is a table of contents at the top. Take a look at that, then either scroll down to your topic of interest or just read along for a good overview of taxation, including types of taxes, how government spends taxes, principles of taxation, history of taxation, and the effects of taxes.

In addition to a very organized article, the MSN site also includes some awesome multimedia links. At the top of the page, click on the "Multimedia" button. Here you will find eight new links, such as images, a list of taxation terms, and charts illustrating U.S. revenues.

TERM LIMITS

Best Search Engine: http://www.google.com/
Key Search Terms: Term limits

Washington Post: Term Limits Special Report
http://www.washingtonpost.com/wp-srv/politics/special/termlimits/
    termlimits.htm

This 1999 special report provides lots of food for thought, from all sides of the issue, on the contentious debate over term limits for elected officials. Use the menu at the left side of the page to access the "Overview" (the home page), "Key Stories," "Opinion," "Resources and Links," and "Special Reports."

"Resources and Links" has great stuff for those of you wanting to explore the pros and cons of this issue. In addition to articles supporting and arguing against the issue, you will find fact sheets on term limits and an article comparing term limits in the states that have already passed laws limiting career politicians.

This is an excellent site for student researchers just beginning to delve into the issue. It's easy and quick to navigate, and it contains an array of resources from many different perspectives.

U.S. Term Limits
http://www.termlimits.org/
middle school and up

The home page of an organization that lobbies for term limits, *U.S. Term Limits* doesn't offer much in the way of a balanced perspective on this issue, but as long as you keep that in mind, you will find some extremely useful information here.

Click on "Information About Term Limits" for an array of facts and figures on the current status of term-limits legislation in various states, as well as a page celebrating presidential term limits and another that explores term limits at the local level of government.

The menu at the left side of the page also offers links to "Press Releases and Publications," "USTL Research Center," "Get Involved," "Online Forum," and "Search USTL Database."

TERRORISM

Best Search Engine: http://www.google.com/
Key Search Terms: 9/11 terrorist attack
                        September 11 + terrorism
                        Osama bin Laden + terrorism
                        World Trade Center + terrorism

America's War Against Terrorism
http://www.lib.umich.edu/govdocs/usterror.html
high school and up

This Web site from the University of Michigan's Documents Center is your best bet for a one-stop resource on the September 11, 2001, terrorist attacks. An exceptionally thorough and reliable research tool, it is a comprehensive index of what happened that day, as well as what was going on in the world of terrorism before September 11 and since. You won't find original material here, but you will find links to the best resources for research on this topic, and they are organized in a logical, easy-to-use format.

The following sections comprise *America's War Against Terrorism:* "September 11th Attack," "Counterterrorism," "Post September 11 Attacks," "Previous Attacks," "Other Countries," "Background Research," and "Related Web Pages." Under each of these are numerous links. The "September 11th Attack" section of the site is by far the largest, with links to the following topics: "Afghanistan," "Airlines," "Al-Qaeda," "Anthrax," "Anti-terrorism Law," "Anti-War Activism," "APEC," "Archives," "Bremer Commission," "Children," "Chronologies," "Comprehensive Sources," "Counterterrorism Measures," and much, much more. The list even includes a link for "Volunteer Opportunities."

The link for "Afghanistan," for example, turned up dozens of sites with a wide array of information—everything from the United States Army's 1986 country study on Afghanistan to an ABC News site on the Taliban to a list of academic links on the history, language, and politics of the country. Other topics covered in depth were women, famine, and mercenary fighters.

How Stuff Works: September 11, 2001
http://www.howstuffworks.com/sept-eleven.htm
middle school and up

If you are pressed for time and just need to get some basic information, skip the previous site and go straight to this one. You won't be able to dig deep here, but sometimes you don't want the temptation of hundreds of intriguing links to distract you from a simple mission.

Although this is a commercial site, with all the annoying flashing windows and distracting ads that entails, you will find answers to basic questions about the September 11, 2001, terrorist attacks, such as "What Exactly Happened When?"; "Who Did It?"; and "Why Did the WTC Towers Collapse?" The answers are brief but useful, and some offer links to other pages on the site, such as a page on Osama bin Laden and another one on terrorism in general.

Terrorism Project
http://www.cdi.org/terrorism/

This site was developed by the Center for Defense Information (CDI) to educate the public about issues concerning terrorism. It "will look at all aspects of fighting terrorism, from near-term issues of response and defense, to long-term questions about how the United States should shape its future international security strategy."

You will find such topics as "Operation Enduring Freedom," "Responding to Terrorism," "Homeland Defense," and "Legislation." Each of these major topics contains analytical articles and factual information that will help you research and understand the issues involved in fighting terrorism. News articles and links to outside resources round out the offerings here.

UNITED NATIONS

Best Search Engine: http://www.google.com/

Key Search Terms: United Nations

Global Policy Forum
http://www.globalpolicy.org/
high school and up

The Global Policy Forum (GPF) was founded in 1993 to monitor global policy-making at the United Nations. Its goal is to promote a more open, accountable, and democratic policy process at the global level and to make the UN more responsive to citizen concerns. The site's main sections provide analysis and links to key documents concerning the following areas or issues: "UN Financial Crisis," "Security Council," "Social/Economic Policy," "Nations and States," "Non-Governmental Organizations (NGOs)," and "UN Reform."

In addition to the main sections described above, you will like the site's "Resources" section. It houses general Web links, tables and charts, GPF publications, and historical UN documents. To find specific information, you can also use the site's A–Z index or its internal search engine.

Non-Members of the United Nations
http://www.geography.about.com/library/misc/blnun.htm
high school and up

This article about the three main nonmembers of the 189-member United Nations has a tiny bit of information on each country's status in regards to UN membership, with links that take you to *About.com* maps and general information sites on Switzerland, Taiwan, and the Vatican City.

United Nations CyberSchoolBus
http://www.un.org/Pubs/CyberSchoolBus/index.html
middle school

This colorful, kid-friendly site is really great if you are looking for information on other countries. Resources include "Information," which lets you compare statistical information on UN member nations; "Country at a Glance," which give you the same statistics on one country at a time; and an "Introduction to the United Nations," which discusses its history and operations. If you want to go more in-depth, try the UN headquarters site reviewed below.

Bells and whistles include "Ask an Ambassador," a link to the "Model UN Headquarters," numerous games and quizzes, and lots of curricular material for teachers.

United Nations
http://www.un.org/
high school and up

Here's the World Wide Web home of the world's foremost international organization. Click on the word "welcome" in the language of your choice, and the rest of the site will follow in that language. The main menu includes links to the following: "UN News Centre," "About the United Nations," "Main Bodies," "Conferences and Events," "Member States," "General Assembly President," "Secretary-General," "UN

Action Against Terrorism," "Issues on the UN Agenda," "Civil Society/ Business," "The UN Works for Everybody," and "CyberSchoolBus."

Most of these pages within the site are self-explanatory from their name, but if you need a little help deciding where to go first, we'd recommend starting with the "CyberSchoolBus." Unlike so many sites designed for students, it's not dumbed down. It offers an introduction to the history and work of the UN, statistical information on UN member states, briefing papers on key issues, information about upcoming Webcast student conferences, and lots of feature articles and reports.

Students involved in Model UN activities at school can access a discussion group under the "Community" section of this page that's specifically for Model UN participants. It has a "Frequently Asked Questions page," a starters' kit, resources, and other links. Search the site for topics that relate to your area of research. Click at the very bottom of the "CyberSchoolBus" page to take a virtual tour of the United Nations.

For substantive information on current activities of the UN, go back to the home page and click on "Issues on the UN Agenda." Here, you will have access to UN documents and reports on more than sixty topics, such as "Governance," "Africa Initiative," "International Finance," "Trade and Development," "Outer Space," and more.

United Nations Scholars' Workstation
http://www.library.yale.edu/un/index.html
high school and up

The *United Nations Scholars' Workstation*, developed by the Yale University Library and the Social Science Statistical Laboratory, is a collection of texts, finding aids, data sets, maps, and pointers to print and electronic information on the United Nations.

You can search the collection by keyword, or you can locate UN information by organizational structure, research topic, geographic area, or biographical information. If you choose to research by topic, you will find a number of economics-related topics here, such as economic and social development, international relations, international trade, and population and demography.

VETO

Best Search Engine: http://www.google.com/
Key Search Terms: Veto

C-SPAN Congressional Glossary
http://www.c-span.org/guide/congress/glossary/pktveto.htm

This URL will take you directly to the definition of "pocket veto," but you can then use the glossary to look up other terms, such as "veto-proof" and "legislative veto." It's strictly a definition site, but this might be the best place to start to make sure you fully understand the meaning of a term.

The Presidential Veto: Touchstone of the American Presidency
http://web.syr.edu/~kacisows/veto.htm

This site is actually a review of a book titled *The Presidential Veto: Touchstone of the American Presidency*, but if you ignore the comments on the book, you will find an excellent, concise summary of the history of the veto and the various types of veto that are exercised.

In reading the review, you will learn about the creation of the veto and its first use by President Washington, as well as the first use of the pocket veto by James Madison, which went virtually unnoticed, and the subsequent debate that began as a result of President Jackson using the pocket veto several times during his time in office. You will also read about the ambiguities that still exist with the pocket veto and contemporary debates on the subject.

WAR POWERS RESOLUTION

Best Search Engine: http://www.google.com/

Key Search Terms: War Powers Resolution + history

War Powers Act + history

Richard Nixon + War Powers Resolution + history

Bill Clinton + War Powers Resolution + history

War Powers Resolution
http://school.discovery.com/homeworkhelp/worldbook/atozhistory/w/
591570.html
middle school and up

Part of *DiscoverySchool.com*'s "A-to-Z History" section, this page contains an easy-to-understand capsule history of the War Powers Resolution (also known as the War Powers Act).

Since this site only contains the essay, navigation is a piece of cake. As you work your way through it, you will learn what the Resolution did, why it was passed, and how it has affected the conduct of foreign policy since its enactment. This site doesn't give you a whole lot of detail, but it makes a great starting point for your research.

The Historical Battle Over Dispatching American Troops
http://www.ripon.edu/Faculty/ShankmanK/130/Leahy.html
middle school and up

This site, which simply contains an article that ran in *USA Today* in July 1999, provides excellent and comprehensive background information on the War Powers Resolution and takes a look at the way the Resolution has been invoked and avoided since its enactment. Just scroll down the page to read the lengthy piece. The site is drab—only two little pictures break up the unnecessarily small text—but the essay is written in a straightforward fashion that makes this complicated topic easier to understand.

War Powers Resolution
http://www.yale.edu/lawWeb/avalon/warpower.htm
high school and up

If you are going to study the War Powers Resolution, you probably need to read it. That's what this site is for. Part of Yale University's massive *Avalon Project*, this site has the entire text of the 1973 law—no frills, no muss, no fuss, just a whole lot of legalese. Since there's no contextual information to be found here, you will probably want to get some background on the resolution from a site like *DiscoverySchool.com* or *The Historical Battle Over Dispatching American Troops* before you tackle this site.

WATERGATE

Best Search Engine: http://www.google.com/
Key Search Terms: Richard Nixon + Watergate

Richard Nixon + impeachment

Watergate + impeachment

Woodward + Bernstein + Watergate

The History Place: Presidential Impeachment Proceedings—Nixon
http://www.historyplace.com/unitedstates/impeachments/nixon.htm
middle school and up

The Watergate break-in in 1972 ultimately led to President Richard Nixon's resignation from office. Amid all of the debates, hype, and hoopla surrounding Nixon's presidency, though, it can be difficult to find a brief and understandable explanation of what happened that June night and how exactly it led to the downfall of a president. This site can help.

This isn't a complicated site, and it doesn't go into a tremendous amount of detail. But it's a great place to get your feet wet as you start your research. The site begins with an essay that provides a *very* brief introduction to Nixon's political career; it then takes you through the events surrounding the break-in and explains how what the White House originally called "a third-rate burglary attempt" snowballed into a scandal bad enough to force Nixon from office. As an added bonus, the site includes the full articles of impeachment drawn up against Nixon (he resigned before Congress could vote on those articles), as well as a couple of audio links where you can hear Nixon's words (including his famous "I am not a crook" quotation) in his own voice. And be sure to click on the essay's hypertext—there are some great pictures of some of the key players in the Watergate scandal.

Watergate 25
http://www.washingtonpost.com/wp-srv/national/longterm/watergate/
middle school and up

While *The History Place* site will give you a brief overview of the Watergate affair, this site—constructed by the *Washington Post* to commemorate the 25th anniversary of the break-in—goes into almost overwhelming detail. But there's not a better place on the Web to find *everything* you need on this topic.

The site is divided into six main sections, two of which are likely to be the ones you will use most: "Watergate Chronology" and "Key Players." Because so many links connect these two sections, your best bet is probably just to start with the chronology and follow the hypertext to the various key players as you read about them. The chronology section also lets you access one of the site's best features—links to top *Washington Post* stories that ran as the scandal was unfolding. (You can also search for these stories directly from a box on the home page.) If you are looking to explore the broader consequences of the Watergate scandal, you might want to check out "The Reforms" section as well, which looks at the adoption of all kinds of governmental ethics rules in the wake of Watergate.

Watergate
http://www.vcepolitics.com/watergate/

Created by an Australian high-school teacher, this comprehensive site about the history of the Watergate scandal contains full texts of speeches and links to a variety of other Watergate resources.

Start with the "Introduction" page, where you will find a chronological listing of events with links to speeches and background information. Go to "Watergate and American Political Values" for an interesting look at the differences between the U.S. political system and a parliamentary system in terms of how the Watergate events unfolded.

WELFARE (STATE AND FEDERAL)

Best Search Engine: http://www.scout.cs.wisc.edu/
Key Search Terms: Welfare

Welfare Information Network
http://www.welfareinfo.org/
high school and up

The *Welfare Information Network* is a clearinghouse for information, policy analysis, and technical assistance on welfare reform. It was created by the Finance Project, a national initiative to improve public- and private-sector financing for education, other children's services, and community building and development.

Updated weekly, the *Welfare Information Network* houses summaries of federal welfare legislation, a catalog of links to welfare-related Web sites, links to more than 9,000 organizations, and publications containing policy analysis, legislative information, and best practices. The site's "Hot Topics" page highlights recent publications, research activities, and discussions of emerging issues. Click on "Promising Practices" to read concise descriptions of projects across the country that serve as models for state and local welfare implementation decisions.

A Pedestrian's Guide to the Economy: Collecting Welfare
http://www.amosweb.com/cgi-bin/pdg.pl?fcd = dsp&term =
     Collecting + WELFARE
high school and up

Humor is often a rare entity in discussions of important economic issues like welfare. That's one of the things we appreciate about *A Pedestrian's Guide to the Economy*. As a handy reference source, it strives to provide answers to "many of the most asked, a few of the least asked, and some of the never asked questions about the economy." *Collecting Welfare* offers solid information, but it manages to do so in a lighthearted fashion. The articles cover the nuts and bolts of the welfare system, tries to dispel four myths about welfare and its recipients, analyzes the pros and cons of the system, and offers a roster of popular suggested alternatives.

WOMEN'S RIGHTS (FOCUS ON GOVERNMENT/LEGAL ISSUES, NOT SOCIAL)

Best Search Engine: http://www.google.com/
Key Search Terms:

Women's Rights 1848 to the Present
http://www.usinfo.state.gov/usa/womrts/
high school and up

In July 1848 a group of men and women met in upstate New York to raise the issue of women's rights. In preparation they issued a Declaration of Rights and Sentiments outlining women's issues and demands. Many historians consider the meeting the beginning of the women's rights movement. To learn more about the Seneca Falls Convention and read the Declaration, which is modeled after the Declaration of Independence, go to this site, which traces the history of the women's rights struggle. Here you can find an overview of the convention, the text of the Declaration of Rights and Sentiments, and a short history of the women's rights movement. You will also find a few short biographies of prominent women's rights reformers, as well as valuable links to other sites.

The site is extremely easy to use. Just choose what you want from the home page. The links to "Official Texts, Speeches, and Remarks" and "Articles, Books, and Reports" offer only very limited late twentieth-century material that you will not find helpful in your historical research. Look at the Declaration as an important document in American social history. It will give you a succinct statement of the position of women in mid-nineteenth-century America.

Votes for Women
http://www.huntington.org/vfw/addinfo.html
middle school and up

This should be the first stop for anyone interested in the history of women's suffrage. It's full of solid information on the people and events important in women winning the right to vote, and it's very easy to use. From the home page you can click on "Eras" for an overview of progress from the Civil War to the passage of the 19th Amendment in 1920, or you can use the "Chronology" for a more in-depth time line of events.

The home page also leads you to information on key women's organizations and publications important in the suffrage movement, as well as discussions of women's suffrage in national and state politics.

Finally, from the home page you can use "Important People" to access biographies of 29 leaders of the fight for equal rights. The entries include women such as Mary McLeod Bethune and Emma Willard, who fought for women's education as well as the vote; Sojourner Truth and Lucy Stone, who advocated the abolition of slavery and women's rights; and President Woodrow Wilson, who pushed the Senate to ratify the 19th Amendment. For some reason, the list of important people includes the Supreme Court case, *Minor v. Happersett,* in which the Court ruled that a woman's right to vote was not protected by the 14th Amendment. The decision prompted the national campaign for the 19th Amendment. The biographies in the site provide only a quick identification of the person, so you will have to look elsewhere for in-depth information on these people's lives. Nevertheless they do introduce you to the key players and enable you to see the range of interests these reformers had.

Votes for Women
http://lcweb2.loc.gov/ammem/naw/nawshome.html
high school and up

This site, part of the Library of Congress's *American Memory* project, is perfect if you want to know what people were writing about aspects of women's suffrage. The site includes 167 books and pamphlets in the Library's NAWSA (National American Women's Suffrage Association) collection. You can read the text of Elizabeth Cady Stanton's "Bible and Church Degrade Women" or Isabella Hooker's 1888 address on the constitutional rights of women. The site allows you to access the documents through keyword searching or by browsing the subject and author. Unless you are very familiar with the subject, it's easier to find the document you want by subject or author than keyword.

The site also contains a very detailed time line of the women's suffrage movement, which you can access from the bottom of the home page and a good bibliography of print resources, also accessible from the home page.

Woman Suffrage and the 19th Amendment
http://www.nara.gov/education/teaching/woman/home.html
high school and up

If you need a quick source for key documents in the suffrage campaign, go to this site developed by the National Archives and Records Administration for the 150th anniversary of the Seneca Falls Convention.

Here you will find nine documents that trace major steps on the road to women's suffrage. Each document contains a short introduction putting it in historical perspective. A review of the introductions will give you a quick summary of the suffrage crusade. You can also get an overview of suffrage history by reading a script entitled "Failure is Impossible," which the National Archives produced on the 75th anniversary of the 19th Amendment.

WORK PROJECTS ADMINISTRATION

Best Search Engine: http://www.google.com/
Key Search Terms: Works Projects Administration

By the People, For the People: Posters from the WPA
http://memory.loc.gov/ammem/wpaposters/wpahome.html
middle school and up

The Work Projects Administration (originally the Work Progress Administration) was the centerpiece of President Roosevelt's New Deal effort to get millions of unemployed Americans back to work. The WPA wasn't just about building dams and houses, though. An integral part of the WPA was the Federal Art Project (FAP). The FAP was created to give work to unemployed artists, but it also had a broader purpose. Roosevelt believed that art was a public good and that the FAP could bring art to everyday men and women—not just to America's elite.

This amazing site from the Library of Congress's *American Memory* project showcases the posters the FAP made between 1936 and 1943. What's especially helpful about this site is that you will learn about the WPA as you look at these cool posters made by some of the country's cutting-edge artists and designers; the FAP made these posters to advertise the services offered by other branches of the WPA, such as the Civilian Conservation Corps. As you view the exhibit, you will get a quick lesson on the different federal agencies involved in the WPA.

This exhibit is huge. You might want to start research here by reading "About the Collection," an essay that gives some background information on the FAP. You will see the link to this essay from the middle of the home page. Near it, there's a link that will take you to an interview with a FAP artist. If you just want to get a sense of this exhibit, click on "Collection Highlights" from the middle of the home page. For those of you who want to find specific posters or to browse the collection to get an idea of all the different WPA programs, you can search the site by "Keyword," "Subject," or "Creator." Look for these links at the top of the page.

3

⸺⚬⚭⚬⸺

Materials and Resources for Government and Civics Teachers

Each of the sites reviewed below reflects the unique needs of teachers of government and civics. Without a doubt, some of these sites will be ones you want to bookmark on your computer. We've arranged the sites in this section into two broad categories: Web Resources and Hands-On Opportunities. However, keep in mind that sites earmarked for teachers are by no means off-limits to other audiences. Parents who are home-schooling their kids, for instance, can use these sites to develop excellent at-home activities, lessons, and field trips. Don't forget to check out the general sites in "The Basics" section found in Volume I of this set.

WEB RESOURCES

About.com: Political Science Resources for the Social Studies Teacher
http://7-12educators.about.com/msub62historypoli.htm

You'll find plenty of material here specifically designed for secondary-school educators. You'll find sections called "How to Hold a Class Debate," "How to Hold a Mock Presidential Campaign and Election," "Picking and Choosing Rights from the Constitution," "Historic Supreme Court Decisions," and links to other useful Web sites, as well as access to *About.com*'s extensive lesson-plan library, organized by grade level and subject matter.

American Memory: The Learning Page
http://memory.loc.gov/ammem/ndlpedu/

The *American Memory* site, created by the Library of Congress, provides access to more than five million historical items, such as unique and rare documents, photographs, films, and audio recordings, many of them relating to the history of our government.

The "Learning Page" section was created to help educators use the *American Memory* site to teach about United States history, government, and culture. Here, you'll find tips and tricks for using the collections, as well as frameworks, activities, and lessons, arranged by grade level, that provide context for their use. Lesson plans, created by *American Memory* fellows, include such topics as "Brother, Can You Spare a Dime?" which uses *American Memory* resources to explore, in this case, the Great Depression and the New Deal programs it spawned. Other lessons include "All History Is Local," "The Constitution: Counter Revolution or National Salvation," "In Congress Assembled," and "Reservation Controversies."

"Resources" can help you answer your students' sticky questions on copyright and citing electronic resources (they do ask those questions, don't they?). Go to "Activities" for game-like exercises that will introduce your students to the collections. One such activity has your students become historical detectives, searching for clues in the death of Billy the Kid.

To delve in further, consider one of the professional development programs offered by the LOC. These include workshops, videoconferences, and the American Memory Fellows Program, all of which offer teachers the opportunity to interact with one another while learning to integrate *American Memory* resources into their classrooms.

AskERIC Lesson Plans
http://www.askeric.org/Virtual/Lessons/

Here you'll find a variety of government-based lesson plans and activities for students in grades 4 through 12. Click on "Social Studies" and then "U.S. Government" to reach plans like "Activities for Learning the U.S. Constitution," "Community Government," "Foreign Policy Simulation," "How Does a Bill Become Law?" "Impact of Government on the Individual," "Mock Congress," "Powers of Government," and many more. You can also backtrack to the list of subjects under "Social Studies," and choose "Comparative Political Systems" instead of "U.S. Government" if you're looking for more international information. Lesson-plan choices here include "Comparing Democracy and Republic," "The Declaration vs. the Communist Manifesto," and "Forming a Government." These are just a few of the high-school-level lessons you might want to check out at this helpful site.

Awesome Library
http://www.awesomelibrary.org/

Here you'll find 18,000 carefully reviewed resources, including the top five percent in education. Enter a door for teachers, students, parents, or librarians, depending on the type of resources you want to access. Or just follow the "Social Studies" link, and you'll see twenty or more topics, including "Countries and Regions," "Current Events," Government," and "Helping Others." Sub-topics under "Government," for example, include "Executive Branch," "Judicial Branch," "Legislative Branch," "Politics and Elections," "Presidential Election 2000," and others.

CivNet
http://www.civnet.org/

This civic-minded international site is an online resource and service for civic-education teachers and students, as well as scholars, policy-makers, civic-minded journalists, and nongovernmental organizations. You'll find a list of joint projects your class might be able to participate in countries around the world, as well as a "Resources" section that's chock-full of curricular materials for teaching international civics, including links to some of the world's greatest historic documents pertaining to civics, democracy, human rights, tolerance, and freedom.

There is also a directory of civics teachers interested in networking with other civics teachers and a list of additional Internet links that's worth a quick look.

The Great American Web Site
http://www.uncle-sam.com/

The citizen's site for every link you need to the U.S. government—that's how this site is billed, and it does a good job of living up to its motto. This is a neatly packaged collection of U.S. government links that you'll find particularly handy in the classroom. The links are organized logically by branch of government—legislative, judicial, and executive, with additional categories for executive departments and independent agencies. Other features of this site include a "Weekly Highlights" column, "Ten Most Visited Sites," "Our Favorite Sites," and "Our Ten Best Lists," which includes "Agency Web Sites," "Individual Web Sites," "History Sources," "Statistical Sources," "Clickable Maps," and other highly useful topics.

Historic Audio Archives
http://www.webcorp.com/sounds/index.htm

Remember the sound of Richard Nixon saying, "I'm not a crook"? Well, maybe not. But you and your students can hear it for yourselves at this site. Audio files of many of America's most famous and infamous personalities can be played in your classroom. You'll also find Joe Mc-Carthy in a scene from a witch hunt, Mayor Daley defending the Chicago police after the 1968 riots, and even George Bush, Sr.'s comments on broccoli.

Historic Supreme Court Decisions
http://www2.law.cornell.edu/cgi-bin/foliocgi.exe/historic

At this Cornell Law School site, you can search by topic some three hundred key Supreme Court decisions. Each decision provides background information and the decision from the court. To access each individual decision, click on the small icon to the left of each case.

History Social Studies Web Site for K–12 Teachers
http://www.execpc.com/~dboals/govt.html

This site received a Britannica Internet Guide award, and it's easy to see why. The URL provided here is the direct link to the "Government/ Politics page" for what is arguably one of the biggest and best indexes for social-science educators on the Web. You'll find everything you need and then some at this site. Government resources are divided into the following categories: "General Resources," "National Executive," "Federal Agencies and Departments," "National Legislative," "National Judicial," "Documents and Archives," "State and Local Government," "Elections and Campaigns," "Current Issues," "Citizen Participation," "Government in Other Nations," "Law and Justice," and "Foreign Affairs/International Relations."

H-Net Teaching
http://www.h-net.msu.edu/teaching/

The *H-Net* system maintains an array of sites on teaching, and this URL is a gateway to many of those sites. Each site includes edited, threaded discussions on topics of interest to list subscribers, as well as archives of previous discussions. You can find the following discussion lists at *H-Net Teaching*:

"H-High-School"—If you're a high-school social-studies teacher, you probably already know about this one. If not, check it out.

"H-Teach"—Here you'll find teachers at all levels engaged in enlightening discussions on a wide variety of topics.

Institute for Citizenship
http://www.citizen.org.uk/education.htm

The Institute for Citizenship works directly with teachers, students, and Local Education Authorities in the United Kingdom to develop, pilot, and evaluate resources that support the teaching and learning of citizenship. Since the organization is based in Britain, its resources are geared toward implementation there, but teachers everywhere will find the lesson plans on 'Learning through Elections" and "Learning through Local Elections"—both of which can be downloaded at this site—to contain lots of valuable information.

Justice for Kids and Youth
http://www.usdoj.gov/kidspage/

This Department of Justice page was designed with the needs and likes of your students in mind, and you'll find plenty here to help them as you cover curriculum on justice-related topics. Click on the button that best matches the age group of your students (grades 1–6 or 6–12) and a list of internal links to Department of Justice pages written and designed for kids will pop up on your screen. You'll see everything from "Civil Rights Laws" to "FBI History" to "History of the US Marshals" to "Internet Do's and Don'ts: The Superhighway Where Kids Drive Too." Each page offers up text and other resources for teaching your kids about the particular topic. The site links are briefly annotated to help you decide where to go.

Parks as Classrooms
http://www.nps.gov/interp/parkclass.html

This is a great site for teachers who want to take their students out of the classroom and into the world. Parks as Classrooms (PAC) programs and materials are the result of a partnership between national-park sites and neighboring school districts. They provide on- and off-site learning opportunities via curriculum-based education programs, audio-visual materials, accredited teacher training, traveling trunks and kits, and teacher and student resource guides.

There are opportunities here for exploration at hundreds of national parks and recreation sites around the country, places like the Eisenhower National Historic Site, which has resources for exploring leadership qualities as well as conflict resolution, and the Women's Rights National Historical Park in Seneca Falls, New York, which sponsors educational programs that highlight the struggle for women's rights and the first women's rights convention in America.

Check out the Park Service's excellent Web site, with links to all participating parks for programs of interest near you. In addition to the

PAC information at this Web site, there's also information you can pass along to your students about Junior Ranger programs.

Social Studies School Service
http://www.socialstudies.com/

This commercial site will entice you to research (and purchase) new teaching materials and texts and explore professional development programs, but its list of activities, broken down by discipline, is the best reason to visit. Go to the "On-line Activities" page, which is located in the "On-line Resources" box at the bottom-left corner of the home page, and click on "U.S. Government." You'll be given 87 links to concise, curriculum-specific activities to teach your students about topics such as the First Amendment to the Constitution, clemency and the death penalty, the growth of regionalism in the first half of the nineteenth century, and the function of congressional committees.

Each activity includes an introduction, a description of the activity, a list of resources to use, directions, an explanation of how to evaluate student work, and the complete lesson plan from which the activity is drawn. Thorough and varied, this site is easy to use and fully searchable.

U.S. Census 2000: Census in Schools
http://www.census.gov/dmd/www/schindex.htm

The U.S. Census Bureau truly thought of everything when it designed its Web site. "Census in Schools" provides excellent teaching materials and tools to help your students understand data on the people of the United States.

Be sure to check out the lesson plans, teaching suggestions, and worksheets, all designed to be used in studying Census 2000 results. These materials supply you and your students with an outstanding opportunity to learn about the demographic changes that took place in the United States during the 1990s.

You'll find an e-mail link to order free packets of additional teaching materials that are targeted to specific age groups. The packet includes a 24-page teaching guide and a 4' × 6' wall map.

U.S. Congress on the Internet
http://thomas.loc.gov/

This Library of Congress site will help you stay on top of what your government is doing. With this, there's no excuse for being out of touch. You'll find current floor activities, pending bills, committee information, links to the Congressional Record, information on the legislative process, historical documents, and the Constitution.

HANDS-ON OPPORTUNITIES

Federal Reserve Bank of New York: Educator-Oriented Initiatives
http://www.ny.frb.org/pihome/educator/initeduc.html

The Federal Reserve Bank of New York offers several programs of interest to government teachers. "The Global Economic Forum," for educators at all levels, is a three-day summer program in which educators gain an international perspective on a wide array of economic and public-policy issues by assuming the roles of policy-makers from various nations.

"In the Shoes of a Fed Policymaker" is very similar, except that the focus is on the making of monetary policy in particular. This is a four-day program. For more information on these programs, which are held in New York City, visit the Web site. If interested in enrolling, you will need to contact the Federal Reserve Bank of New York by phone or e-mail.

The First Amendment Schools
http://www.socialstudies.org/profdev/profdev1.html#opportunities

Interested in learning more about the First Amendment? This annual three-day teachers' workshop in Washington, D.C., will let you learn from national experts the meaning and significance of the First Amendment. Conducted in cooperation with the Newsweek Education Program, the project is cosponsored by the First Amendment Center and the Association for Supervision and Curriculum Development. All expenses, including travel and lodging, will be paid for up to 30 teachers. Check the Web site for an online application and workshop details and dates.

Green World Center Study Retreat
http://www.greenworldcenter.org/content.html

Here's a more contemplative, low-key opportunity for those of you who might want some time to work on writing a book or article or developing new curricula. A residential program in the Appalachian Mountains of Quebec, the Study Retreat brings together students, teachers, scholars, writers, artists, and others who need to take some time for themselves and their work. The Center is especially interested in environmental civics; human ecology; literature and philosophy; cinema; photography; multimedia; peace studies; animals and society; anthropology; nature writing; and environmental education.

Click on "Study Retreat" on the home page to read more about the Center's resources and the faculty, which includes such folks as Jane Goodall, Noam Chomsky, and Francis Moore Lappe.

NEH Projects
http://www.neh.fed.us/projects/si-school.html

Summer institutes abound for teachers, but the ones offered by the National Endowment for the Humanities are among the best. The topics are intriguing, the locales diverse, and the stipends generous. Eligible applicants must teach full-time in an American K–12 school or, if teaching abroad, a majority of their students must be American.

Topics for the recent Seminars and Institutes included "Boundary Lines: Women Rewriting the American South," "Four Centuries of Struggle: The History of the Southern Civil Rights Movement," "The Vietnam War: Morality and Politics," "Greek Values in Crisis: Thucydides, Sophocles, Plato," and "Social Justice, Identity, and Human Rights." Take a look at the complete list, and start planning now. Applications are due by March 1 each year.

Working with Historical Documents at the National Archives
http://www.nara.gov/education/classrm.html

This summer workshop offers you the opportunity to gather primary-source material from the nation's premier storehouse of history. During the National Archives' one-week "Primarily Teaching" program, teachers research a topic of their choice, create classroom materials from historical records, and discuss how to present primary documents to students. Teachers have their pick of the complete Archives collection. Graduate credit is available from the University of Virginia for an additional fee.

4

—⊶∞⊷—

Museums and Summer Programs for Government and Civics Students

In this chapter, we've scouted out the best Web sites for museums and summer programs for government and civics students. This part of the book is designed to help you learn about government and civics in a more hands-on style. We'll describe Web sites where you can view the original U.S. Constitution right from the comfort of your very own room, take a virtual tour of the White House, or explore the history of women's suffrage. Also, check out the general sites in "The Basics" section in Volume 1 of this set.

MUSEUMS

Colonial Williamsburg
http://www.history.org

If you can't get there in person, this Web site is the next best thing. It's especially good for younger students who may be studying colonial government for the first time and teachers looking for resources that are easily used in the classroom. From the home page, click on "History" and you'll be given the following choices: "Resources for Teachers and Students," "Electronic Field Trips," "The History Explorer," "The Libraries of Colonial Williamsburg," "Research," "The Museums of Colonial Williamsburg," and "The Williamsburg Institute."

There's so much here that it's hard to decide where to start, but we recommend "The History Explorer," "Meet the People," See the Places," "Colonial Dateline," "Experience Colonial Life," and "Additional Resources" are the five sections you'll have to choose from. Opt for "People" and you'll be presented with the following: "African Americans," "Colonial Children," "Families" (and there are several specific families to choose from), "Founders," and "People of Williamsburg." You can read biographies and descriptions of these varied folks until you're thoroughly acquainted.

You'll probably be drawn to "Electronic Field Trips," back on the home page, but beware that while these offer more live and multimedia resources, they do take place on a specific date and time and require that you register in advance.

National Archives and Records Administration
http://www.nara.gov/

Click on the "Online Exhibit Hall" at the *National Archives* home page, and you'll be able to view the American originals of the Declaration of Independence, the Constitution, and the Bill of Rights. There's also the online exhibit called "Designs for Democracy," which showcases more than 100 designs from 200 years of U.S. government drawings. You'll find just about every medium represented and a vast collection of subjects as well. "American Originals: Treasures of Congress" highlights a sampling of landmark documents created by or delivered to Congress.

National Civil Rights Museum
http://216.157.9.6/civilrights/main.htm

If you're studying the Civil Rights movement, you won't want to miss the "Interactive Tour" at this museum. Click on "Interactive Tour" on the home page, and you'll begin a journey, called Voices of Struggle, that will introduce you to some of the many African Americans who fought for civil rights and give you an overview of civil-rights history. The tour covers slavery, the Civil War, the Emancipation Proclamation, the many Civil Rights Acts passed between 1866 and 1875, the migration of blacks away from the South, Jim Crow laws, education, Booker T. Washington, philanthropies, the vote, Ida B. Wells, W. E. B. DuBois, race riots, and many other topics. Click on the names at the bottom of the page when you first begin the "Interactive Tour" if you'd like to read brief biographies of key individuals.

In addition to the tour, this site offers plenty of information about the museum and its activities, as well as directions for visiting the museum, which is located in Memphis, Tennessee.

National Museum of American History
http://americanhistory.si.edu/

One of the most popular museums in the country, the National Museum of American History is part of the Smithsonian Institution, the largest museum in the world. Its Web site offers numerous virtual exhibits, including "A More Perfect Union: Japanese Americans and the U.S. Constitution," "The American Presidency: A Glorious Burden," and "The Disability Rights Movement."

Another section that might be interesting and useful is "Not Just For Kids," which has a "Hands On History Room," where, among other activities, you can send a telegraph. Perhaps you'd just like to use the "Timeline" to explore, for example, the Civil Rights movement using the Museum's collections. Click on the picture of African Americans at the Woolworth's lunch counter in Greensboro, North Carolina, and find yourself in 1960, sitting for justice. A picture of Barbara Bush in an evening gown will take you to a brief display on First Ladies and their fashion.

National Women's History Museum
http://www.nmwh.org/

The online exhibit, "Motherhood, Social Service, and Political Reform" will walk you through the history of women's suffrage and show you more than fifty historical images associated with the suffrage movement.

Click on "Featured Exhibit" on the home page, and you'll enter the exhibit with a page that offers you the option of taking an "in-depth journey through the history of women's suffrage" or a "walking tour through the image gallery." There's also a time line, a quiz, a list of additional resources, and dozens of interesting articles to support lesson plans in this subject.

Choose the in-depth journey, and you won't be disappointed. The historical overviews are well illustrated with photographs of suffragists and other significant images, as well as primary source material, such as the 1848 Report on the Seneca Falls Women's Rights Convention. The in-depth journey begins with the Seneca Falls Convention and covers much terrain, including women's involvement in the Civil War, the various organizations founded to campaign for women's right to vote, the impact of the Progressive Era on the suffrage movement (don't miss the suffrage songs link on this page), the creation of a female political culture and imagery, and mainstream use of domestic images and motherhood, among other topics.

The White House
http://www.whitehouse.gov/history/

If you've always wanted to set foot in the White House, here's your virtual chance. At the "History and Tours" page of the White House

Web site, you'll find an online historical tour that leads you through 11 rooms in the Presidential residence. You'll see the famous Blue Room, the State Dining Room, the China Room, and eight others, all with full-color photographs accompanied by intriguing histories. No tour guide needed.

This site also boasts a trivia quiz; "Presidential Hall," which contains biographies of all the presidents as well as trivia questions; a "First Ladies" section; and a "Facts" page, among other offerings. The site is fully searchable, available in Spanish, and contains a "Contacts" page with e-mail addresses for the President and Vice President, just in case you've been meaning to write.

SUMMER PROGRAMS

American Institute for Foreign Study
http://www.aifs.org/

AIFS offers summer programs for college students in France, Germany, Italy, Japan, Mexico, Russia, Spain, and the United Kingdom. For high school students, see the "Summer Enrichment Programs" section of the Web site for a description of programs in England, France, Italy, Russia, and Spain.

For students of government, there are numerous options, many of them focusing on the study of foreign relations and foreign policy. Students live in host cities, where they can study not only politics, foreign relations, and government, but also foreign languages, business, economics, computers, fine arts, communications, and history.

These are all-inclusive trips, with airfare, housing, meals, excursions, and cultural activities included in the tuition. See the Web site for more details. You can download an application or call the American Institute for Foreign Study using their toll-free number.

Congressional Interns
http://www.house.gov/paul/interns.htm

If you've ever wanted to intern in the office of a U.S. congressional representative or senator, here's your chance. This is the Web site for Senator Ron Paul of Texas, chosen for inclusion here because it was the first to pop up on our Web search. Each senator or congressional representative has his or her own Web site for interns. There is no one central place to search for information on these internships. But if you type in the address listed above and replace "paul" with the last name of your representative or senator, you should arrive at the section of that person's Web site that is devoted to internships.

Another way to search for these opportunities is to type "congressional interns" as the keyword in your favorite search engine and peruse the Web sites that are returned. We searched on Google and found the Web sites of numerous senators and representatives, as well as some sites for specific organizations and agencies in Washington, D.C., that are associated with the government.

Department of State Internships
http://www.state.gov/m/dghr/hr/intern

The Department of State manages several student employment programs for students to get experience in a foreign-affairs environment through firsthand knowledge. Some students work in Washington, D.C., and others have the opportunity to work at an embassy overseas. Positions are both paid and unpaid, and many are available during spring, summer, or fall. See the Web site for complete information.

Education World's Countdown to Summer: Free Summer Programs for Teens
http://www.education-world.com/a_curr/curr074.shtml

Interested in an academically enriching summer program in government, even though you may not have the funds? Here you'll find a list of freebies, including Governor's Honors Programs. Although most states offer such programs, not all of them are free.

Each state's Governor's Honors Program differs a little from the next, but most are month-long, residential programs for academically motivated students who have just completed their junior year. Apply online to the free programs listed here, or contact your state's Governor's Honors Program for more information.

Landmark Volunteers
http://www.volunteers.com/

Travel to one of 55 nationally renowned historic landmarks to work for two weeks. Opportunities in 2001 included working in Plimoth Plantation in Massachusetts, with The Boston Symphony in their summer residency at Tanglewood, or in Colonial Williamsburg in Williamsburg, Virginia. This nonprofit community-service organization for high-school students will house and feed you while you're on the job, but you'll have to pay your own way to your volunteer site. Check out the Web site for a complete list of summer volunteer opportunities and a free brochure. You can even apply online if you decide this one's for you.

Lisle International: Intercultural Volunteer Programs for Global Citizens
http://www.lisle.utoledo.edu/

The Lisle Fellowship offers short-term experiences around the world that focus on cooperative, democratic leadership and participation. The programs seek to exemplify multicultural/multiracial decision-making, planning, and administration.

In 2002 programs were held in Turkey, Bali, the USA, and India, and addressed topics such as building a sustainable future, the creative experience of arts and community, and women's voices. Programs in Costa Rica and Holland, as well as other places, were held in 2003.

See the Web site for complete descriptions of these programs and the host countries, and note that although these are month-long programs in wonderful, far-flung places, they are extremely reasonable in price. If budget is a factor, you'll definitely want to check out these opportunities.

NASA Lyndon B. Johnson Space Center Oral History Project Summer Intern Program
http://www.jsc.nasa.gov/

Established by the Center Director in 1996, the Johnson Space Center (JSC) Oral History Project's primary goal is to research and interview individuals who enabled the exciting and challenging space programs of yesterday and today. This program provides temporary summer work only and is limited to undergraduate and graduate students.

As an Oral History Program Summer Intern, you will have the unique opportunity to participate in documenting the history of U.S. human space exploration. You will be responsible for researching biographical information on key contributors to NASA's Mercury, Gemini, Apollo, Skylab, and Space Shuttle programs. In recent years, the application deadline for the summer program was February. For information on the upcoming summer program, contact Bill Larsen (281.483.4062) or Glen Swanson (281.483.6924), or e-mail glen.e.swanson1@jsc.nasa.gov.

National Archives and Records Administration Internship Program
http://www.nara.gov/professional/intern/intern.html

The National Archives and Records Administration invites undergraduate- and graduate-level students to submit applications for its voluntary internship program. The program is available to students regardless of major, but these internships offer wonderful opportunities to students in political science, history, American studies, library science, and other related disciplines who wish to gain firsthand experience in archives and history-related work, while also developing an invaluable reference for future employment.

Peterson's Summer Opportunities
http://www.petersons.com/summerop/select/a068se.html

Here you'll find 99 sponsors with summer programs offering classes in government. Most are traditional academic programs, so use this list if you're looking to beef up your transcript for college. There are prestigious programs at places like Phillips Andover, Harvard University, the University of Chicago, and many other excellent schools. You'll also find programs like the Junior Statesman Foundation Seminars, which offer numerous academic programs around the country that are focused specifically on American government, constitutional law, debate, leadership, and U.S. foreign policy; and The Experiment in International Living, which offers, among its many programs, one in Poland that includes community service, a homestay with a Polish family, and travel.

ProPeru
http://www.properu.org/

Interested in international relations? This internship opportunity in Peru is great for those of you interested in international development, in particular. You can earn valuable professional and international experience while immersed in a small community, performing meaningful work, and exploring the cultural and historical richness of Peru.

Through the Intern in Peru Program, each student works on a focused development project with one of 40 affiliated nongovernmental organizations (NGOs). The focus of the development project is determined by the specific skills of each student and the community where you are placed. Projects often involve building a school, providing medical services, developing housing, or doing a public-works project.

Check out the Web site for a list of programs and projects, photos from previous projects in Peru, reviews from previous participants, and all the application information you need, including a downloadable form.

Russian Language, Culture, and Society Program
http://www.knowledgeexchange.org/cis/russia/msu/rlcs/frameset.htm

For undergraduate, graduate, and postgraduate students, this program at Moscow State University offers intensive Russian and Slavic language training and coursework in political science, international relations, history, sociology, anthropology, literature, education, journalism, business, economics, and education. Knowledge of Russian is not necessary as all classes are conducted in English. You'll enjoy excursions in Moscow, St. Petersburg, and Novgorod, while earning up to twenty undergraduate or graduate credits. Programs run in fall, spring, summer, and the academic year.

See the Web site for a list of program highlights and a toll-free number to call for more information.

USAJOBS' Guide to Student Internship Programs with the Federal Government
http://www.usajobs.opm.gov/EI13.htm

The federal government is interested in finding people from diverse backgrounds who have the skills needed to meet its future employment needs. While some federal agencies have developed agency-specific programs, this internship listing is limited to special programs that can be used for hiring in all federal agencies.

You'll find such programs as the Congressional Hispanic Caucus Institute's Fellowship Program (CHCI), the Presidential Management Intern Program (PMIP), and the White House Fellows Program.

5

⬤⬤⬤

Careers

Whether you're simply gathering information to help you turn your passion for government and civics into a livelihood or you're actively searching for your first job in the field, the World Wide Web can play an integral role in the development of your career.

Your idea of a perfect job in government or the public sector may involve running for office at the local, state, or national level, teaching political science, or serving as a foreign diplomat. Or perhaps you're interested in becoming a public school administrator or joining the military—the choices are remarkably varied. Regardless of the specific field you're interested in, you'll discover numerous Web sites with tools to help you determine your career aptitudes, match your academic interests with a university program, locate funding for a research project, find online peers, register for professional conferences or student workshops, and of course, you'll encounter dozens of job database sites, including those specific to government-related careers.

We've selected what we consider to be the best career-building government Web sites, with the needs of upper-level high-school and college students firmly in mind. These sites, which include professional organizations and societies, federal and state agencies, private companies, nonprofit groups, and academic organizations should give you a good jump start on your career.

PROFESSIONAL ORGANIZATIONS AND SOCIETIES

American Political Science Association
http://www.apsanet.org/

This is the major professional society for people who study politics, government, and public policy in the U.S. and around the world. You'll find the usual resources—publications, conferences, teaching resources, and a very helpful section on "Jobs/Careers."

There's an extensive "Guide to Jobs in Political Science," an article on the benefits of the political-science major, a section called "Finding and Advancing Your Political Science Career," and another called "Questions to Ask When Thinking About Pursuing a Ph.D."

This page also can hook you up with a subscription to the Personnel Service Newsletter, which is a pretty decent resource for locating academic and nonacademic jobs in political science around the country.

American Society for Public Administration
http://www.aspanet.org/

This professional society has a membership of more than 10,000 government and nonprofit administrators, scholars, teachers, and students. It's extremely student-friendly, which means that you'll find a wealth of goodies geared specifically to your current and future educational and occupational needs.

The "Careers in Public Administration" section features public administration job openings in government and nonprofit organizations and several universities in a service called "The Recruiter Online." You can also access "Career Links," which will help you search more careers in government, academia, consulting firms, health services, and more. "Internship Programs" is the section of the site that will help you learn more about governmental internships, including federal and state internship programs, as well as local government programs in the Washington, D.C., area. Other sections of interest at this site include information on trends within the field, a section devoted to international resources, and a section specifically on nonprofit resources.

The heart of the site for students, however is the "Students' Area," which you can access from the main menu. Try the following link—http://www.aspanet.org/students/resource_frm.html—to ASPA's "Student Resource Center," where you can submit a question about academics, your future career, or public administration in general. There's also information at the Students' Area on student grants, questions to ask when looking for a first job, universities where you can major in public affairs or a related discipline, and much more.

National Association of Schools of Public Affairs and Administration
http://www.naspaa.org/publicservicecareers/index.htm

This is the organization for all those colleges and universities that offer advanced degrees in the field of public affairs and administration. The URL provided here takes you directly to the section of the page devoted to students, where you'll find such resources as "What Is Public Service?" "Find an Internship," "Education and Public Service," "Starting Your Career," and "Links and Resources." Each of these sections contains embedded links to other sites that expand on what this site has to offer, which is actually quite extensive. You'll find definitions and ruminations about working in the field, as well as practical tips and guidelines for finding your first job or applying to graduate school.

National Council for the Social Studies
http://www.ncss.org/

Defined as an information service for educators, this organization's Web site contains sections on conferences, standards, teaching resources, awards and grants, meetings, membership, and more. If you're considering a career as a teacher, you'll find lots to think about here, and if you're already headed down that career path, you'll be able to take advantage of all the resources offered. Click on "Professional Development" to learn more about educational and work opportunities as a government/civics teacher.

FEDERAL AND STATE GOVERNMENT ORGANIZATIONS

America's Career Infonet
http://www.acinet.org/acinet/library.htm

"Dream it. Find it. Get it" is the motto of this career service that's geared to help you along the path as you try to figure out what you want to do. If you're looking for ideas, give this site a try. It can connect you to resources that will help answer all your career-related questions. Just type in a keyword, and let the search begin.

Sections of the site include "Job and Resume Banks," "Job Search Aids," "Occupational Information," "Relocation Information," and "State Resources." For government-related careers, try searching under "Explore by Occupation," which is located logically in the "Occupational Information" section.

BLS Career Information
http://stats.bls.gov/k12/html/edu_over.htm

This Bureau of Labor Statistics page for kids is a great general resource for exploring career options in all fields, with sections on "Music/Arts," "P.E./Outdoors," "Science," "Social Studies," "Reading," and "Math"—but it also includes some excellent resources for exploring government-related careers. Click on "Social Studies" at the bottom of the page to learn about the following career positions that are recommended for kids who like social studies: police officer, politician, real-estate agent, urban planner, and clergy. Click on "politician," for example, and learn lots of details about the profession, including what politicians do, where jobs are located, what types of future possibilities exist in the profession, what politicians earn on average, and more.

Bureau of Land Management: Student Career Experience Program
http://www.nc.blm.gov/jobs/SCEP/SCEP.htm#About the Student Career
    Experience Program

In case you think BLM stands for some kind of sandwich, it's time for a proper introduction. The Bureau of Land Management (BLM) is an agency within the Department of the Interior that administers 264 million acres of America's public lands, located primarily in 12 western states. If you happen to live in one of those 12 states—or wish you did—read on. Like many other government agencies, the BLM offers two employment programs to help students build their careers while still enrolled in school.

The Student Temporary Employment Program (STEP) places students in temporary (up to one year) jobs that are not necessarily related to their academic fields. The Student Career Experience Program (SCEP) hires students—often those with STEP experience—to work in their academic field. SCEP students generally attend college on a regular semester or academic quarter schedule and work for the BLM during summer vacation and holiday periods. You'll find specific and current info about both programs' openings at BLM's Web site.

Defense Link: U.S. Department of Defense
http://www.defenselink.mil/other_info/careers.html

This Web site is your top source for locating U.S. Department of Defense jobs as either a service member or as a civilian. You'll find job postings and sections on "Frequently Asked Questions," "General Military Information," "Issues and Policies," and "People and Records."

FirstGov
http://firstgov.gov/

"Your first click to the U.S. government" is this Web site's motto, and it's true that you'll find all parts of the government neatly organized into three main sections—"Citizens Interacting with Government," "Businesses Interacting with Government," and "Governments Interacting with Government."

You'll be most interested in the "Citizens" section, which contains links to online government services, such as "Find a Government Job," "Apply for a Student Loan," "Volunteer," "Find a School, College, or Library," and "Find a Job or Find an Employee: America's Job Bank," to name just a few of the links provided.

Peace Corps Master Program
http://www.peacecorps.gov/volunteer/masters/index.html

Trying to decide between graduate school and the Peace Corps? The Peace Corps has come up with a way that you don't have to choose. Thanks to partnerships with more than forty campuses across the United States, the Peace Corps Master's International (MI) program allows you to incorporate Peace Corps service into a master's degree program.

Students apply to both the Peace Corps and the participating graduate school, and must be accepted by both. You would typically complete one year of graduate studies before starting a Peace Corps assignment. Your Peace Corps assignment then serves as the foundation for a thesis or other culminating project.

You can use the Web site to learn more about the participating graduate schools and the specific areas of study, which include government-friendly subjects such as business, public policy and administration, intercultural management, and urban planning.

Students.gov
http://www.students.gov/link_search/listlinks.cfm?&Topic=0404

This is an index to U.S. government career sites. You can search for internships, fellowships, student job programs, and plain old regular jobs. You can also find links to government services that assist you with financial aid, taxes, and finding a job.

U.S. Census Bureau Jobs
http://www.census.gov/hrd/www/

If you have an interest in demographics, it's easy to use this Web site to investigate career possibilities with the U.S. Census Bureau.

From this Web site, click on "Professional Jobs: Student, Entry, and Mid Career" to see areas of interest, such as "Statistics, Economics, Business Administration" and "Sociology, Psychology, Demography." Each area offers a description of the type of work and job responsibilities involved.

After you've ascertained your own interests and aptitudes, click on "Nationwide Positions" to view a list of jobs available with the Census Bureau. There's even a special section for "Student Employment," where you'll find information on summer internships and cooperative work programs for government students. If you're further along in your education, and drawn to statistics and demography, you'll also find info here about the Census Bureau's postdoctoral research program.

U.S. Department of State: Student Programs Index
http://www.state.gov/www/careers/rstudprogindex.html

If you're interested in a career in foreign affairs, you'll want to visit the U.S. Department of State's comprehensive Web site.

The department manages several student employment programs that can provide you with invaluable on-the-job experience in a foreign-affairs environment. If selected for one of the programs, you could work in Washington, D.C., or at an embassy overseas. Positions are both paid and unpaid and are available during spring, summer, and fall.

Use the comprehensive Web site to learn details about the various programs, which include a cooperative education program; a graduate fellowship program; the Presidential management intern program; domestic and overseas student internships for university juniors, seniors, and graduate students; and student-worker trainee opportunities for high school, vocational school, and undergraduate students.

NONPROFIT AND ACADEMIC ORGANIZATIONS

Campus Outreach Opportunity League
http://www.cool2serve.org/

This organization is dedicated to educating and empowering college students to strengthen our nation through community service. The Web site can tell you all about its programs, the COOL Movement Summit, the COOL Annual Conference, membership in the organization, and more. You can also access the COOL On-line Resource Center.

Career Services: Political Science
http://career.asc.ohio-state.edu/careers/sbs/Poli%20Science/polisciintro.
    htm

This Ohio State University site answers your questions about career options for political science majors, internship opportunities, salaries for political science graduates, and graduate school possibilities. You'll also find a working definition for "political science" and helpful links to organizations and associations in the field.

Under "Options," explore career possibilities in government/politics, law, business, education, and retailing. Under "Salaries," use the special search engine to find salary statistics by major and by year of graduation. The Internships section is geared specifically to Ohio State University students, but its list of organizations that offer internships will be helpful to anyone interested in the field.

Idealist.org
http://www.idealist.org/

This Web site is filled to the brim with great ideas for teens who want to work for the betterment of humanity. You'll find sections on "Organizations," "Jobs," "Volunteer Opportunities," "Services," "Resources," "Campaigns," "Events," "Internships," "Career Fairs," and more, and all of these contain information from around the globe—more than 153 countries—in case travel figures prominently in your dreams.

Go to any one of the above to search for opportunities, or if you'd like to contemplate your options a little more, go to "Community," where you can talk to folks from around the world about your interests, or "Kids and Teens," where you can hunt down resources for a neighborhood project, explore human rights issues at kid-friendly sites, or visit organizations started by kids—groups like the Care Bags Foundation, started by 11-year-old Annie Wignall of Iowa, to provide essential, fun, and safe things to kids during difficult times in their lives. Annie delivers more than 800 care bags each year. There's also Kids Konnected, which was started by 11-year-old Jon Wagner-Holtz when his mother had breast cancer. Jon couldn't find other kids with sick parents to talk to about the experience, so he started Kids Konnected in California. It now has programs all across the States, as well as a 24-hour hot line, e-mail newsletter, monthly meetings, resources, and summer camps.

Independent Sector
http://www.independentsector.org/

This is a coalition of leading nonprofit organizations, corporations, and foundations who are interested in strengthening not-for-profit initiatives, philanthropy, and citizen action. If your future career path is likely to cross the nonprofit sector, you may want to take a look at this site for the information it provides about that world. You'll find sections at the site devoted to exploring corporate-nonprofit partnerships, taxes, fundraising, e-philanthropy, accountability, volunteering and giving, and many more issues. "Research and Public Policy" may also contain information that you will find interesting. "Joblink" at the bottom of the menu contains a very few job postings from member organizations.

Student Conservation Association
http://www.sca-inc.org/

If you want your public service to be in the woods instead of in an office, check out the Student Conservation Association (SCA). Dedicated to "changing lives through service to nature," this group's Web site is bursting at the seams with listings of volunteer and internship spots across the country.

Click on "Volunteer and Internship Opportunities" to learn how you can lend a hand in month-long team projects for the National Park Service, the U.S. Forest Service, the Bureau of Land Management, and other agencies. This site makes finding an unpaid internship or volunteership almost too easy: you can access a list of current positions, get information, and request an application, all online.

Paid internships in areas such as endangered-species protection, archaeology, environmental education, wilderness patrol, and marine biology are also available by tapping SCA's searchable online database. You may also be eligible for SCA's Diversity Internship Program, which offers paid seasonal internships to college students who traditionally do not work within the conservation field (ethnic populations, women, and others).

Index

Page numbers in bold indicate main discussion of a topic.

About the Authors

ELIZABETH H. OAKES is the author of more than 15 books, including *Career Exploration on the Internet* and *International Encyclopedia of Women Scientists*.

JEFFREY D. GREENE is Professor of Political Science at the University of Montana.